Christ at the Center

The Westminster History of Christian Thought

Other Books Available in This Series:

Christendom at the Crossroads: The Medieval Era,
by J. A. Sheppard

Crisis and Renewal: The Era of the Reformation,
by R. Ward Holder

CHRIST AT THE CENTER
The Early Christian Era

Lisa D. Maugans Driver

WESTMINSTER
JOHN KNOX PRESS
LOUISVILLE · KENTUCKY

1st edition
Published by Westminster John Knox Press
Louisville, Kentucky

09 10 11 12 13 14 15 16 17 18—10 9 8 7 6 5 4 3 2 1

Book design by Sharon Adams
Cover design by Lisa Buckley
Cover illustration: Christ Among the Doctors, *detail from panel one of the Silver Treasury of Santissima Annunziata, c. 1450–53 (tempera on panel) by Fra Angelico (Guido di Pietro) (c. 1387–1455) Museo di San Marco dell'Angelico, Florence, Italy/The Bridgeman Art Library Nationality*

Library of Congress Cataloging-in-Publication Data

Driver, Lisa D. Maugans.
    Christ at the center : the early Christian era / Lisa D. Maugans Driver.
        p. cm. — (The Westminster history of Christian thought)
    Includes bibliographical references (p.   ) index.
    ISBN 978-0-664-22897-2 (alk. paper)
    1. Church history—Primitive and early church, ca. 30–600.   2. Theology—History—Early church, ca. 30–600.   3. Christian life—History—Early church, ca. 30–600.   I. Title.
    BR166.D75   2009
    270.1—dc22

                                                                                        2009001925

PRINTED IN THE UNITED STATES OF AMERICA

⊗ The paper used in this publication meets the minimum requirements of the American National Standard for Information Sciences—Permanence of Paper for Printed Library Materials, ANSI Z39.48-1992

Westminster John Knox Press advocates the responsible use of our natural resources. The text paper of this book is made from 30% postconsumer waste.

To Steve, Nathaniel, and Zoë

Contents

Series Introduction   ix
Acknowledgments   xi
Abbreviations   xiii
Introduction   xv

Part I   Why Christ? (Second Temple Period, ca. 520 BC–AD 70)   **1**

  1. "The One to Redeem Israel" (Luke 24:21)   5

  2. "Are You the One Who Is to Come?" (Matt. 11:3)   25

Part II   The Pillars of the Faith (ca. AD 50–324)   **45**

  3. "Go Therefore and Make Disciples" (Matt. 28:19)   49

  4. *Christianus/a Sum:* I Am a Christian   69

  5. Scripture: From Jewish to Christian   91

  6. Heresy: Congregational Dynamics and Theological Method   115

Part III   A Dynamic Golden Age (Fourth and Fifth Centuries)   **139**

  7. *Ekklēsia:* The People of God   145

  8. Cultivating Life in Christ   167

  9. Cultivating Humanity   185

 10. Jesus Christ: Divine and Human   205

Epilogue: Partings   227
Notes   231
Index of Names of Persons   243
Index of Subjects   249

SERIES INTRODUCTION

The Westminster History of Christian Thought series provides a set of resources for the study of the history and development of Christian thought from the period of the early church to the present. The books are designed to be accessible introductory studies. They focus on the issues that were important questions and the theological expressions that emerged during the various eras. Strong attention is also paid to the historical and cultural contexts in which the theology developed. The studies are written by superb teachers who present their work in clear and energetic ways. These experts are committed to enhancing the teaching and learning tasks.

We hope this series will be of help to those who want skilled guidance to the development of Christian thought from the days of early Christianity to contemporary times.

The Publisher

Acknowledgments

I never intended to write a book. It seemed God's will, and only as such was it finished. Don McKim set the ball rolling. His trust, patience, and encouragement kept me in the project through times when I was on the verge of faltering. Valparaiso University graciously supported research leaves and a sabbatical dedicated to this project. However, it has been family and friends who brought the book to completion through their prayers, childcare, and reading through chapters. Special thanks go to my husband, Steve, and Susie Hord for their editing efforts. Finally my parents deserve recognition for instilling in me a love of God and of learning from my childhood.

In accord with the Rule of Saint Benedict (4.42–43), I fully own the errors and infelicities of this work and give glory to God for whatever good issues from these pages.

Abbreviations

ANF	*The Ante-Nicene Fathers*
c.	century
ESV	*English Standard Version*
KJV	King James Version
NASB	*New American Standard Bible*
NPNF[1]	*The Nicene and Post-Nicene Fathers*, Series 1
NPNF[2]	*The Nicene and Post-Nicene Fathers*, Series 2

Introduction

While the primary focus of this volume might be called Christian theology, it must be said up front that the first generations of Christians did not use the term "theology." Nor did they call themselves "Christians" or what they believed "Christianity." Instead, they called what they believed "the Way" (as in Acts 19:9), and how they lived was simply to follow that way. Followers of Jesus embarked upon a way of understanding reality that required substantial adjustments both in how they looked at the world and in how they lived in it. What they believed about God, Jesus, themselves, and the world around them shaped how they lived. Conversely, how they interacted with each other, worshiped, welcomed strangers, and cared for the poor shaped how they understood God.

It is necessary for the reader to understand this very basic point if one is to understand this book as a whole. Early Christians believed that there could be no increase in knowledge of God without a corollary increase in moral likeness to God. There could be no moral life without adhering to the knowledge that they had gained of God. Thus theology was not a rational dissection of "god" that could be conducted by believers and unbelievers alike. Instead, theology, or thinking about God, required the active involvement of the whole person in pursuit of a relationship with God. This relationship was experienced in the community of believers and in the world as a whole. Thinking about God was practical (in that belief and the practice of belief were inextricably tied together) and communal (in that belief was shaped by conversation with fellow believers and lived out among those believers).

The reciprocity between knowledge (or faith) and practice is crucial for understanding the history of Christian thought. It also is crucial for the thematic coherence of this book. Early Christian thought was experiential and

communal. Thinking about God occurred in varied and far-ranging communities, separated by time, space, language, and culture. The questions these
believers asked and the treatises they wrote were not systematic, but pertained
to their particular situations. Early Christians and the ideas to which they
gave birth were as varied as the times and places in which they lived.

This rich variety bedevils any attempt to represent the development of
early Christian thought as a single narrative. While individual stories will be
told, the inclusion of any event, person, or idea must lead inevitably to the
exclusion of many others. What united the early Christians was not their own
particular story, but their belief in the overarching story of God's gracious
offer of everlasting life. Regardless of their particular contexts, they all faced
the same two questions: Who is Jesus? What does it mean to follow him?
While particular contexts would shape the form of these questions and how
they would be answered, these two basic questions nonetheless provide an
enduring coherence to what early Christians thought and how they lived.

This survey thus attempts not a narrative, but a collage. The images contained in this collage may sometimes tell a story, but the unity of the collage
will arise from the questions it reveals. Who is Jesus? What does it mean to
follow him? What will unfold is not a neat story with a tidy ending, but a way
or method of thinking about God. Early Christian thought about God was a
communal rather than a solitary experience. It involved the careful scrutiny of
what had been handed down as well as thorough consideration of what ideas
might imply for the future. Finally, this thought was experiential. Christians
wrestling with these questions were united in the belief that they had somehow encountered the risen Christ.

The first part is particularly concerned with the question of Jesus' identity.
How did the Jewish followers of Jesus come to the conclusion that Jesus was
indeed the Christ? We will see that such a conclusion required reassessing
both the idea of messiah and the nature of God's covenant. It was therefore
necessary for the earliest believers to reread Scripture (Jewish holy writings)
through the good news of Jesus born, died, and risen. Having established that
Jesus was (and is) the Christ, they then could explore what the "Christhood"
of Jesus might mean for them and for all humanity, whether Jew or Gentile.

Moving into the second and third centuries, the second part samples the
speculations of believers as they reflected further upon how their belief in
Jesus' identity shaped their own. The potential for persecution lent urgency
to their discussions, as did the tensions among believers who showed different
levels of commitment to, and understanding of, the faith. Experimentation
characterized how believers shaped an identity founded on Christ. Christians
differed on the extent to which they interacted with Jews and Gentiles, both
socially and intellectually. Because he brought together God and humanity,

heaven and earth, Jesus Christ was a persistent conundrum for believers and nonbelievers alike. How could these opposite dimensions ever fully meet? How could evil, change, and suffering accord with a good and perfect God?

The third part opens the door onto developments in Christian belief and practice after the persecutions. The communal element of Christian identity remained central to entering, living, and learning in the church. Greater contact of Christians with each other across the Roman Empire and beyond encouraged attempts at synthesis while respecting variety. These encounters also prompted heated debates about how best to frame the way Christians negotiate the boundaries between the uncreated God and created humanity.

The reader should keep in mind that there is no tidy resolution to these debates. Disputes about the divinity and humanity of Christ that arose in the fifth century continue to fracture the church today. As new peoples have encountered the story of salvation through Christ, they have added their own images, thoughts, and contexts to this collage of Christian thought. Nevertheless, even as the collage of Christian thought continues to grow, this particular study of it must come to an end. It does so by taking up the difficulties inherent in trying to synthesize various understandings of Jesus into a single creedal formula, and in exploring how the development of this formula fostered both unity and ever-hardening divisions in the body of Christ. The tensions evident in these christological controversies indicate the divergent paths that knowing and following Christ would take in the medieval and Byzantine periods.

PART I

Why Christ?
(Second Temple Period, ca. 520 BC–AD 70)

ISSUES

Jesus the Christ is the Alpha and the Omega of all Christian thought. Christians begin their reflections by encountering him, and they direct their lives toward him as their ultimate goal. In order to situate Jesus' coming and reception as the Christ or Messiah (Anointed One), it is important to appreciate how many visions of salvation that title could encompass. This part serves as a prologue, exploring how and why good Jews could embrace Jesus as the Christ: a Christ who completed Israel's history and initiated a return of all humanity, even the Gentiles, to the God of covenant and creation.

Examining this pivotal shift to Jesus as God's salvation involves a daring sweep of history, from God's relationship with ancient Israel to his covenant activity in Jesus during the Roman Empire's first century. The story journeys through Israel's remembered and relived experience of the exodus, the exhilaration of the kingdoms, the harrowing and confusing destruction of the kingdoms, and then it lodges in frustration, waiting for God's full restoration of Israel's purpose as God's people (chap. 1). Pondering the claim that Jesus was truly God's Christ requires some attempt to see things from the eyes of multiform Judaism of the first century AD. Jewish identity rested upon God's formative rescue of his people in the exodus and his gift of a national "constitution" in the law. Further reflection upon the base story governed interpretations of the Israelites' continuing experiences as a kingdom (late 11th c. BC–586 BC) and then as a defeated and scattered people (Diaspora). By Roman times (beginning in 63 BC) Jews had experienced subjugation under four different empires over seven centuries and a disappointing period of their own self-rule. These events left Jews eager both to understand why God had not yet restored them and to dream about how God would still do so one day.

The journey continues along a tricky route through Jesus, who lived, died, and rose again to new life (chap. 2), before hitting the roads of the Roman Empire and beyond as the good news of Jesus the Christ, that is, Christianity. These first believers rejoiced that somehow God and the covenant people (now understood more universally than ethnic Jews) met in the Christ. Taking Jesus as God's Christ necessitated claiming Israel's past for all Christians, even while leaving behind some traditional ways of relating to God (e.g., temple and king) that Christ fulfilled in his person.

HISTORICAL CONTEXT

Jesus lived at the beginning of the Roman Empire, when Augustus Caesar ruled as the first emperor (31 BC–AD 14), followed by Tiberius Caesar (AD 14–37). As Christians in the first two centuries of the faith reflected, the time seemed particularly ripe for God to act. The Pax Romana (Roman peace) initiated by Augustus resulted in unusual civil and economic stability, travel opportunities, and freedom from serious external threats to Roman territories until the end of the second century. Roman roads may have all led to Rome, but in doing so the empire integrally connected large parts of Asia, Africa, and Europe for the first and last time. With piracy radically reduced, the Romans could call the Mediterranean *Mare nostrum*, "Our Sea." Although travel was still difficult, the apostle Paul and nameless others could trudge and sail hundreds of miles across the empire while spreading the gospel, less anxious about safe travel than about how their message would be received.

The empire consisted of a basic division (culturally and linguistically) between the Latin West and the Greek East. Today the line would pass through the Balkan Peninsula; for instance, Serbia was a "Greek" area and Croatia was a "Latin" area. To the south and through the middle of present-day Libya, eastern Libya (ancient Cyrenaica) was Greek while western Libya (Tripolitania) was Latin. All native populations fell under one of these two cultural/linguistic influences as heirs either of the Hellenistic kingdoms, begun by Alexander the Great (d. 323 BC), or of Roman conquests. Business, politics, and education were conducted in one of these two languages.

The empire's success brought even greater diversity to existing urban centers like Rome. Roman authors at times recorded their dismay at the hubbub and the erosion of good Roman values. Religions from exotic eastern (oriental) conquests became very popular for their emotionalism and for individual salvation, such as Isis and Osiris/Serapis from Egypt, and Cybele/Astarte/

Great Mother from Asia Minor and Syria. The Roman Senate and emperors anxiously sought to keep Roman citizens from extending their allegiance to nonnative gods and engaging in orgies or mutilation. Non-Romans could continue to worship their native gods, but they had to honor Rome's deities and tone down any wild or immoral practices. Influences from Egypt (part of the empire from 31 BC) and Persia (Mesopotamian areas variously under Roman and Persian authority) pushed emperors increasingly to accept divine honors from eastern nations accustomed to acknowledging their chief rulers as gods.

Into this matrix came Jesus of Nazareth, killed for being "King of the Jews," whom his followers called "Lord" in seeming antagonism to "Lord Caesar," the emperor. Romans were already dismissive of Judaism, although forced by its antiquity to grant it legitimate status (for Jews only). Odd by ancient world standards for its monotheism, circumcision, and food restrictions, Judaism at least had an old tradition among a recognized ethnic group, sacred writings, a temple, and sacrifices. Romans had little patience for the occasional uprisings by Jewish rebels, who were intent upon Jewish self-rule as a divine right in their homeland. Even the last straw, the Jewish War of 66–70, which resulted in the destruction of the temple, was not the last straw. Romans put down serious Jewish revolts not only in Judea (Simon Bar Kokhba, 132–134), but also, alarmingly, in provinces with large Jewish populations: Africa, Egypt, and Cyprus (115–117). From the Roman perspective, Christians, following a known and executed rebel, were thus already part of a suspect population.

1

"The One to Redeem Israel"

(Luke 24:21)

SOME BASICS ABOUT GOD
AND THE CHOSEN PEOPLE

Jesus of Nazareth appeared among the Jews as an enigma, a riddle. He provided plenty of data for unraveling his identity and purpose. He preached and confronted; he healed and disrupted. The problem remained that the data did not seem to fit any coherent pattern, either for those opposing or for those supporting the man. Jesus himself polled his disciples about his reputation, which ranged from John the Baptist to Elijah or Jeremiah (Matt. 16:14; Mark 8:28; Luke 9:19). Peter answers on behalf of the disciples that Jesus is the Messiah, the "Anointed" (Mark 8:28–29). The despair that hung over the disciples in the wake of Jesus' death came from their dashed hope "that he was the one to redeem Israel" (Luke 24:21).

Why do they answer the way they do? Isn't there a background story that shaped reactions to Jesus? Judaism of the early first century AD certainly, as now, took shape from some foundational stories and experiences within the history of the Israelites. Likewise, Judaism of this period exhibited numerous variations on the basic themes. The confusion and conflicting expectations

---

NAMES OF THE CHOSEN PEOPLE

Israelites: descendants of the patriarch Jacob, renamed by God "Israel" (Gen. 32:28). *Hebrews:* Name used in the exodus for the Israelites in Egypt. *Jews:* People of Judah, the southern Israelite kingdom; after the exile this term identified all remaining Israelites. Scripture also uses tribal names to indicate the northern kingdom, such as Ephraim.

---

which the Gospels hint at in response to Jesus had a very real basis in the lived experience of Jews at that time.

The first "Christians" thought about Jesus within the patterns preserved in the story of their God's relationship with the chosen people of Israel. There is no "Christian thought" which is not grounded within the God of Abraham, Isaac, and Jacob, who revealed himself to Moses in the burning bush as "I AM" (YHWH, Exod. 3:14). Thus, we begin here with the structure and motifs of the Jewish Creator God's interaction with his people as expressed and understood in the period leading to Jesus' day.

How did first-century Jews think about their own religion? "In lots of ways" is the short answer. A quick flip through the Gospels and Second Temple Jewish writings makes it clear that there were several competing or complementary perspectives on being a pious Jew. Holding these various views and lifestyles together was allegiance to the One God, YHWH. Jews worshiped YHWH in daily prayer in the home and through appointed sacrifices at the temple in Jerusalem.

Judaism, unlike most religions in the Greco-Roman world yet somewhat like the philosophical schools, was also a way of life. Worship of YHWH involved a life shaped in some way by Scriptures. Scriptures laid out a story of the people's origins, which gave meaning to their moral and social responsibilities. Torah (law or teaching) repetitively reminds the people to act in certain ways because YHWH is the one who saved them from Egypt

> **SECOND TEMPLE**
>
> Solomon's Temple was the first. The temple created by the Jews who returned from exile to rebuild Jerusalem was called the Second Temple. It designates the time period from ca. 520/516 BC to the destruction of the temple by Rome in AD 70.

and because the exodus experience should make them more sensitive to others who are oppressed and powerless. Festivals and rituals teach important moments in that story even as they renew the community's identity and relationship with YHWH. Passover invites reliving the release from Egypt as one who was there. Circumcision celebrates the increase of the people of God, marked as his special possession in fidelity to the covenant made with the first patriarch, Abraham. Being a Jew assumed an ethnic connection to Abraham. In the Second Temple period, complete conversion of non-Jews (Gentiles) was quite rare and, in some circles, controversial.

In Palestine, priests were the experts and teachers of Scripture- and temple-oriented Judaism. Most lived outside Jerusalem and only visited the holy city when their family group was scheduled for a week of service at the temple. Priests functioned as the learned teachers of the faith in many communities outside of Jerusalem, whether there was a synagogue or not. In the early first century AD, synagogues tended to be more common outside of Palestine, but their purposes were similar: a community center where Jews could engage in communal prayer, listen to Scripture and commentary, and at times host pilgrims.[1]

Scripture itself had comprised a fairly standard set of writings since the mid-third century BC.[2] Of chief importance was Torah (or Pentateuch, meaning "five volumes"), which included Genesis, Exodus, Leviticus, Numbers, and Deuteronomy. These books recounted the origins of Israel's relationship with the God of creation. The story spotlights God's choosing of Israel as his special covenant partner, culminating in rescue from Egypt and gift of his laws and teachings on Mount Sinai. A second, yet still authoritative, group of writings was called Prophets. Confusingly for many today, these writings cover both the oracles of prophets as well as the stories of the kings of Israel and Judah. Finally, there was a rather porous group of Writings that encompassed Wisdom literature (Proverbs), adventure/romance (Esther), and hymns (Psalms).

There was never any legislation that decreed what official Jewish Scripture was. Torah was Scripture; the Prophets and Writings had a secondary authority. The Septuagint of the mid-third century BC contains thirty-nine writings that correspond to the contents of the current Hebrew Bible, together with an appendix of writings variously considered authoritative or edifying but generally written in Greek rather than Hebrew. It is clear that the text of many of the Prophets and Writings was still evolving in the first century AD and beyond. Some Septuagint texts differ from those found among the Qumran Scrolls (most date from the 1st c. BC), which also show variations from the current base text for the Hebrew Bible, the Masoretic text (standardized in the 8th to 9th c. AD but reflecting much earlier texts).

Scholars debate how widespread literacy may have been among Jews in the Second Temple period, and in what languages (Greek, Aramaic, Hebrew). Furthermore, it remains uncertain how many communities had the resources to invest in a library of scrolls, even the five of Torah, let alone the other thirty-four. Yet through festivals, piety in the home, temple-related worship, and occasional access to readings and interpretation of Scripture, many ordinary Jews had a good grasp of the basics of their religion as a worldview and a way of life.[3] They learned about their faith by living it: whom they could marry (only Jews), what they did not eat (unclean), how they divided time (every seventh day for rest), twice-daily prayer (paralleling morning and afternoon sacrifices at the temple). In many cases early Christian thought follows this pattern as well; early Christians did things in response to Jesus and over time contemplated the meanings within their Christ-ward actions of worship and imitation.

ISRAEL'S FORMATIVE STORY AND EXPERIENCES

Exodus

Across the first-century world (Roman Empire, Eastern Africa, Persia), Jews continued to locate the roots of their identity in the story of the exodus and the promised land of Israel. Jews relived this momentous story of salvation annually in the Passover festival. The children of Israel enslaved in Egypt were brought out of captivity through mighty acts of the God who promised fidelity to their ancestors Abraham, Isaac, and Jacob. This nation of nobodies received its identity in being rescued and designated God's "treasured possession," "a priestly kingdom and a holy nation" (Exod. 19:5–6). The covenant was sealed through God's gift of teachings or law, by which the chosen people are to live out their national and religious identity. They must not abandon, but rather embrace, their prior "nobody" status in the way they deal with other potential "nobodies" in their community: non-Israelites, widows, orphans, poor (22:21–24; 23:9). God promised dire consequences to those who oppress such vulnerable people in the community because of a key item in the story: the "cry." God heard and responded to the cry of the oppressed and enslaved Israelites. He threatened his chosen people with the fate of Egypt if they took the role of oppressor. Israelite behavior is to be governed by their founding story in the exodus experience: God's fidelity and action, their limitations and dependence.

The core story contains these central elements: God's founding of a special people, their eventual rescue from slavery, and the gracious gifts of teachings and homeland. Jews in Jesus' generation knew from Scripture how the pattern operated in Israel's subsequent and often stormy relationship with this God "who brought [them] out of the land of Egypt, out of the house of slavery" (20:2). Scripture recounted and interpreted the people's uneven fidelity, first as a kingdom and then as a conquered and scattered people. First-century Jews also used the pattern to understand what God might do next in their subordinate status under a succession of empires.

End of the Kingdoms and the Exile

Trust in God's gracious choosing and rescue generated many strains of hope when the Israelite kingdoms lost their political existence. The glory of David's kingdom barely lasted through his son Solomon. Civil war under David's grandson Rehoboam resulted in two kingdoms: Israel in the north (capital Samaria) and Judah in the south (capital Jerusalem). While the economic situation of the two kingdoms was often rosy, the Deuteronomistic Scriptures looked back upon persistent sloppiness in the kings' and people's fidelity to God. This retrospective analysis paralleled segments of Israel's story told by prophets and sages and manifested the gloomy assessment of the chosen people. Prophets such as Isaiah and Jeremiah despaired over the path the kings and people chose. Israel adulterously extended its trust in alliances with other nations and those nations' gods. The powerful of Israel disregarded the cry of the vulnerable and even committed gross injustices. Idolatry and injustice were faithless counterparts to the Israelites' calling to love God and their neighbor. This was the prophets' critique and warning. The people of God were on the brink of receiving "No Mercy" and becoming "Not my [God's] people" (Hos. 1:6–9), thus reversing God's pledge in the exodus covenant (Deut. 29:13).

DEUTERONOMISTIC HISTORY

Biblical scholars have categorized the books Joshua to 2 Kings as a composite history of Israel that builds on Torah themes made explicit in Deuteronomy (literally, the "second law" or "repeat" presentation of "the law"). Among other themes, it interprets Israelites' endeavors to be God's people in light of their fidelity (or not) to the covenant portrayed in Torah. It may have been initially compiled and written during the reign of Josiah to celebrate his reforms to return the people to covenant fidelity and worship at the temple (late 7th c. BC). Most scholars hold that the history underwent editing (ranging from significant to minimal) during the Babylonian (mid–6th c. BC) exile as the Jews sought to understand God's activity in this bleak situation.

The conquered Israelites/Jews of the sixth century BC may have had mixed feelings about whether things were all that bad. But the impact of an authoritative body of Scripture as it emerged during the Persian period presented some basic patterns for contemplating the whole of Israel's past and looking toward the future. The Torah and prophetic writings, including histories, relayed a framework of God's unfinished rescue of a people who perpetually failed and needed rescue. This conceptual framework holds true even though the majority of Israelites stayed put in the land. Whether in the land of Israel or not, the people were not entirely at home anymore.

Psalms 105 and 106 illustrate the tensions in surveying Israel's heritage as well as emphasizing one foundational pattern underlying both. Psalm 105 celebrates God's fidelity to the covenant he made with Abraham, as reported in Genesis. God orchestrated Joseph's rise to power in Egypt although he was sold into slavery by his brothers. God then made the Israelites honored guests in Egypt. He manifested his power and faithfulness to the Israelites when they were later enslaved by the Egyptians. After mighty signs convinced the Egyptians to release Israel, God then kept proving himself as Savior by miraculously providing water, food, and protection in the wilderness. The psalm concludes with Israel's purpose as a chosen and rescued people in the promised land:

> So he brought his people out with joy,
>   his chosen ones with singing.
> He gave them the lands of the nations,
>   and they took possession of the wealth of the peoples,
> that they might keep his statutes and observe his laws.
> Praise the LORD!
>
> (Ps. 105:43–45)

Following the upbeat recitation of God's gracious fidelity and power, Psalm 106 delves into the people's response. The psalmist painfully confesses Israel's short memory of God's salvific acts. The people see plagues strike the Egyptians; they cross the Red Sea and see Pharaoh's army drown, only to grumble that they want more proof of God's intentions toward them. In reference to several episodes, the psalm depicts the Israelites as perennially disobedient and ungrateful. God, on the other hand, keeps trying to beat some sense (e.g., Isa. 1:1–6) into his unruly children even as he keeps rescuing them from the consequences of their sins. At last God lets his people go their way, abandoning them to conquest by foreign nations:

> Many times he delivered them,
>   but they were rebellious in their purposes,
>   and were brought low through their iniquity.
> Nevertheless he regarded their distress
>   when he heard their cry.
> For their sake he remembered his covenant,
>   and showed compassion according to the abundance
>   of his steadfast love.
> He caused them to be pitied
>   by all who held them captive.
>
> (Ps. 106:43–46)

The psalm ends in a communal "cry" for rescue and regathering of the dispersed people of Israel.

LORD

Jews respectfully did not pronounce God's name given to Moses in Exodus: YHWH. Wherever the text had YHWH, they would read "Lord." In English translations YHWH is indicated by capitalizing LORD.

When the ancient Israelite kingdoms fell to the Assyrian and Babylonian Empires (late 8th and early 6th centuries BC respectively), the exodus experience came chillingly alive. Heart-wrenching laments were raised to a God that many feared had utterly abandoned them:

> Why have you forgotten us completely?
>   Why have you forsaken us these many days?
> Restore us to yourself, O Lord, that we may be restored;
>   renew our days as of old—
> unless you have utterly rejected us,
>   and are angry with us beyond measure.
>   (Lam. 5:20–22)

Survivors of the siege of Jerusalem were burdened by the bleak memory of starvation, a desolate city, and the temple as a heap of rubble. The leaders of the kingdom of Judah, political, religious, and artisan, were shipped off to Babylon. The bulk of the population was left as lowly serfs to Babylonian lords. Once again Israel was enslaved, once again separated from their promised land, or at least governance of their own land. By ancient standards, a conquered people could look forward to national extinction through resettlement and mixed marriages. This was largely the fate of the Israelites who were conquered and resettled under the Assyrians. Voilà: No more covenant people, for there was no longer a promised land, no temple, no Davidic Son of God on the throne, and the bloodline of Abraham seemed destined for dilution and pollution. To all appearances, God had abandoned his covenant.

Such a dismal picture of Israel's identity formed a poignant refrain for Jews in Jesus' day, as many wondered why God had not yet returned in power nor reassembled his "treasured possession." Some seemed quite satisfied in their new homes, particularly the large communities in Egypt and Persia that had been home to Jews for over five hundred years. Regardless of this scattered existence, Jews identified themselves with the land of Israel by the story of its gift from God and their ethnicity. Scriptures familiar to first-century Jews (Torah, Prophets, and other Writings) provided paradigms for hoping that God in his faithfulness would redress a variety of conditions key to preserving the covenant people.

THE SETTING FOR HOPE: THE EXILE TO THE FIRST CENTURY AD

Hope for Restoration

An unbroken line of prophets refused to bow to inevitable oblivion. Some, recalling Israel's foundation story in the exodus, offered hope for God to act again on behalf of his people, ushering in a second, glorious exodus out of captivity. Others pointed to equally potent symbols of a renewed relationship with God such as the temple, the land of Israel, and human leaders assisting in God's deliverance.

Isaiah proclaimed that God is the one "who makes a way in the sea, a path through the mighty waters" (crossing the Red Sea in the exodus) and destroys "chariot and horse, army and warrior" (the destruction of Pharaoh's army when the Red Sea waters returned). This God will once again "make a way in the wilderness" (43:16–17, 19).

Jeremiah urged those about to be defeated by Babylon to trust in God's new covenant. He envisioned a Sinai episode where instead of presenting the law of the covenant to Moses, God "will write [the new covenant] on their hearts" (31:33). Even as Jeremiah described God's commitment to hand over Judah and Jerusalem to Babylon for Israel's infidelity, the prophet held out a magnificent reconciliation in words that continued to stir hope centuries later. After a purifying suffering and dispersal under Babylon, God promises:

> See, I am going to gather them from all the lands to which I drove them in my anger and my wrath and in great indignation; I will bring them back to this place, and I will settle them in safety. They shall be my people, and I will be their God. I will give them one heart and one way, that they may fear me for all time, for their own good and the good of their children after them. I will make an everlasting covenant with them, never to draw back from doing good to them; and I will put the fear of me in their hearts, so that they may not turn from me. (32:37–40)

Ezekiel, an exiled priest and prophet, relayed vivid images regarding God's sure intent to restore his people with a true king, a new life in their homeland, and a restored temple. God himself will be the true shepherd (king), replacing the string of other shepherds (kings) who had abused God's beloved flock and led them astray (Ezek. 34). God promises the breath of new life to the dead Israelites, depicted as dry bones: "You shall live, and I will place you on your own soil" (37:14). Finally, in an extravagant vision (chaps. 40–48) Ezekiel described the glorified temple, where God's glory will once again reside, and the proper relationship with God can be maintained through sacrificial worship. Throughout the description, God warns that restoration of the temple, to precise measurements, coincides with the people renouncing their sins.

Yet the view that Israel somehow deserved such desolation was not uncontested. In Psalm 44, Israel resolutely rejects that defeat has anything to do with abandoning God. "All this [humiliating national defeat] has come upon us, yet we have not forgotten you, or been false to your covenant" (44:17). In fact, the psalmist accuses God of abandoning his covenant duties. The lament challenges God to wake up and fulfill his saving promises precisely because the people depend upon God to continue what he began in the exodus and settlement of the promised land (44:1–3).

Even Isaiah, while accepting that some of the suffering was a just discipline for covenant infidelity, pointed out that what Israel actually experienced in the destruction of the kingdoms went well beyond what God required. Babylon, God's tool of punishment, will in turn be destroyed by God's "anointed," Cyrus the Persian, because the Babylonian conquerors did not play by God's rules:

> I was angry with my people
>   I profaned my heritage;
> I gave them into your [Babylon's] hand,
>   you showed them no mercy.
>   (47:6)

Thus God announces that rescue is at hand because Israel has more than paid for her prior covenant failures.

> Comfort, O comfort my people,
>   says your God.
> Speak tenderly to Jerusalem,
>   and cry to her
> that she has served her term,
>   that her penalty is paid,
> that she has received from the LORD's hand
>   double for all her sins.
>   (40:1–2)

Hope in and after the exile focused on a belief that Israel's circumstances were incompatible with God's desires for his chosen people. Explanations for the seeming inconsistency between God's promise and the people's lived experience ranged from a theory of just retribution (punishment for covenant infidelity) to one of justice not yet accomplished (punishment of the nations/Gentiles for dishonoring God and for causing suffering among his people).

When and how God would complete the new covenant was envisioned in many ways as the people lived through the following centuries. The people had survived as a nation beyond expectation, but they remained under the rule of Gentiles. From the Assyrian and Babylonian exiles to Jesus' day (seven hundred years), prophets, sages, and other religious leaders lived in hope of God's restoration of Israel. They believed that YHWH, whose steadfast love or mercy (*hesed* in the Hebrew Scriptures) in the past prompted saving acts, would act again.

The Babylonian exiles enjoyed something of a protected existence and some even held positions at the royal court. Settled in large groups, which facilitated ethnic survival and the continuation of their traditions, the exiles from Judah and Jerusalem escaped the gradual disappearance suffered by the Assyrian deportees. Even Judah's rebellious and next-to-last king, Jehoiachin, joined the Babylonian court after thirty-seven years in prison. When Cyrus of Persia conquered Babylon (539 BC), he was hailed as God's "anointed," divinely commissioned to initiate the new exodus (Isa. 44–45).

Things were not quite that glorious when some of the Jews returned to Jerusalem with Cyrus's blessing. In fact, return seemed so unattractive that most of the exiles remained in exile by choice. Jerusalem was a mound of rubble, including Solomon's Temple; old Israelite territories in the north and south were peopled with foreigners and peasant descendants of the Judeans who were left behind to work the conquered lands for the Babylonians. The books of Ezra and Nehemiah show how the returning Jews treated the existing inhabitants as Gentile or corrupted by intermarriage with Gentiles. While an altar was raised and sacrifices began quickly upon return, work on the Second Temple stalled for over a decade. Not until 515 BC was the temple dedicated.

Persian overlords were replaced by Greek ones following Alexander the Great's accumulation of Persian territory in the mid-fifth century BC. Then came the Hellenistic rulers, heirs to Alexander's short-lived empire, and eventually Rome in 63 BC. Temple leadership under the high priest and leading priestly families functioned as the political liaison to the ruling empires. The high priest basically ran the territory of the Jews as an administrator for the Persian or Greek kings and was appointed by the kings. Neither God himself nor a decisive human agent had reestablished Israel to the extent that many hoped.

Pursuing the Political Kingdom: Maccabean Interlude

From around 140 to 63 BC, the land of Israel experienced some level of political independence. Beginning with a revolt led by Judas Maccabee (the Hammer), his family, the Hasmoneans, proclaimed themselves to be high priests and kings of Israel. At first it seemed that God's full restoration was at hand: the Jews achieved a substantial period of political autonomy. Later Hasmonean rule merely enhanced the feeling that exile, and the sins that precipitated exile, still hung over the nation.

In a move uncharacteristic for the practice of ancient empires, Antiochus IV Epiphanes, the Greek ruler of the Seleucid Empire (which included Judea), decided to snuff out distinctive Jewish worship and practice. He thought it was time for the Jews to wake up, lose their parochial quirks, and join the civilized world of Greek culture. Granted, Antiochus was cooperating with

Jewish leaders who hoped to align Judea more closely with Greek culture. Elite Jerusalem youths could become urbane "Greeks" through the Hellenistic education system and gymnasium established in the city by Jewish leaders. Many sought out the procedure for reversing circumcision.

Smoldering resentment toward those who would diminish key elements of Jewish identity broke out into rebellion against the Hellenizing Jews and their Greek supporters. In response Antiochus sought to suppress rebellion by staunching its sources in uniquely Jewish practices. Particularity appeared parochial and dangerous to Greek rulers; in contrast, Hellenism stood for universalizing and cosmopolitan culture. In 167/166 BC Antiochus outlawed Torah and Torah-prescribed practices, such as circumcision and food purity laws. He also established pagan worship within the temple. This was the "abomination" and "desolation" decried in the books of Daniel and 1 Maccabees. Hellenizing Jews may have convinced themselves that Zeus and Baal were the cultural equivalent to the God of Israel: same God, different names. This was a common Hellenistic understanding, known as syncretism. Subsequent Jewish history, especially as recorded in 1 and 2 Maccabees, viewed such close cultural and political cooperation with Gentile culture as an abomination.

Antiochus's strategy backfired. Pious resentment was hardened by systematic persecution. Judas Maccabee and his forces reclaimed and purified the temple. Its rededication in 164 BC is celebrated by Jews today in the Feast of Dedication (Hanukkah). The Hasmoneans claimed the high priesthood and slowly declared themselves kings as they continued their wars of purification and expansion. First and Second Maccabees extol Hasmonean leadership for removing "the disgrace brought by the Gentiles" (1 Macc. 4:58). Judas Maccabee was depicted as an agent of God, imitating pious kings of old and enjoining God's help in a campaign committed to reclaiming Jewish identity in the face of persecution and cultural assimilation. By about 140 BC, the Hasmoneans had achieved independence from the Hellenistic kingdom in Syria.

Despite the promise of self-rule, Hasmonean rule did not sit well with many Jews. The Hasmoneans were not descendants of David and thus not legitimate kings. They were not descendants of Zadok (high priest under King Solomon) and thus not legitimate high priests. They too eventually adopted many elements of Hellenistic culture and feuded violently. Consequently, few Jews saw Rome's intervention in another Hasmonean civil war as a bad thing. When Pompey took charge of Jerusalem in 63 BC, Judah returned to a situation analogous to the Persian and Greek periods: internal affairs governed by a Jewish high priest approved by the ruling empire. Client kings (such as the Herodian family) and Roman officials (like

Pontius Pilate) also had their place in the complicated political landscape. Theologically, though, hope for a more concrete restoration continued to brew among Jews, be it a Maccabean-style revolt or a direct appearance of God to set things right between the "sons of light" and "the sons of darkness," on an intertwined spiritual and political plane (vision in the Qumran Scrolls).

If this strikes you as a history lesson and far from Christian thought, you are right on the first but wrong on the second. Jewish and later Christian thought presumes a God who acts and reveals himself in the world. For both the Jews and Christians, history *is* theology. The exodus is a key example of the formative event (story) of God's saving and forming a people for himself. It becomes a lived history through prescribed rituals. The exodus experience formed a community that also is perpetuated through text: Torah (the story in Torah ends with the death of Moses). Yet further reflection upon the base story in Torah as well as the lived experience of the people of the exodus prompted further stories (both oral and written traditions) and rituals (e.g., the new festival of Hanukkah). Attempts to spiritualize Christian belief and practice are generally doomed to failure because the God of the covenant, the God of Jesus and Christians, is a God of action. He created, acts in his creation, and continually reaches out to his special creation of humanity. Theology is reflection on God's relationship with humanity as lived out in time and experienced in this world.

LOOKING FOR GOD'S SALVATION

Covenant Themes

Having laid out the political experience of Jews under successive Babylonian, Persian, Greek, and Hasmonean rules, let us turn to the hopes that developed in this period. Hope developed along the lines of the covenant promises established with the patriarch Abraham (Gen. 12:2–3; 17:1–8) and renewed under Moses with the giving of the law at Mount Sinai (Exod. 19–24):

   a. a populous nation
   b. a free nation subject to God and no others
   c. a nation that will be a source of blessing to other nations
      This could be taken to mean that Israel will be the source of good things coming to noncovenant peoples. It could equally mean that the glory and power of Israel would become a standard blessing along the lines of "May it go with you as with Israel."
   d. a geographic home for the nation
   e. a nation bound to God, who will be especially present to them

In the postexilic and Second Temple period, covenant hope looked toward God to act decisively in fidelity to the covenant. There was no single Jewish expectation, but rather variations in the degree of emphasis on the original promises in the context of the Jews' current situation.

Two adaptations occurred during the period of national sovereignty under a king. King and temple (built by King Solomon) were indicators of God's ruling presence among the people, functioning in much the same way as had the pillar of fire/cloud, the tabernacle, and the ark of the covenant in the exodus memories. Postexilic and Second Temple Jewish texts modified hope in the covenantal promises as follows:

a & c. National integrity: regathering of the scattered Israelites; reestablishing ethnic purity and circumcision; ambivalent relation to Gentiles
b & d. National autonomy: political independence in the territory of the ancient Israelite kingdoms; self-regulation of religious identity
   e. Holiness: restoration and purification of central symbols that would coincide with the returned presence of God (the temple, priesthood, kingship, use of Torah)

Hopes for national integrity raised two seemingly opposed scenarios with regard to the chosen people's relationship with noncovenant people. Texts from the period indicate hope either for the utter destruction (or at least bondage) of Gentiles at the hands of Israel, or for some integration of Gentiles with Israel as fellow people of the one and only God. Postexile Jewish identity was problematic since Israel could not be linked to an existing geopolitical entity. Without clear membership in a polity, questions abounded about how communities or individuals qualified as true Israel: physical and dietary markers? purity of the blood of Abraham? submission to the God of Israel through Torah? temple?

The concept of holiness covered a range of paradigms for imagining what God's presence would look like and how the people might prepare for his presence. Certainly God was not present in such an overwhelming way that other nations stood back in awe, allowing God (or God with his king/priest) to rule his people in peace. In the Second Temple, appointed sacrifices and festivals took place, a priesthood

> *Diaspora*, meaning "scattered" or "dispersed," refers to the Jewish people who no longer lived in their homeland as a result of the various invasions of Israel and Judea.

functioned, and a high priest presided. But some wondered whether God was really present as promised. Was something in present temple leadership preventing God's full restoration, something like corrupt priests or a priesthood from the wrong lineage? The scrolls from Qumran indicate that community's bid to replace the existing temple regime with their own pure Zadokite personnel.

By the time of Jesus, these themes persisted. While not universally appreciated, John the Baptist's raucous call for repentance in preparation for God's reign and his terrifying day of judgment was perfectly intelligible to Jews familiar with Israel's prophets (e.g., Matt. 3:1–10). John's message reflected layers of prophetic tradition that linked Israel's situation to its former or even current sins. To prepare for God's action, the nation needed to purify itself from characteristic sins of idolatry and injustice. Other Jewish texts targeted temple personnel or leaders for repentance and purification. Last, many Jews in Judea and the Diaspora speculated upon what role Scripture should play. How could common folk learn and live the law, especially now that it was available in the relatively stable collection of Torah, Prophets, and Writings? In the Diaspora, many Jews relied upon the Torah as the symbol of God's presence and the personification of God's wisdom when living at a distance from the temple (e.g., Sirach 24, written before 180 BC in Jerusalem).

Chronic disappointment in the religious-political leaders after the exile spurred abundant criticism and hope for purified leadership expressed in promise e (above). Hope for multifaceted restoration sometimes envisioned a human agent whose job description varied enormously. The array of possibilities illuminates why there was such confusion surrounding Jesus' identity.

God's Agent

Christians often assume that messianic prophecy in the Jewish Scriptures pointed clearly to a single image and person whom most Jews refused to recognize in Jesus of Nazareth. That is not the case. *Messiah/Anointed* was only one of several titles or roles associated with some human helper in God's next act of deliverance. Even the term *messiah* itself carried different connotations. Peter's witness in the Gospels that a messiah must not suffer and die (Mark 8:32–33) is linked to others' expectations that Jesus should be (or was attempting to become) a rival to Herod Antipas or even Caesar. By the Second Temple period, messiah as an anointed one traditionally referred to the king (as adopted son of God) and the high priest.

Reflecting on Jesus' questions about his identity and the responses he received from his followers, it is clear that hope for God's conclusive acts of restoration for Israel embraced more than one model. Jewish texts, including Scripture, exhibit similar variety throughout the Second Temple period. They do not consistently envision that God would engage a human helper. When he does, the titles and roles varied. Twin messiahs were an option, especially during Persian rule, when the grandson of the next-to-last king of Judah, Zerubbabel, was appointed governor of Judah; and a Zadokite, Joshua, held the high priesthood around 520 BC (Zech. 3–4). If one believed the temple to be central to God's presence and restoration, then God's central agent was cast as a high priest. To a certain extent it could be acceptable to have a Gentile overlord as long as temple worship and leadership were left unhindered. It is possible that the Sadducees and elite priestly families viewed Israel's situation in this way under the Romans.

If one were drawn to a preexilic model of kingdom, then a king would fit the bill. This would require opposing both the Herodians and the Romans in violent rebellion. Both those roles (king and priest) were also recognized as anointed. God's agent might be a wise teacher who would embody and expound the Torah, so the covenant would truly be written on people's hearts, as Jeremiah had described (31:31–34). This could extend God's presence even without a change in political regimes.

Revolt was by far the most visible shape to Jewish hope from an outsider's point of view. The Jewish historian Flavius Josephus (ca. AD 38–100) noted a series of troublemakers whose lives and revolts met the same dead end from the death of Herod the Great (4 BC) to the end of the Jewish War (AD 70). Josephus tried hard to lay the blame of the Jewish War on a few unruly malcontents in order to construct an image of generally good citizenship for other Jews, both in Palestine and in the rest of the Roman Empire. Yet it would seem that Jews' underlying hopes for something better from God prompted sporadic support for would-be divine agents of God's vindication. One so-called robber preferred to kill his children, wife, and himself rather than capitulate to Herod the Great, whom he cursed for being of low birth. Herod the Great descended from Idumeans (Edomites) who had been conquered and converted by force under the Hasmoneans. It was not hard for covenant-sensitive Jews to find fault with Herod; he was neither ethnically Jewish nor of the house of David.

Prophets denouncing religious and social conditions, Robin Hood-like brigands seeking justice for the oppressed, would-be kings elevated from the

---

Qumran, on the northwest shore of the Dead Sea, where a library was discovered in 1947. In addition to Scripture, the scrolls included texts that revealed a Jewish sect dedicated to purifying Israel through replacing the temple leadership. They were the "sons of light," led by the "Teacher of Righteousness." They lived apart in prayer and purity, thus to engage in a cosmic struggle against Israel's enemies, "the sons of darkness," both Gentiles and ethnic Jews who had compromised their covenant membership and no longer belonged to true Israel.

people: few opponents of established religious and political leaders were specifically called *messiah*. Yet all seemed to have believed or played upon the existing hopes for a warrior or prophet who would work with and for God's kingdom, against the Gentiles or the powerful who were in league with the Gentiles. Most were considered enemies of the state for threatening order and the rule of the one acclaimed as the ultimate lord and king: Caesar.

Broadly speaking, some Jews saw the Hasmonean priest-kings, the Herodian kings, and the high priests as somehow illegitimate (neither of royal lineage of David nor of the priestly lineage of Zadok). One did not have to go to the extremes evident in the Qumran Scrolls to hope that God would purify the leadership of his people when he accomplished the nation's full salvation. Elsewhere the prophet Malachi, an adamant critic of Second Temple worship and the priesthood even before the Hasmoneans, described the "messenger" who would prepare for God's coming. The messenger would cleanse the corrupt priesthood and is equated with the prophet Elijah (3:1–6, 4:5).

On the other hand, the temple clearly was of central importance for most Jews. Even while hoping for a "cleansing," they continued to trust God's reception of the regular sacrifices and worship offered at the temple regardless of occasionally fallible priests and Levites. The most caustic critiques of the priesthood may have arisen precisely because people cared deeply about the temple.

Since Jesus clearly referred to himself as "Son of Man," the title's traditional resonances must be reviewed. Generally Hebrew Scriptures use this designation to contrast humble humanity with the holy God, such as God's title for the prophet Ezekiel and in Psalm 8:4 (ESV): "What is man that you are mindful of him, and the son of man that you care for him?" (see also Ps. 144:2–4 ESV). Another key to the way Jesus would be understood comes from the imagery of Daniel 7. The book of Daniel was written in the context of threats to Jewish identity under Gentile rule, especially the challenge of Antiochus IV Epiphanes (3rd to 2nd c. BC). Its accounts of righteous resistance at the risk of death in chapters 1–6 show the vindication of potential martyrs. At the climax of each story the Gentile persecutors conclude that the God of Israel is the one, true God. Daniel 7 pictures Israel's vindication after a succession of empires. Then "one like a son of man" (7:13 ESV), also described in the plural as "the holy ones of the Most High" (7:18, 21, 22, 25, 27), arises in the midst of beastly monsters, whom the Ancient of Days destroys. Like the human Adam exercising dominion in the midst of the beasts of creation, God gives his "holy ones" charge over all the other wild kingdoms (7:27).[4] Two collective images are used to communicate Israel as agent of God in this vision: the "son of man" and "holy ones." To both are accorded "kingship" and "dominion" over peoples that will not end (7:14). Jesus' use of the "Son of Man" designation certainly draws upon this imagery, but in ways initially foreign to its original context. Daniel's message offered hope during a crisis for vindication of Israel by God, the Ancient of Days. Jesus used Daniel 7 in a way that pointed to a threat to covenant fidelity arising within Israel rather than externally (see chap. 2).

Interestingly for Christians, suffering, particularly the image of the Suffering Servant in Isaiah 52–53, carried divine-agent overtones only indirectly. The four so-called Servant Songs of Second Isaiah refer sometimes to Israel personified or a prophet of the people. The corporate images (Isa. 42:1–9; 49:1–7; 52:13–53:12) depict an exiled, humiliated servant-nation whom God will exalt and use as a tool of revelation to the Gentile nations. The individual-prophet image (50:4–11) emphasizes the classic suffering of prophets who speak God's word and endure rejection among those they are called to encourage. Even when the Isaiah passages are used to indicate God's expected agent of deliverance (as in the sections of *1 Enoch* from the 1st c. AD), suffering is definitely not part of the package. The servant in *1 Enoch* is depicted in Isaiah's language: a "righteous one" (38.2; 92.3) and "chosen one" (chaps. 39–62), known from before his birth (even before creation itself), opposing the enemies of God's holy ones. Suffering was linked to salvation only insofar as it reflected the condition of the nation while it awaited God's deliverance.

Resurrection

Resurrection imagery and beliefs emerged within the exile and Second Temple Judaism, but not every Jew jumped on the resurrection bandwagon. The Second Temple party of the priestly elite, the Sadducees, maintained the traditional stance that death is the end for the individual and that eternal life consists in the continuation of the family. Nevertheless, prophets used language about God reviving and bringing his people back to life for the purpose of encouraging the exiles that God would be faithful and rescue his people (e.g., Isa. 26:19, corpses will rise; Ezek. 37, the dry bones returned to living people). Rising to the challenge of the Maccabean crisis, Daniel 12 takes the vindication metaphor even farther into a reviving of the dead at judgment, followed by assignment into "everlasting life" or "everlasting contempt" (12:2). Later reflection on the Maccabean Revolt produced a strand of bodily resurrection hope in the mouths of the martyrs (2 Macc. 7). The mother urges her sons to remain faithful to God so that by their faithful death she may receive them back. One brother sneers at Antiochus's tortures because "the King of the universe will raise us up to an everlasting renewal of life, because we have died for his laws" (2 Macc. 7:9). The martyrs submit to having body parts cut off with the hope that the God who made the parts will restore them. The author of 2 Maccabees associated God's vindication of the martyrs with the eventual deliverance of the nation.

While Jews broadly believed in some sort of resurrection of the dead, just what that meant, predictably, could be murky: is it only the soul or spirit? does it include the body? where will the resurrected ones exist? will it be only for righteous individuals or for the whole covenant people? While much contempory Greek philosophy highlighted the innate immortality of the soul, Jewish belief focused upon God as the source of all life, even after death. The shadowy existence of the dead in Sheol or the grave emphasized that life without the body was not true human existence at all. There seemed to be general hope for a final raising of the dead at the end of the age, especially for those who died in defense of covenant fidelity, such as the Maccabees. Whatever its specific shape, resurrection was regarded as a sign of God's vindication of the righteous, and of his covenant people at the end of the age. It was not the same as going to heaven and usually seemed to assume a type of replanting of the people in the land, in paradisaical circumstances (Isa. 27).

CONCLUSIONS: THE SHADES OF HOPE

That God would be faithful to his covenant was the core of Jewish belief. How and what that would look like reflected the variety of emphases within the primary covenant themes deemed most crucial to Israel's past and future identity. The variety that existed in Palestinian Judaism in the first centuries BC/AD gave different priorities to the main themes:

1. National integrity: How would God reassemble and purify Israel? Would the Gentiles be gathered and integrated too?
2. National autonomy: How would God achieve Israel's independence? Who would lead the new Israel (king, priest, both)?
3. Holiness: How would new Israel manifest holiness morally and ritually? What role would the temple have? How would God's presence alter temple, priesthood, kingship, Torah?

Jewish Scripture and the precedent of David's kingdom, as well as the dissatisfaction with the current leadership, lent strength to hopes for a godly king and warrior, a legitimate and faithful high priest, perhaps introduced by a prophet. But ultimately, longing for God's own presence is the most powerful and widespread yearning related in the Second Temple Jewish traditions. There was no standard messianic expectation, but there was fairly uniform desire to have God dwelling among the people as in the exodus and ruling them with or without a human assistant, even with or without conventional war. And when God returned, he would usher in not necessarily the end of the world, but surely a new age in the world he had created.

TIME LINE (BC)

722	Fall of Samaria (capital of northern kingdom, Israel) to Assyria
586	Fall of Jerusalem (capital of southern kingdom, Judah) to Babylon
539	Persians conquer Babylon
539–333	Persian period
538	Cyrus of Persia allows Jews to return and rebuild Jerusalem
333	Hellenistic rule of Judea (Alexander and subsequent rulers) begins
333	Alexander the Great conquers Persia
323	Death of Alexander the Great
167	Seleucid ruler Antiochus IV Epiphanes outlaws Torah practices
167	Maccabean Revolt begins
164	Rededication of the temple (Hanukkah)
140s–63	Independent Hasmonean Judea
63	Roman period begins: Pompey annexes Judea/Palestine

QUESTIONS FOR DISCUSSION

1. How were the exodus experience and the later exile linked in Jewish thought?
2. After the exile, why did Jews in Judea and beyond think that they needed saving? How did Jews expect God to save them?
3. In the Second Temple period, what components were important for identifying Jews as Israel, the covenant people? How did Jews put these together in different ways?
4. What were the competing or overlapping "job descriptions" for the Messiah? How were these related to differing interpretations of covenant fulfillment and Israel's identity?

SUGGESTED FURTHER READING

Fitzmyer, Joseph A. *The One Who Is to Come*. Grand Rapids: Wm. B. Eerdmans Publishing Co., 2007.

Grabbe, Lester L. *Judaic Religion in the Second Temple Period: Belief and Practice from the Exile to Yavneh*. New York: Routledge, 2000.

Sanders, E. P. *Judaism: Practice and Belief, 63 B.C.E.–55 C.E.* London: SCM Press, 1992.

Stegemann, Ekkehard W., and Wolfgang Stegemann. *The Jesus Movement: A Social History of Its First Century*. Translated by O. C. Dean. Minneapolis: Fortress Press, 1999.

Wright, N. T. *The New Testament and the People of God*. Vol. 1 of *Christian Origins and the Question of God*. Minneapolis: Fortress Press, 1992.

2

"Are You the One Who Is to Come?"

(Matt. 11:3)

Jesus of Nazareth lived and preached good news out of elements common to Jewish hope but in a shape often as hard to recognize by fellow Jews as Jesus was after his resurrection. Ancient hopes made the people wonder: Is Jesus the one through whom God will regather, purify, and vindicate Israel? Will Jesus sit on the throne of David after kicking out the Romans? Will Jesus usher in the new age of God's presence among us, holding the Gentiles subject to us, for a change?

This chapter examines Jesus' quirky messiahship and the "good news" (or gospel) in the New Testament. Many hailed Jesus as the Messiah, the "one to redeem Israel" (Luke 24:21), even before his death. The Gospels show how at every turn specific expectations about the people, their nationhood, and God's activity underwent significant revisions. Temple and Torah were replaced or probed for a deeper meaning in Jesus. Regathering had less to do with the geographically scattered Israel than with those spiritually lost and straying from God the Father. Speculation about the kingdom and the promised land solidified into the experience of a community detached from a specific geography or ethnicity but directly attached to Jesus. The rest of the New Testament builds upon interpretive insights that came not merely from Jesus' teaching, but also from his actions, especially his troubling death and resurrection.

Before jumping in, it is worth knowing some technical details about "good news." The Gospels are the books in the Christian Bible that describe the life of Jesus as "good news." The word *gospel* comes from an Old English translation (*god-spel*) of the Greek *eu-angelion* for "good news." Scholars have studied the many similarities found in the Gospels of Matthew, Mark, and Luke. These three are called "Synoptic" Gospels because one can easily "look"

(Greek root *opt-*) at them "with" (Greek preposition *syn-*) each other. Mark is assumed to be the earliest Gospel (ca. AD 65–75), whose order and material were followed by Matthew and Luke (ca. 80–95). Material that Matthew and Luke share, but is not in Mark, has been called "Q" (German *Quelle*, source). The source Q is a hypothetical document to explain the shared material in Matthew and Luke. Finally, scholars have generally agreed that the Gospel of John was the last of the four, around 90–100. It has much material independent of the Synoptics and is characterized by long discourses following seven pivotal signs. Later works not used regularly within Christian worship took the "gospel" title for reflections on Jesus. Some of these noncanonical works will be addressed in part 2.

PRO: WHY LINK JESUS TO MESSIAH?

The Gospels (especially the Synoptics: Matthew, Mark, and Luke) retain the flavor of surprise, discovery, and dispute experienced by the first witnesses to Jesus: Jews who were awaiting God's reign over Israel. Although committed to their present form thirty to sixty years after Jesus' death, the Gospels open a door to the way Jews began to think as "Christians." They relay a good bit about the uneasy transition from multiple expectations about God's next move in the covenant story to the specific fulfillment offered by and in Jesus.

What did people see in Jesus that prompted speculation about God's new age and Jesus' potential role as the Messiah? The Gospels show that Jesus aroused hope because his "good news" (gospel) accorded with many traditional signs of God's gracious presence. Interestingly, the very things suggesting that Jesus was indeed God's Messiah also alienated others whose vision of covenant fulfillment emphasized similar elements in different ways. We will examine the disputed points after reviewing evidence in favor of Jesus' role as agent of God's deliverance: prophet and teacher.

Prophet

After the clear announcement "The beginning of the good news of Jesus Christ, the Son of God," the Gospel of Mark quotes representative hopes in the prophets Isaiah and Malachi that in turn incorporate exodus imagery of a path through the wilderness. The good news is "God is coming! His messenger is here! Get ready!" Jews hearing this message could situate it within the range of covenant hopes described in chapter 1 (above). Getting ready included what the new prophet, John the Baptist, was preaching: repentance from sins, which still interfered with God's full and glorious return to Israel.

Rather than depending on the right Abrahamic genes, John reprised the classic theme of prophecy. Salvation requires "turning back" to God by sharing with the needy and by doing one's job honestly and justly (Luke 3:10–14). Jesus' preaching carried on the call: "Now after John was arrested, Jesus came to Galilee, proclaiming the good news of God, and saying, 'The time is fulfilled, and the kingdom of God has come near; repent, and believe in the good news'" (Mark 1:14–15).

THE PHARISEES

Ancient references to Pharisees (Josephus, New Testament, rabbinic writings beginning in the 3rd c. AD) highlight their care for oral traditions in addition to torah ("tradition of the elders") and their attempts to apply torah prescriptions of cultic purity for the temple to as much of daily life as possible. Thus table fellowship, food preparation, family relations, and avoidance of pollution in social contacts typify their concerns. Pharisees shared the popular Jewish belief in resurrection and final judgment. Disputes in the Gospels, as well as the apostle Paul's particularly "zealous" (Gal. 1:14; Phil. 3:6) example of Pharisaism, point to variations among Pharisees themselves.

When Jesus went public, crowds sensed a great prophet whose critiques of the religious authorities, attention to religious outcasts, and healing miracles were enormously attractive. Who would not enjoy hearing Jesus dress down fussy Pharisees as whitewashed tombs, externally clean and tidy while internally polluted by stinginess (Matt. 23:27; Luke 11:39–41)? Just like the prophetic rabble-rousers of old, Jesus spoke harsh truths to leaders, warning them that their supposed devotion to God was instead a covert attempt to manipulate God. Just like the classic prophets, Jesus found himself on the wrong side of the powerful, who threatened his life. When Jesus defended his mingling with "sinners," he explained his actions as a physician reaching out to the sick or a prophet recalling sinners to righteousness. Jesus pointed out the ironic reality that those who considered themselves healthy and righteous had blinded themselves to their own neediness before God. In the tradition of Israel's ancient prophets, Jesus cried "woe" against those who used knowledge of God's law to keep righteousness and power to themselves rather than to open the way of righteousness to the whole nation (Matt. 23:1–36). Such a stunning and hypocritical failure of righteousness mirrored Judah's and Israel's leaders at the cusp of the exile, as lamented by Isaiah and Jeremiah: all used their positions for their own benefit rather than to lead the people to God (woes; Isa. 5:8–23; 9:16; Jer. 2:8).

A lot of people felt themselves to be "sitting in darkness" of illness, deformity, impurity, sin, and death (see Luke 1:79). To them Jesus announced his fulfillment of Isaiah's promise "to bring good news to the poor" and "to proclaim release to the captives and recovery of sight to the blind, to let the oppressed go free, to proclaim the year of the Lord's favor" (Luke 4:18–19, quoting from Isa. 61:1–2; 58:6). Matthew presents a threefold shape to Jesus' good-news ministry: teaching in synagogues, proclaiming God's kingdom, and healing. Jesus supported his oral presentation of the good news with concrete acts of deliverance for those "afflicted with various diseases and pains, demoniacs, epileptics, and paralytics" (4:24). Crowds "praised the God of Israel" (Matt. 15:31) in wonder at Jesus' compassion and deeds of power. Surely the God of the covenant, who rescued lowly Israel from Egypt, was in their midst once again through Jesus the prophet.

Teacher

All the Gospels agree that close followers, crowds, and antagonistic religious authorities alike understood Jesus to be a teacher. Inquirers engaged Jesus as "teacher" or "rabbi" more often than in any other role. In his encounters with religious leaders, Jesus always is a teacher to the teachers. The Gospel of Luke indicates this role beginning with Jesus' first visit to the temple when he went AWOL from his parents as a twelve-year-old in order to engage teachers "in [his] Father's house" (Luke 2:41–50). His authority in speaking and acting astounded (or infuriated) his audiences. Out of surprise people often extrapolated that he was something more than a teacher of Israel. Some connected him with wisdom figures like King Solomon or the wise lawgiver Moses, but the wisdom that the Gospel memories recall show Jesus steering Israel's law and lifestyle in distinctive and often controversial ways.

Crowds remembered his confrontations with authoritative teachers of the law where Jesus' ingenuity discomfited his interrogators. In the mode of classic prophets, Jesus refused to water down obedience to the law, and thereby covenant fidelity, to mere scorecard-keeping. This prophet-teacher repeated God's perennial critique that scrupulosity in details "neglect[s] the weightier matters of the law: justice and mercy and faith" (Matt. 23:23). Jesus refused to lighten the requirement of righteousness; he challenged covenant righteousness to spring from an interior commitment to God through the law. The Gospel of Matthew associates Jesus with teaching the law on a mountain, like Moses (Matthew's Sermon on the Mount). Curiously Jesus claimed his own authority for interpreting the law in a series of statements that begin, "You have heard that it was said, . . . but I say to you" (Matt. 5:21–48). Jesus could use the undisputed importance of observing the Sabbath as central to covenant fidelity in order to lead others to consider how best to honor God. Does a true Israelite honor the Sabbath through "resting" from all activity, or by prioritizing the preservation of life (healing, snacking on field grain), which God created before the initial Sabbath? As an accomplished teacher, Jesus pressed Jews to consider more deeply what was at stake in "turning back to God" through the requirements of torah: seeking and doing the will of God.

Though Jesus accepted titles of teacher and prophet in the Synoptic Gospels, he utterly rejected attempts by others to pin *messiah* on him. Demons proclaimed the truth about Jesus, and disciples might glimpse it, but Jesus hushed them all. On this point, the hopes of many for Israel's salvation foundered in confusion. Doubts raised about the legitimacy of Jesus as a teacher and prophet were exacerbated when Jesus refused to be the Messiah so many wanted him to be.

CON: JESUS AS A FAILED MESSIAH

Jesus Cannot Be a Prophet-Teacher from God

Jesus the prophet seemed too good to be true. Religious authorities, claiming their role in protecting the people from being misled, were wary about Jesus' self-referential teachings. Certainly Elijah and Elisha, great wonder-working prophets of old, had healed and even raised the dead. However, these men in whom God worked so powerfully never tried to forgive sins as well. Torah laid out covenant loyalty and lifestyle; temple priests mediated forgiveness of sins from God. A Moses or Abraham might argue with God to have mercy on those deserving destruction, but no human could forgive sins apart from the temple institution and torah instruction. Yet Jesus casually forgave sins and healed, flippantly challenging his opponents: "Which is easier, to say to the paralytic, 'Your sins are forgiven,' or to say, 'Stand up and take your mat and walk'?" (Mark 2:9). For the "Son of Man," Jesus announced, "has authority on earth to forgive sins" (2:10).

There were enough concerns over Jesus' orthodoxy to warrant doubt as to the source of his amazing powers. This so-called teacher healed on the Sabbath, apparently to make the religious authorities look bad before the common people. Ordinary acts of piety, such as fasting, had little place in the life of Jesus. Jesus himself recognized his reputation as a party boy, but he observed that strict piety would not have won him acceptance either: "For John [the Baptist] came neither eating nor drinking, and they say, 'He has a demon'; the Son of Man came eating and drinking, and they say, 'Look, a glutton and a drunkard, a friend of tax collectors and sinners!'" (Matt. 11:18–19). Yet the doubters had a point: if Jesus really were from God, would he not rather manifest the greatest combination of interior and exterior holiness expected by torah?

Nowhere did ambivalence about Jesus agitate leaders more than his relationship with the temple. Although observant in some ways, Jesus had no qualms about bypassing the temple altogether. At times Jesus healed and forgave sins without also referring the individual to the normal mediator of God's forgiveness, the temple (and its priests). Jesus was also regarded by many to be a direct source of purity. He easily engaged uncleanness as something he himself dispelled with no contagion to himself. Sinners, Samaritans, Gentiles, lepers, a bleeding woman, demons, and the dead—nothing bothered Jesus, though it did upset others. Torah is exceedingly clear about honoring God through attention to purity, which was necessary for participation in temple worship and thus for drawing near to God. Practically speaking, one who lived as though the temple were extraneous threatened the central economy of Jerusalem and the stability of its leadership.

Establishing Jesus' source of authority then became a priority since it pointed, for better or worse, toward a nonhuman origin. Jesus' control over demons led to suspicions that the lord of demons was using Jesus as a ruse to draw the people from God, impersonating the coming "son of David" (Matt. 12:22–24). Near the end of his ministry, religious authorities directly asked Jesus to state the nature of his authority. In shock over Jesus' interference with normal temple practice during the busy season preceding the Passover, angry officials demanded to know how and why Jesus cleared out the merchants who provided the animals necessary for the people's gifts and sacrifices to God (Matt. 21:12–16; Mark 11:15–18; Luke 19:45–48). Furthermore, too many people remembered Jesus' announcing the destruction of the temple for temple authorities to ignore this incident (Mark 13:2; Luke 21:6). Jesus' intentions toward the temple became the central issue investigated by the authorities who arrested and tried Jesus. Obviously a messiah who threatened the temple was inconceivable. Only Gentiles and the forces of evil would do that.

Jesus Cannot Be the King-Messiah

Jesus' unique, authoritative presence as a teacher of the law and as a prophet in word and deed led observers toward another conclusion: God's warrior-king Messiah. By the Roman period many Jews, like Zechariah, longed for God to raise "up a mighty savior" from David's royal line to "give light to those who sit in darkness and the shadow of death" (Luke 1:68–79). On the popular level many Jews hoped for a glorious national kingdom, headed by a descendant of David. They chafed until the time when they could worship at the temple without Roman troops polluting the sacred temple courts with their unclean Gentile eyes as they peered down from the adjacent Antonia fortress. The historian Josephus recorded a riot that broke out after a soldier "mooned" the worshipers below (*Wars* 2.12). Most Jews took satisfaction in a scenario where Gentiles were destined to judgment by Israel and its God.

From John the Baptist, to the cross-examining high priest, everybody was asking Jesus, "Are you the Messiah/Christ?" All were rather sure of what the Messiah should be doing, and Jesus did not seem to be doing it. Fiery John the Baptist kept looking for signs that Jesus was gearing up for the great day of the Lord's wrath, where true and false Israel would be clearly demarcated and the latter "burn[ed] with unquenchable fire" (Matt. 3:12). Imprisoned by Herod, John sent a dispirited question via his disciples to Jesus: "Are you the one who is to come, or are we to wait for another?" (Matt. 11:3). Elsewhere the Gospel of John reports that Jesus had to run away from the feeding of the five thousand because the crowd started to surmise that not only was Jesus "the prophet who is to come into the world," but also that they should "take him by force to make him king" (John 6:14–15).

The disciples had their own view of Jesus the Messiah and eagerly awaited his public announcement of the fact. Sure, Jesus said strange things about "taking up your cross" to follow him, but the disciples (through Simon, nick-named Peter/Rock) were all ready to set Jesus straight about a nonsuffering messiah (Matt. 16:13–28; Mark 8:27–38; Luke 9:18–27) who would lead his chosen followers to thrones of power and judgment (Matt. 19:28, Luke 22:30; seats of honor for James and John: Matt. 20:20–23; Mark 10:35–40). What really unsettled them was Jesus' outraged rebuke that such a royal, warrior image of the Messiah emerged not from the God of the covenant, but from Satan and the powers of evil. They fell into despair when Jesus was arrested and crucified, having lost all hope that he could be "the one to redeem Israel" (Luke 24:21).

Just before Jesus was crucified, a jubilant crowd shouted, "Hosanna! . . . Blessed is the coming kingdom of our ancestor David!" at his entry into Jeru-salem (Mark 11:9–11). Entranced, they trailed him to the temple, perhaps to see whether this "Son of David" would finally announce his rule over the kingdom. Likely they were as surprised as the temple authorities, though not as offended: instead of proclaiming himself king, Jesus threw out the money changers and merchants of sacrificial animals (Matt. 21:12–16; Mark 11:15–18; Luke 19:45–48). By the end of the week, Jewish leaders were rid of a theo-logical and political threat. They could feel vindicated at witnessing yet one more false king-messiah revealed and removed. A dead messiah was no mes-siah at all for Jesus' friends or enemies. The promised land continued under Roman rule; the people remained scattered; God seemed no more present among the people than before Jesus' career.

A NEW VIEW: GOD'S MESSIAH JESUS

Let us examine how the earliest Christians came to call Jesus the Messiah by looking at both God's story and Jesus' mission with vision corrected by the cross and resurrection. As important as covenant traditions were to Jesus' brand of the good news, he nevertheless dared to occupy a role in the good news that challenged accepted ways of being in covenant with YHWH. For many, the good news ceased to be good, and to be of God, when Jesus placed himself at the heart of the covenant relationship with God. "And blessed is anyone who takes no offense at me," says Jesus (Matt. 11:6). Some certainly did take offense at both Jesus and those who would follow him. The disciples struggled with the possibility that God would put "messiah" and "cross" together. Jesus' response is unequivocal: be embarrassed at my way, the way of the cross, and you will find yourself left out of the kingdom: "Those who are ashamed of me and of my words, of them the Son of Man will be ashamed when he comes in his glory and the glory of the Father and of the holy angels" (Luke 9:26). The identity of the people of God is their response to the good news. The covenant challenge to choose life over death, the God of Israel over other gods in the wake of the exodus (Deut. 30:11–20), is transformed into choosing not merely Jesus' message, but especially Jesus himself.

Perspectives Before and After the Resurrection

There are two trajectories for examining the way the earliest believers wrestled with their responses to Jesus as depicted in the Gospels. First, given that the earliest believers were Jews, we have looked at Jesus from the perspective of actions and conditions associated with God's past faithfulness to the covenant. Jesus presented a mixed message in his life and in his death as Prophet, Teacher of the law, and King-Messiah. The second trajectory involved a massive reevaluation of Israel's story and Israel's God among those who accepted that Jesus was the long-expected act of God. This perspective takes Jesus, including his death and resurrection, as the starting point for

> *"In accordance with the scriptures"* (1 Cor. 15:3) became a standard phrase among early Christians to underline their basic belief that Jesus as the suffering and dying Messiah was actually part of God's plan throughout covenant history. This usage parallels the Gospel citations of Jewish Scripture, which Jesus "fulfilled." "Scriptures" assumes the Jewish holy writings.

reading a new shape onto the past and future, which we will see in part in the Gospels, but even more in the Letters of Paul. Looking back, Christians discerned how Jesus is the Christ "in accordance with the scriptures," where the story of God and Israel were preserved. Looking ahead, the Christ opened new possibilities for being the people of God.

The Synoptic Gospels take the first perspective in telling the story of Jesus as a mystery that is understood only after the crucifixion. Jesus is a puzzle in the Synoptics because he does not quite fit the expectations by which all stripes of Jews tried to understand him. The disciples are in the same boat with Jesus' opponents: they do not understand. The elements of hope that Jesus embodies combine in ways previously unnoticed. Jesus constantly warns people and demons not to tell anyone who he is or what signs he has accomplished. In part he seems anxious to keep a lid on news of his messianic ministry that might be taken to rival Herod's kingship (not wanting to lose his head, like John the Baptist) or the temple leadership. It may also be an attempt to keep unreliable witnesses from adding to the knots of confusion that Jesus is trying to untangle.

Confident of God as revealed in Jesus, the Word of God, the Gospel of John and the rest of the New Testament writings present Jesus entirely from the perspective of Easter. Insiders in the Gospel of John, like Nathanael, already recognize Jesus to be "the Son of God!" and "King of Israel!" (1:49). They already benefit from accepting Jesus' transformation of God's story with Israel: becoming friends of Jesus (John 15:14–16), children of God (1:12; 11:52), and children of light (12:36)—even as they still struggle in a world that rejects Jesus and his followers. In contrast, outsiders struggle, sometimes tragicomically, with Jesus' identity and message. Think of Nicodemus, obtusely asking about how one might crawl into his mother's womb to be reborn (3:4); or the Samaritan woman, challenging Jesus to get "living" water from a well without a bucket (4:11–15).

Death and Resurrection Reveal Jesus at the Center

The Gospels make clear that only with his death and resurrection did Jesus' centrality begin to make sense. The events from Jesus' final visit to Jerusalem to his death and resurrection comprise the longest continuous narrative unit in each of the Gospels and provide the basis for reevaluating both Israel's and Jesus' own prior story. In the Synoptic Gospels, variety and confusion in viewing God's covenant faithfulness to Israel give way to a new clarity so that Messiah can be rightly understood in Jesus. Indeed, the Gospel of Luke shows Jesus' calling himself Messiah only after his followers have witnessed his death. Only then can he walk them through the Scriptures to understand that "the Messiah should suffer these things and then enter into his glory" (Luke 24:26; see also 24:46).

The Gospel of John illustrates this transformation by means of reflective recollection. After the resurrection as the disciples "remember" various incidents or words that previously left them confused, they find insights within Scripture as to the true meaning of Jesus' words and actions. When Jesus drove animals and money changers from the temple area, "His disciples remembered that it was written, 'Zeal for your house will consume me'" (John 2:17; see Ps. 69:9). Likewise, Jesus' claim that he would raise up the destroyed temple in three days made sense when they could link the temple with Jesus himself. "But he was speaking of the temple of his body. After he was raised from the dead, his disciples remembered that he had said this; and they believed the scripture and the word that Jesus had spoken" (2:21–22). This same process occurs with the entry into Jerusalem before Jesus' death (12:16) and the empty tomb (20:9). Furthermore Jesus is shown warning the disciples that they will not understand what he is doing right away when he washed the disciples' feet (13:7) and prepared them for persecution and the coming of the Holy Spirit (16:4). Through this remembrance motif, the Gospel of John underscores that knowing Jesus requires living through the climax of his death and resurrection.

Resurrection set the stage for mission rather than a self-satisfied rumination on the good things coming to the beleaguered faithful or the thrones of judgment promised to the Twelve. In the Gospels of Matthew, Luke, and John, Jesus' resurrection begins the age of Israel's proclamation that Jesus really is the "light for revelation to the Gentiles and for glory to [God's] people Israel" (Luke 2:32). Even in the breathless flight of the women at the empty tomb, with which the Gospel of Mark originally ended, the command is to "go, tell" (16:7–8). The empty tomb marvelously initiates a new open-ended story of going and telling in contrast to the earlier commands to "tell no one."

Formerly confusing, distressing, or insignificant incidents and teachings take on new or deeper significance after the disciples are reunited with the resurrected Jesus. Inklings of Jesus' identity become the confident proclamations that introduce the Gospels: Jesus the Messiah/Christ, Son of God, the Word who is God. Memory of his story and experience of his abiding presence allow later followers to find new meaning and applications for Scripture in new circumstances that yet remain "in accordance with the scriptures," that is, in harmony with the story of God's salvation in Israel's Scriptures.

RE-VIEWING THE COVENANT: JESUS MESSIAH IN THE GOSPELS

More Than a Prophet or King

The gut reaction of those who perceived a unique authority in Jesus as prophet and teacher and king proved correct, even if their picture of these roles needed refining. In the wake of the resurrection, early Christians believed that Jesus was a prophet, but even more that he was the author and the fulfillment of all Scripture. When Jesus revealed his divine glory to Peter, James, and John, the whole of Scripture in the persons of Moses and Elijah bore witness to their support of and subordination to the transfigured Jesus as he was acclaimed to be God's Son (Matt. 17:1–9; Mark 9:2–10; Luke 9:28–36). Before the resurrection, Jesus counseled the disciples to keep this to themselves; but after the resurrection, the disciples could incorporate this into their overall reinterpretation of Scripture and Israel's story that Jesus himself initiated.

In Matthew, the longed-for Davidic king and the promised new Moses (Deut. 18:15–19) combine in Jesus only to be surpassed by him. In five discourses, reflecting Moses' five farewell speeches in Deuteronomy, Jesus is shown to have the God-given authority to correct and intensify the law, rather than merely to teach it. He is torah itself. The magi search him out as the king of the Jews, but demonstrate by their own worship that his kingship exceeds the geographical and ethnic bounds of David's kingdom. Jesus is of the line of David, but he rules as King of the Universe, who will sit in judgment over all nations (Matt. 25:31–46). Jesus' good news of Israel's restoration by its faithful God was aimed at Israel's repentance and reformation, not against Rome or any other Gentile overlord. God's rule and Jesus' kingship would be magnified beyond anything that people had experienced, even during David's reign. When Jesus discoursed about his messiahship (understood as "king" by Roman authorities) with Pontius Pilate, the Gospel of John shows him at pains to distinguish God's rule, which exists on the plane of truth, where geographical boundaries and fighting forces are irrelevant (John 18:33–38). Jesus' authority originates outside of this world, even as his rule encompasses this world.

God's Mighty Savior of the Covenant

Luke frames the good news in the extravagant outpouring of the Spirit that signals God's kingdom or reign. As in a Broadway musical, figures keep breaking into song, glorifying the God of Israel (Zechariah, Elizabeth, Mary, angels, Simeon). Even before Jesus is born, the prophetic songs insist that God is already saving Israel in his current baby-making acts (i.e., the miraculous pregnancies of aged Elizabeth and the virgin Mary). Take, for example, the way the old priest Zechariah celebrates the birth of his son John the Baptist:

> [68]Blessed be the Lord God of Israel,
>   for he has looked favorably on his people and redeemed them.
> [69]He has raised up a mighty savior for us
>   in the house of his servant David,

⁷⁰as he spoke through the mouth of his holy prophets from of old,
  ⁷¹that we would be saved from our enemies and from the hand of all
    who hate us.
⁷²Thus he has shown the mercy promised to our ancestors,
  and has remembered his holy covenant,
⁷³the oath that he swore to our ancestor Abraham,
  to grant us ⁷⁴that we, being rescued from the hands of our enemies,
might serve him without fear, ⁷⁵in holiness and righteousness
  before him all our days.
⁷⁶And you, child, will be called the prophet of the Most High;
  for you will go before the Lord to prepare his ways,
⁷⁷to give knowledge of salvation to his people
  by the forgiveness of their sins.
⁷⁸By the tender mercy of our God,
  the dawn from on high will break upon us,
⁷⁹to give light to those who sit in darkness and in the shadow of death,
  to guide our feet into the way of peace.

(Luke 1:68–79)

This is a Christian text. But read in relation to the Jewish covenant, this familiar text might seem odd in its depiction of salvation and hope. Salvation focuses upon the restoration of the covenant nation of Israel (v. 68), the descendants of Abraham (vv. 72–73). Rescue envisions the ability to worship freely, to live righteously and without fear of interference from enemies (vv. 71, 74–75). This will be accomplished by a divine agent, a savior from the royal family of David, as announced by Prophets (Scripture), and a new prophet (the baby John). The exilic lament that the captive people still "sit in darkness" (v. 79; see Ps. 107:10; Isa. 9:2; 42:7) gives way to hope of a new dawn of restoration. Salvation (v. 77) is the sign of forgiveness; it is God's public announcement ("knowledge") both to the children of Abraham and to the enemies from whom Israel has been redeemed.

The three broad themes of covenant hope are addressed here. National integrity will be restored when God keeps his promise to Abraham and his descendants to save the people as a whole. Gentiles would seem the most likely identity of enemies whom God will prevent from interfering with worship until Jesus' trial proved otherwise. National autonomy is in the works because God has already raised a savior as heir to David. This carries potentially political implications of a restored kingdom. Finally, God's merciful actions will produce a people who may live righteously and in peace with God in their midst, without threat to torah practice or temple worship. The people's holiness and God's presence complete covenant fulfillment.

Such a vision of covenant hope leaves out whether a massive emigration to the geographic land of Israel is expected and what specific role the temple or torah might play in the people's fearless worship and holy living (vv. 74–75).

Nonetheless, Zechariah's song reflects the conclusions of early Christians, who were convinced that God's long-awaited covenant salvation had come in Jesus.

Jesus as Vindicated Israel

Looking back over Jesus' career from the perspective of the resurrection, believers could point to God's vindication of Israel in Jesus. Israel was essentially represented in the single person of Jesus, who succeeded in covenant fidelity on the very points where Israel failed at the beginning of its wilderness journey.

The threefold testing in the wilderness at the outset of Jesus' ministry set the stage for understanding Israel as personified in Jesus (Matt. 4:1–11; Luke 4:1–13). The Israelites regularly complained that God was not providing for their physical needs; Jesus refused to make bread out of stones. The Israelites suffered from chronic memory loss at God's miraculous acts of salvation; Jesus refused to ask God to prove his power. After leaving Egypt, Israelites bowed down to a golden calf; Jesus refused to bow to Satan. Each of Jesus' answers was drawn from Deuteronomy (6:13, 16; 8:3) where Moses challenged the people to be faithful to their faithful God. They were not faithful, but Jesus was.

At the conclusion of Jesus' life, his trial before Caiaphas the high priest reveals the fatal differences in vision about God's salvation of true Israel. Jesus' alleged bid to destroy the temple and replace it with one "not made with hands" takes center stage (Mark 14:58). The high priest immediately demands, "Are you the Messiah, the Son of the Blessed One?" (14:61). The Gospel of Mark shows Jesus baldly accepting the titles for the very first time. Jesus' audacious reply (14:62) connects him as "Son of Man" (from Dan. 7:13), who is the true Israel. His future position "at the right hand of the Power [i.e., God]" (see Ps. 110:1, a royal psalm) will be to judge Israel's enemies. Jesus aligns himself with the vindicated Son of Man, Israel personified and shrunk to Jesus alone. God will appoint him to command angels to regather his people "from the ends of the earth to the ends of heaven" (Mark 13:26–27). Early Christians viewed Jesus' resurrection to be God's vindication, proving Jesus truthful and revealing his opponents as Israel's enemies.[1] Tragically, many of Israel's leaders and caretakers would not share in Israel's vindication because they had set themselves against God's kingdom. With the hindsight of the resurrection, believers understood better why Jesus spoke bluntly about the end of the temple as a means of relating the nation to God. Jesus now stood at the center of God's salvation, fulfilling Israel's covenant duties and, through rising from the dead, leading the way for others.

YHWH Dwells with Israel Again

With Jesus' disturbing death and resurrection firmly in sight, the Gospel of John goes back to the very beginning, to look for the Messiah with the corrective lenses of Jesus' life, death, and resurrection. The connection with Israel's story is rich. Echoing the majestic creation story of Genesis, this Gospel starts "in the beginning," with creation brought into being by God the Word. This moving prologue (John 1:1–8) clearly sets forth how the God of creation, the God of Moses, comes to creation in the Word. Jesus, the Word of God, is himself God's faithful revelation and presence. God the Word-made-flesh "pitched a tent with us" (1:14, my trans.) just as he camped with Israel in the mobile temple of the tabernacle. The Word is and reveals the "glory" of God, using the same Greek term that the Septuagint (Greek translation of Hebrew Scripture; see chap. 5) used for God's presence in the temple, the tabernacle, and Moses' face-to-face meeting with God on Mount Sinai. Unlike the unbearable divine glory reflected on Moses' face, the Gospel proclaims, "We have seen his glory" in the Word, the Son of God (1:14–18). Furthermore, John claims that "the law indeed was given through Moses; *grace and truth* came through Jesus Christ" (1:17, emphasis added), who alone knows and has come from God the Father. This too reflects the Septuagint's terminology for God's merciful covenant love and his trustworthiness. The Gospel of John plainly understands Jesus to replace the temple in his person (2:19–22) and makes this an interpretive key for other passages where Jesus is shown to be the definitive place to encounter God (e.g., 4:23; 14:20). The Gospel of John leaves no doubt: in Jesus one encounters YHWH. This being the case, then God has truly fulfilled his promise to dwell intimately with his people. God's renewed presence indicates that Israel's "sins" have been forgiven and that the Messiah has ushered in a new age in the covenant.

Regathering the People of God

The question of who comprised the kingdom of God directly challenged popular images of physically herding all Israelites back to Judea. Hope for national return in Jesus' ministry shifted to stress on rescuing the lost.

Jesus as the instrument of God's regathering focuses upon the vulnerable poor of the Law and Prophets: the blind, the lame, the deaf, widows, and Gentiles (aliens). Among those of "lost" or "outsider" status were Gentiles (Canaanite woman, Roman centurion, the Gentile from whom a "Legion" of unclean spirits were expelled), children (Jairus's daughter), women (Samaritan woman at the well, woman with a bleeding disorder). More remarkable yet were his interactions with uncleanness: lepers, tax collectors, and the dead.

Jesus reached out to those who knew they could make no claim to be among the pure or righteous of Israel. All these cases illustrate Jesus' insistence that becoming like a child (Matt. 18:1–6) or a slave (Mark 10:44 NASB) or a sheep (Luke 15:4–6)—thus recognizing one's own littleness and propensity for getting lost—are far more important to one's membership in the kingdom of God than a genetic connection to Abraham.

Some of Jesus' most challenging stories drew a picture meant to warn current leaders that their place in the kingdom truly was fragile. Membership in Jesus' version of the people of God jarred the sensibilities of other existing images of the true Israel. There was his parable about the younger son who insulted his father, sold his share of the family property, idled away his inheritance among Gentiles, and became an unclean swineherd. The sinner is reinstated as an honored member of the Father's house (understood as the family of God) while the respectable, stay-at-home elder son's position is left in doubt (Luke 15:11–32). This offended the audience ("the Pharisees and the scribes") of the three Lost-Found parables (Luke 15). They disagreed with Jesus' representation of God's deliverance as a search-and-rescue mission geared toward the worthless folk with whom Jesus fraternized ("tax collectors and sinners," v. 1). Jesus scandalously suggested that the stay-at-home brother (the leadership) had fallen into the role of ethnic but not observant Jews, virtually Samaritans. Meanwhile the sinner brother (true Israel) returned from exile among the Gentiles to a celebratory banquet as a full member of the Father's household again.[2]

Jesus' parable of the vineyard and the tenants is even more inflammatory. While attitudes toward Jesus are at stake, the parable targets the tenants: Israel's caretakers. Recall that the vine itself is Israel. Just as leaders of old mistreated God's prophets, so it is with Jesus, the murdered son of the landlord. The vine is not destroyed (as in Isa. 5), but the tenants are. Within the passage (related almost verbatim in all the Synoptic Gospels: Matt. 21:33–46; Mark 12:1–12; Luke 20:9–19), this is clearly a strike against the "chief priests, the scribes, and the elders" (Mark 11:27; 12:12). Jesus had been arguing about the nature of his authority following his entry into Jerusalem and driving the merchants from the temple. Readers of the Gospels, knowing at last who Jesus is, sadly understood that Israel's leadership failed to prepare the people for God's presence and thus could not welcome the kingdom announced in Jesus.[3] This kingdom, depicted as banquet, will consist of those who respond to God's invitation, a motley population, dragged from the streets and unable to repay their host's kindness (Matt. 22:1–10; Luke 14:12–24). Those who could have been most prepared to recognize God at work instead risked missing out on the kingdom by failing to embrace it in Jesus.

RE-VIEWING CHRIST AND COVENANT
BEYOND THE GOSPELS

Despite being committed to writing after years of telling stories about Jesus, the Gospels open a fascinating window into the challenges of reevaluating the story of God and Israel amid the variety of hopes cherished in the Second Temple period. Writings beyond the Gospels, mostly letters of encouragement and troubleshooting, help us observe how first-generation Christians re-viewed Israel's story and the covenant in light of Jesus, the crucified and risen Lord. The earliest Christian writings are the apostle Paul's Letters (from ca. AD 50–62). His unsought experience with the resurrected Jesus had a profound impact upon his way of thinking about being a Jew and about God's plans for Israel and the world. In a way, Paul claimed that there is no Israel without Jesus the Christ. With Paul one can observe the adjustment from a life conformed by one radical view of God's story (the Pharisees) to a life conformed to God's story in Jesus the Christ, crucified and raised.

PAUL'S LETTERS

Many scholars limit Paul's authorship to the letters directed toward the Christians at Rome, Corinth, Galatia, Philippi, and Thessalonica. For this book's purpose, which is to consider what early Christians thought, we will take as a whole the dossier of Letters to seven congregations, which traveled together by the beginning of the second century. This collection includes those listed above together with Letters to Ephesus and Colossae (including Philemon).

Paul and the Christ

Self-described as a rabid traditionalist, Paul went on the offensive against followers of the dead Jesus within three years after the crucifixion. Something happened. Paul's Letters describe his meeting with the risen Jesus as a vision or revelation. Whatever happened became the basis of his authority and irrevocably changed his mind about Jesus, about what a Christ is and who the people of God are. "Christ" in Paul's Letters is no longer a job description; it is a name for the resurrected Jesus.

Paul called his primary message "gospel." Unlike the Gospels, which are at pains to show the connection between the covenantal good news and Jesus himself, Paul's "gospel" is clearly about Jesus. In his earliest letter to the Thessalonians (ca. 51), Paul assumes that his audience is already familiar with

PAUL AND THE PHARISEES

Paul may represent an extreme position that advocated making the land of Israel into temple by means of the covenant people personally observing cultic purity. Certainly Paul's depiction of his pre-Christian life focused upon how distinctive the covenant people should be, even while setting himself apart from covenant people who failed to be properly distinctive.

the gospel: "We believe that Jesus died and rose again" (1 Thess. 4:14). Introducing himself to the Jesus-believers in Rome (ca. 57), he again summarizes the "gospel of God" "concerning his Son, who was descended from David according to the flesh and was declared to be Son of God with power according to the spirit of holiness by resurrection from the dead, Jesus Christ our Lord" (Rom. 1:1, 3–4). A widely recognizable pattern of thought and worship was thus established within thirty years of Jesus' death: death and resurrection, humiliation and exaltation.

Paul cited a hymn (either his own composition or one known already) to the Philippians (early 60s) that portrays Christ exalted by God and receiving universal worship on the basis of voluntary humiliation. Beginning in the "form of God," Christ took slavelike human form and suffered a wretched slave's death on the cross (Phil. 2:6–11). The central valley of humiliation, between the two peaks of glory, is the cross. In the mid-fifties Paul characterized the difficulty of this saving paradox: "For the message about the cross is foolishness to those who are perishing, but to us who are being saved it is the power of God. . . . We proclaim Christ crucified, a stumbling block to Jews and foolishness to Gentiles" (1 Cor. 1:18, 23). The cross gave believers a spectacular glimpse into how God works through weakness and foolishness as humanity generally defines them.

Beyond the recognizable though altered covenant hopes, first-generation Christians such as Paul and his network of communities honored Jesus in the same breath as God and believed that God wanted Jesus to receive worship previously accorded to YHWH alone. The Philippians' hymn noted above ends with God's command to worship Jesus: "Therefore God also highly exalted him and gave him the name that is above every name, so that at the name of Jesus every knee should bend, in heaven and on earth and under the earth, and every tongue should confess that Jesus Christ is Lord, to the glory of God the Father" (2:9–11). Belief in the extent of Jesus' authority and glory contributed to the confessional slogan "Jesus is Lord" (Rom. 10:9; 1 Cor. 12:3) in a society used to the imperial claim that "Caesar is Lord." Honoring Jesus with the title "Lord" also scandalized Jews used to reading LORD in their Greek translation of Scripture as an honorific replacement for YHWH, God's name revealed to Moses and deemed too holy to pronounce. Further, Paul the Jew and Christian felt justified in both recalling and altering the chief confession of the Jewish faith, the Shema, "Hear, O Israel: The Lord is our God, the Lord alone" (Deut. 6:4). In reassuring the Corinthians about the powerlessness of the many "so-called gods," Paul wrote, "Yet for us there is *one God*, the Father, from whom are all things and for whom we exist, and *one Lord*, Jesus Christ, through whom are all things and through whom we exist" (1 Cor. 8:5–6, emphasis added). The lordship of Jesus, the crucified and risen Christ, revealed a new way to relate to the God of Israel.[4]

Paul was convinced that this Jesus was truly God's Christ despite the inconsistencies with many previous covenant hopes, especially the Christ who was supposed to conquer the Gentiles. Instead of military and royal actions, Jesus the Messiah was understood as Lord, whose saving task was reconciliation between God and all humanity. Apart from Romans 1:3, Paul's Letters are unconcerned to connect Davidic hopes to Jesus Christ. Paul was much more impressed by Christ's victory over death and the powers of evil. Christ did provide deliverance, restore relationships with God, and inaugurate God's kingdom in more universal terms than few since Isaiah had hoped.

Paul regularly explained salvation in Jesus Christ in terms of reconciliation, recalling traditional hopes for the restoration of Israel with God. Paul furthered the barrier-breaking words and actions of Jesus. To Paul, all nations now had the almost unbelievable opportunity to be Israel through Christ's reconciling work. Struggling to describe the relationship of Gentiles with the original people of God, Paul proclaimed that Jesus' death transformed Gentiles from enemies of God into friends (Rom. 5:6–11). God grafted Gentiles into the nation of Israel, from which root they take nourishment (11:11–24).

Given Israel's mixed tradition about the fate of Gentiles, it is no surprise that Gentile membership in the Christ's Israel surfaced as a problematic issue among early Christians. At one extreme, Paul confronted those who taught the ethnic privilege of Jews as the original people of God (Galatians). Paul attacked the view that true Christians must adopt the old covenant and ethnic markers that used to give concrete evidence of one's allegiance to the one YHWH (e.g., circumcision, dietary restrictions, abandonment of all other gods). At the other end, Paul sought to halt a reverse superiority complex among Gentile Christians tempted to glory over the unbelief of many Jews (Romans).

Paul's attempts to defuse the situation led him to emphasize Christ's role in reconciling groups across previous barriers that marked those who were or were not God's people. Those who could confess that "Jesus is Lord" are one people of God: "For there is no distinction between Jew and Greek; the same Lord is Lord of all" (Rom. 10:9, 12). Likewise, the Letter to the Ephesians used highly visible covenant language to emphasize the completeness of Jewish and Gentile unity in Christ (2:11–21). Instead of the vulnerable "strangers" and "aliens" set apart from covenant Israel, Gentiles in Christ are full "citizens" with the original "saints" (or "holy ones"), "members of the household of God" (2:19). Even as Israel had been depicted as true humanity amid the beastly Gentiles in Daniel, Ephesians points out that Christ does "create in himself one new humanity in place of the two, thus making peace" (2:15). God in Christ has opened the household to reembrace the family of humanity.

CONCLUSIONS

From Jesus' mission in Palestine to the last generation who heard the stories from eyewitnesses (ca. 27–90), the first Christians thought about Jesus through God's covenant with Israel. Even Gentile converts had to become part of Israel's story, no longer through ethnic markers such as circumcision or purity practices, but through a worldview that saw God's work of salvation in Jesus on a continuum with the covenant experience of Israel. The multiple scenarios that Jews of the Second Temple period had posited for God's salvation were reduced to the pattern of Jesus' life, death, and resurrection. In Paul the cross broke through the former national, privileged relationship with God so that all humanity might have life as the people of God in the body of Christ. Jesus' followers now looked to him to define covenantal salvation by a thorough reassessment of Jewish Scripture. God's presence was in and through Jesus rather than through torah or temple. In the wake of resurrection, believers spread the good news of God's new covenant and confidently invited others into the kingdom of the Christ.

QUESTIONS FOR DISCUSSION

1. What is good news/gospel? What makes it "good"? For whom is it "good"?
2. How did Jesus fall short of expectations for the Christ and for God's covenant fulfillment? What was troubling about Jesus and his representation of God's covenant?
3. Why did Christians think that Jesus himself was the good news?
4. After the resurrection, how did the first Christians understand God, Israel, and the covenant differently as a result of recognizing Jesus to be the Christ? What stayed the same?

SUGGESTED FURTHER READING

Dunn, James D. G. *Jesus Remembered*. Grand Rapids: Wm. B. Eerdmans Publishing Co., 2003.

Cambridge Companion to St. Paul. Edited by James D. G. Dunn. New York: Cambridge University Press, 2003.

Gorman, Michael J. *Apostle of the Crucified Lord: A Theological Introduction to Paul and His Letters*. Grand Rapids: Wm. B. Eerdmans Publishing Co., 2003.

Hurtado, Larry W. *One God, One Lord: Early Christian Devotion and Ancient Jewish Monotheism*. 2nd ed. Edinburgh: T&T Clark, 2003.

Wright, N. T. *Jesus and the Victory of God*. Vol. 2 of *Christian Origins and the Questions of God*. Minneapolis: Fortress Press, 1996.

Part II

The Pillars of the Faith
(ca. AD 50–324)

ISSUES

Over the second and third centuries, Christians established a recognizable identity and distinctive expressions of faith. As individuals and communities, they struggled to fulfill Paul's recommendation: "If it is possible, so far as it depends on you, live peaceably with all" (Rom. 12:18), including the civil authorities, whom God appointed to maintain order (13:1–7). Peaceable living, including a reluctance to serve in the army, hold public office, or attend blood-sports, ironically provoked violence against Christians for opting out of normal society. Attempts by Christians to explore their faith in greater depth enriched the faith; yet at times believers squirmed uncomfortably at new conceptual images of Christ that did not accord with the faith their communities had received. Christian efforts to negotiate persecution and heresy depended upon developing methods to determine whom to trust, what to believe, and how to live faithfully.

Three pillars emerged to direct the young church: martyrs, the Scriptures, and the rule (or canon) of faith. Chapter 4 examines the practical difficulties of living peaceably without sacrificing key elements of Christian identity, such as exclusive monotheism, in the midst of a polytheistic culture where religion implied civic duties. In their life and death, martyrs illustrated the limits to which one could be Christian and Roman, a son or daughter of God and an upstanding citizen of Rome. Chapter 5 looks at how early Christians handed down their beliefs and way of life through the integrally related streams of tradition and Scripture. Of primary importance to believers in this period was remaining faithful to the story of God with Israel, as revealed in Jesus Christ. At the same time Christians were also sorting out which of their own writings might be used in worship alongside traditional (Jewish) Scripture. The sorting process depended upon the memory of local Christian assemblies in consultation with neighboring and distant ones. Beginning with what they often had in common, Christians built their interpretation of both Scripture and the faith upon God—the Father, Son, and Holy Spirit—as known through the Son who was born, lived, suffered, died, and rose again in glory. The threefold God revealed by means of the actual life of Jesus the Son of God lay at the center of early Christian belief and theological method.

HISTORICAL CONTEXT

Gentile converts could expect their families and neighbors to assume that they had joined a cult putting adherents at risk socially and legally. Non-Christians considered Christians to be aberrant; their Christ-God required unthinkable allegiance, disrupting civic, religious, and familial relations. It certainly was an exceedingly odd cult, without temples or shrines or sacrifices, which suggested an exceedingly odd and perhaps dangerous god. Jews at least had an ancient tradition of worshiping only one God. Christians, as became clear over time, claimed Jewish monotheism and Scripture, yet introduced a man recently executed under Roman law to be worshiped in tandem with the Jewish God. The inconsistency and novelty upheld suspicions.

Second-century persecution of Christians took place in an unprecedented era of political and economic stability. This accounts in great part for the local and rare nature of incidents against Christians. It also explains something of the optimism expressed by many Christian writers that common sense would prevail to protect Christians once Rome's leadership understood the moral and intellectual basis of Christianity. Only five emperors ruled from Nerva (96–98) to Marcus Aurelius (161–180), each carefully chosen and then adopted as successor to the purple.

In contrast, over eighty emperors or imperial hopefuls fought their way to the top from 192 to 285. Cycles of bad weather, crop failure, resulting famines, and susceptibility to disease exacerbated the third-century political instability. Marcus Aurelius's troops brought back smallpox from their Mesopotamian campaigns, a disease that spread rapidly across the empire, with devastating results. In the East, Persians under their Sassanian rulers were ready to take over Rome's border provinces and more. Many Germanic peoples thought this to be a good time to move to the empire for protection from fiercer peoples, or to profit from easy pickings along the northern border, where troops were in short supply. Small wonder that Romans tried to figure out what had offended the gods!

Third-century emperors deliberated how best to limit violence against fellow Romans in the pursuit of good order. They weighed the threat of instability from offending the gods against the instability of persecuting a sizable percentage of the empire. Decius (249–251) sought only to persuade citizens to show solidarity with the empire; executions were rare, though sentencing to slavery or the mines, or disfigurement and death by the tools of persuasion (torture and imprisonment), were the norm.

By the end of the third century, the emperor Diocletian (284–305) succeeded in imposing order upon the mayhem that had threatened the very existence of the empire. Diocletian's vision for setting the empire on a solid foundation included establishing orderly administration of the sprawling empire and planning for imperial succession. He formalized the eastern and western divisions of the empire (Greek and Latin, respectively), each ruled by a senior emperor ("Augustus"). The two Augusti each chose one "vice-emperor" ("Caesar"), who would rise to the position of Augustus in due time. This system mirrored the one that contributed to the peace of the second century. Diocletian's Tetrarchy (rule of four) was composed of himself and Maximian, a fellow soldier, plus the Caesars Galerius and Constantius Chlorus, father of the future emperor Constantine I. Diocletian planned for Augusti to serve a number of years, then abdicate together in order to allow the Caesars to take over. This did not work as well in practice as in theory; soon after Diocletian abdicated in 305, the sons of the new Augusti rebelled when not chosen as Caesars. The most successful rebel would be Constantine.

Diocletian, who initiated the "Great Persecution" (303–312), at first resisted outright bloodshed. In the name of traditional Roman gods and mores, the Tetrarchy had restored much political and economic stability in the nineteen years before the persecution. The remaining threat seemed to come from those who persisted in withholding their allegiance to the empire's welfare, refusing to honor its gods: Manicheans (a Persian, dualist religion) and Christians. After controlling the Manicheans, Diocletian turned his attention to the Christians. He tried to appease the gods by dismissing Christians from the army and his government in 302. In the end this was not enough for the other members of the Tetrarchy. Christian observers, such as the scholar Lactantius (ca. 260-ca. 330), attributed the persecution both to alarm over bad omens and to indignation that brazen Christians had built a fine church within sight of Diocletian's palace in Nicomedia (modern Izmit in Turkey). Diocletian's relatively mild persecution (reduction in civil status, destruction of church buildings, confiscation of church books and valuables, torture to encourage Christian leaders to recant) devolved into a bloody hunt at the urging of the Caesar Galerius in 304, who became Augustus in 305.

During this time, Christianity continued growing in membership, public awareness, and sophistication. Non-Christians, such as the second-century Celsus, might speak contemptuously of Christianity but recognized it as a unified movement worthy of intellectual attack, calling it the "Great Church" (Origen, *Contra Celsum* 5.59). Already an empirewide organization, Christianity emerged from the peculiar stresses of the second and third centuries equipped to become the favored religion of the empire. It had clearly defined ideals for personal and communal identity in worship, sacraments, martyrs, and ascetic disciplines, balanced by procedures to restore those who fell short of the ideal. By weathering serious challenges to its core worldview, the Great Church developed methods for exploring and supporting its stances. Belief was grounded in Jesus' story according to the Scriptures and in the understandings and practices of living communities. Non-Christian learning became "plunder" for Christians, who nonetheless consciously tested scholarly methods and insights against the authority of Scripture and the creedal story of Christ.

3

"Go Therefore and Make Disciples"

(Matt. 28:19)

Over its first two hundred years, Christianity spread steadily across the Roman Empire, into Persia and Ethiopia. Establishing cells along major land and sea routes, early Christians went "to the Jew first and also to the Greek," meaning Gentiles (Rom. 1:16). This chapter reviews the message carried by early Christians from about 50–250 and the aspects that drew outsiders into this community shaped by the Jesus story. In the first place, Christians had a particular message about a specific God. They used several methods of communication, including moral witness and access to supernatural power. Some sources allow us to identify what non-Christians found convincing in the Christian message: beliefs and a way of life that converts in turn felt impelled to impart to still others. Once convinced, new believers entered into the story of Jesus as part of the people of God. Worship and rituals, such as baptism and the Lord's Supper, provided the setting for learning and practicing this new identity in community. Within such communities, Christians eagerly sought to understand more deeply their Lord and the hope they had in him. Theology thus arose from experiences of Christ in the worshiping community.

THE MESSAGE

Early Christian writings assume that people will be drawn to Jesus. Christians did not discuss mission strategies but instead occupied themselves with forming a Christian identity and worldview among inquirers as well as established disciples. Like Jesus' own proclamation of good news, the early Christians "spoke" with both words and actions formed within their church families.

Christians' embodiment of the risen Jesus and his teachings carried the message to the world.

For those familiar with Israel's story, the good news of Jesus as God's covenantal Messiah/Christ occupied the central position. Indeed, Jesus himself comprised the core good news. Explaining this to non-Christians required an act of translation, both of Israel's covenant and of Jesus' role in God's extended covenant.

"Repent, and Be Baptized" (Acts 2:38)

The good news after the resurrection of Jesus sounds much like that preached by both John the Baptist and Jesus. Luke's account in Acts (late 1st c.) delivers the proclamation to Jews in Jerusalem and beyond in familiar tones. A good example is Peter's address to the Pentecost crowd who witnessed the gift of languages granted to Jesus' followers (Acts 2:14–39). Peter explains that God is indeed present in the outpouring of the Spirit (as promised in the prophet Joel) and in his vindicating resurrection of Jesus, exalted at God's right hand. In sum Peter announces, "God has made him both Lord and Messiah, this Jesus whom you crucified" (2:36). When the distressed crowd asks, "What should we do?" Peter gives the classic advice of generations of prophets, though with a Jesus twist: Turn back to God, and "be baptized . . . in the name of Jesus Christ." While some local and Diaspora Jews in attendance might have been present during the fateful Passover fifty days earlier, Peter's message is not geared toward laying the blame of Jesus' death on these or any other Jews. Peter points toward the continuity of a God who has saved his people in the past and is doing so now through Jesus the Christ. The message is to return to covenant fidelity by means of Christ.

Later, Acts shows Paul and Barnabas at a synagogue. They recount God's acts of salvation in the exodus and David's kingdom in order to point to David's successor, Jesus, through whose life, death, and resurrection "forgiveness of sins is proclaimed to you" (13:16–43, esp. v. 38). Here "sins" function in a typically Jewish way, indicating the failures in covenant fidelity that have hung over generations of Jews: "Everyone who believes is set free from all those sins from which you could not be freed by the law of Moses" (13:39). God has demonstrated his fidelity with his people, past and present, "by raising Jesus" (13:32–33).

The Story of Jesus

Scholars have identified other early missionary sound bites within New Testament texts from around 50–80. Scattered phrases and passages work as summaries of the basic message, slogans meant to remind believers of the story into which they have been "written" (see 2 Cor. 3:2–3). Some are exceedingly brief, such as the reminder to the Thessalonian Christians, a primarily Gentile group. Paul acknowledges their pagan origins, "how you turned to God from idols, to serve a living and true God, and to wait for his Son from heaven, whom he raised from the dead—Jesus, who rescues us from the wrath that is coming" (1 Thess. 1:9–10; ca. 51). This sounds a lot like John the Baptist: "Repent, God is coming." "Turn to God before he throws the chaff and unfruitful trees into the eternal fire" (see Matt. 3:1–12; Luke 3:1–17). The Thessalonians' primary act in conversion is the basic requirement for becoming Jews: moving from bondage under false, dead gods to the protection of the "living and true God"—a phrase prevalent in Jewish antipagan polemic of the period.

Above all, the proclamation invited hearers into a new way of understanding one's place in the universe. While not denying the formative Jewish story of exodus, Christians gave priority to the story of Jesus' life, death, and resurrection to shape their understanding of what Israel's experience with the God of the covenant now meant for all. Paul left an extended example of the core proclamation in 1 Corinthians 15:1–8 (ca. 54):

> Now I would remind you, brothers and sisters, of the good news that I proclaimed to you, which you in turn received, in which also you stand, through which also you are being saved, if you hold firmly to the message that I proclaimed to you—unless you have come to believe in vain.
>
> For I handed on to you as of first importance what I in turn had received: that Christ died for our sins in accordance with the scriptures, and that he was buried, and that he was raised on the third day in accordance with the scriptures, and that he appeared to Cephas, then to the twelve. Then he appeared to more than five hundred brothers and sisters at one time, most of whom are still alive, though some have died. Then he appeared to James, then to all the apostles.

Paul called this the good news, or gospel, which gave the Corinthians their identity, their very salvation (15:2). The resurrection of Jesus meant the resurrection of the believers, which is Paul's focus for the rest of chapter 15. Doubts in the resurrection undermined the entire proclamation, "misrepresenting God" and founding a "futile faith," which left its duped disciples dead in their sins (15:12–19). Accepting the proclamation of the resurrection involved being shaped by and benefiting from Jesus' life story. The story was not set in a murky, mythic past, but reveals God's activity now.

Christians viewed God's salvation according to a cosmic plan whose ripples were transforming the entire creation. By contextualizing Israel's past within the panorama of creation, both Jews and Gentiles could appreciate the enormity of Christ's work, which amazingly reached to their very own lives. The "Christ psalm" of Colossians 1:15–20 echoes themes throughout the New Testament: Creator as Savior (John 1:1–18) and the exaltation of the crucified Christ above all of creation (Phil. 2:6–11). Everything has its origins and continued existence through "the beloved Son" (Col. 1:13), who "himself is before all things, and in him all things hold together" (1:17). Israel's master story unfolds the subplot of Jesus the crucified Christ, which in turn reveals the cosmic master story of the Creator Savior. This is the "mystery" at the heart of Colossians' good news, now at work among even the Gentiles (1:27): "Through [Christ] God was pleased to reconcile to himself all things, whether on earth or in heaven, by making peace through the blood of his cross" (1:20).

Even as the literary (rather than preached) Gospels were gaining wider circulation (late 1st c.), the gospel-in-a-nutshell or core proclamation remained central: Jesus Christ, Son of the Father, born of the virgin Mary, baptized by John, preacher and healer who suffered and died under Pontius Pilate, rose again, and ascended to God's right hand until he returns as judge. In this way Ignatius of Antioch (ca. 110–130) in his letters reminded the Christians at Magnesia (chap. 11), Tralles (chap. 9), and Smyrna (chap. 1) of the true teaching preserved and passed down through their trustworthy leaders. Later Christians would use this story in two ways: to seal initiates in the faith, calling it a creed (Latin *credo*, "I believe") or symbol, and to measure the legitimacy of teachers and writings against the tradition of the apostles, calling it the rule (or canon) of faith (see chaps. 5 and 6 below).

Messengers

Christians attributed the missionary impulse to the power of God. Luke (his Gospel and Acts) portrayed God's Spirit empowering the spread of the good news from lowly Galilee to Jerusalem, the center of Judaism, and finally to Rome, the center of the world. The Holy Spirit blocked Paul and his companions from going to the provinces of Asia and Bithynia and directed the missionaries by a vision to proceed to Macedonia instead (Acts 16:6–10). Around 110 Ignatius of Antioch perceived God's will in his captivity as an opportunity to encourage other Christians along the way to his trial in Rome. He also sought to be an example of Christlikeness to the ten "leopards," his guards (*To the Romans* 5).

Although not accounts of the actual apostles, the apocryphal acts at least convey images of missionaries' struggles to follow the Spirit obediently as understood in the second and third centuries. The Spirit's bidding entailed risks at which even apostles balked. The apostle John (*Acts of John*, mid to late

2nd c.) received both a vision and a heavenly voice sending him to Ephesus, while an Ephesian citizen also experienced a divine nudge to seek out John. Much to John's chagrin, the man expected the apostle to raise his wife from the dead. When the distraught husband also dropped dead, John suspected that God had set him up for a brief, violent engagement in Ephesus (both were brought back to life). The early third-century *Acts of Thomas* describes Thomas as so reluctant to take his allotted mission to India that Jesus had to sell the defiant disciple as a slave to a merchant of the Indian king. Messengers could be reluctant; nonetheless, Christ and the Holy Spirit kept pushing the message and messengers.

So what was it like when a Christian missionary entered a town? What were the heralds of the good news doing? In Paul's example, the message and the messenger were clearly evaluated as one, and together they experienced great vulnerability. Paul sarcastically listed his qualifications to the Corinthians as an authentic apostle: hard and dangerous travel, hunger, beatings, scourging, stoning, imprisonment, rejection, shipwreck (2 Cor. 11:23–28). Despite the popular image of Paul addressing the Athenians in philosophical debate, most often Christian announcement of the good news was less public. Paul's missionary activity and the outreach described in the Gospels and Acts show individuals or small groups visiting synagogues or holding conversations in hosts' homes. Paul the Tentmaker likely set up shop and chatted with curious passersby and with those who had the leisure to follow up on discussions begun in the synagogue or at a household meeting. Furthermore, he was rarely alone; he headed a well-organized missionary team. His letters name over three dozen coworkers, both men and women.[1]

Strictly speaking, early Christian writings never use the term "missionaries." Instead, there were several titles associated with the intentional dissemination of the gospel both inside and outside the community of believers. Titles were given to Christians with particular charisms or spiritual gifts for the edification and maturation of the church. Apostles, literally, messengers or ambassadors, were granted a particularly high level of authority among believers. Usually these were individuals closely associated with and commissioned by Jesus during his earthly ministry. The apostles in Jerusalem, especially the "pillars" (Peter, James the Just, and John son of Zebedee; Gal. 2:9) exerted authority in discerning and recommending appropriate methods of spreading the gospel into the 60s.

When the first Christians spoke of the many roles in the church, they recognized that all believers bore witness to the good news: some by their everyday lives within their local community and others by taking Christ on the road. Though confusing for us today, the titles usually appear in groups without specifying what an apostle or prophet or evangelist actually did. After all, the initial recipients of the letters and other writings knew what the author meant. Paul in 1 Corinthians 12 lists the Spirit-bestowed gifts operating among the believers in Corinth: prophecy, teaching, miracles, healing, helping, leadership, language, and interpretation. The linguistic gifts were useful in a multicultural port like Corinth. Ephesians 4 mentions apostles, prophets, evangelists, pastors, and teachers. The variety of gifts and roles resulted at times in attempts to figure out which were the more important gifts (and therefore people), a struggle particularly traumatic for Paul in his relationship with the Corinthian Christians. The New Testament Letters portray genuine concern that all the members, not just a single-point leader, bear a responsibility to employ their charisms for building up the church (1 Cor. 12; Eph. 4). This included attracting outsiders for their salvation (1 Cor. 10:31–33). The Letters to Timothy and Titus recommend that an overseer (Greek *episkopos*, "bishop") should manage the believers' gifts without excluding or supplanting members' responsibilities.

From the piecemeal picture that remains of the earliest Christian communities, we know that they bustled with activity. Itinerant Christians were so common that by 100 at least one community (likely in Syria) adopted regulations about visitors' comings and goings (*Didache* 11–13). Christians valued itinerant apostles, prophets, and teachers (again not clearly differentiated), who could be expected to share a revelation in the Spirit. At the same time, these Christians realized that blind credulity neither honored God nor protected the community. Visiting instructors demonstrated their authenticity by teaching nothing in conflict with the community's core tradition, by staying no more than two or three days, by living what they taught, and by not seeking to profit from their visit. False teachers and prophets would reveal themselves by doing the opposite. On the other hand, the *Didache* (11–12) warns against judging too quickly lest the community offend the Spirit. The visitor was to be "welcomed as the Lord," but the community must use its own powers of observation to assess the prophet's legitimacy. To early Christians, the message and the messenger were entwined: both had to be tested before being enjoyed.

CONVERSION TOWARD THE MESSAGE

People do not generally convert, or turn, to a new worldview or religion because of its overwhelming intellectual power. Instead, most people join a group because of the dynamics of the group and the people through whom they learn about the group. It was no different for the majority of converts to Christianity in the first centuries.

Christian families raised their children in the faith. The *Martyrdom of Polycarp* claimed that the old bishop had been faithful to Christ his entire eighty-six years, establishing that his adherence to Christianity took place within his family in the mid–70s. Among the directives of the *Didache* (4.9) is the traditionally Jewish emphasis on the parents' responsibility to raise up their children in the "fear of God" in parallel to admonitions regarding Christian households (cf. Eph. 6:4). In the court proceedings of Justin Martyr's trial (ca. 165), the Roman official tried to track down the sources of his prisoners' conversion and was surprised that so many of them had learned the faith from their parents.[2] In contrast to sensational or intellectual conversions, Christian literature of the second and third centuries rarely highlighted domestic growth because it was not unusual. However, by the fourth century, many Christians took pride in their pedigrees (e.g., the family of Basil of Caesarea in Cappadocia), especially when family members heroically withstood persecution.

From the outside, non-Christians might try to dismiss the broad appeal of Christianity by associating it only with the dregs of society, but a number of non-Christians liked Christians and wanted to be part of a community that lived and hoped for the things that Christians sought. To those highbrow literati who were not impressed, some well-educated Christians "translated" the faith in search of common ground for peace and—rather a long shot—conversion (more in chap. 4). The major attractions of Christianity were moral excellence, access to divine power, and philosophical fulfillment.

Moral Community: Practicing What They Preach

Christians liked to boast of the power of God to change lives from worse to better. According to Justin Martyr, Jesus Christ became man "for the conversion and restoration of the human race."[3] He claimed that Christians demonstrate this transformation on a daily basis in ordinary circumstances: neighbors noticing how Christians remain calm, how they refrain from anger when cheated, how unusually honest they are in business (*1 Apology* 16). While intellectual non-Christians criticized Christians for their irrational, blind faith, Christians replied that at least faith in Jesus led to changed lives among all classes, not just the elite with time and money to be philosophical (Origen, *Against Celsus* 1.9).

Early Christian writings anchored behaviors and communal identity in the risen Jesus Christ. The patterns that described Christ's exaltation and explored the implications of his death and resurrection formed the rationale for Christian identity. The words and deeds of those who entered into Christ would be judged on the basis of their Christlikeness. Paul considered Christians themselves to be "a letter of Christ," "written on our hearts, to be known and read by all" (2 Cor. 3:2–3).

In the following centuries, Christians continued to hearken back to the fundamental choice offered to Israel to choose life or death (Deut. 30:15–20) and the path of the righteous over that of the wicked (Ps. 1). Deriving from a Jewish moral landscape, the "Two Ways" instruction informs the teaching of the *Didache* (ca. 100), *Shepherd of Hermas* (90–150), and *Epistle of (Ps.) Barnabas* (ca. 130). The *Didache* begins the way of life by quoting scriptural directives to love God and neighbor, including the Golden Rule. Life in the *Didache* proceeds from behavior shaped by the Ten Commandments, demonstrated in caring for the vulnerable (poor, orphans, widows, children, and unborn) and manifested in humility, nonretaliation, and radical, interior righteousness (closely related to the Sermon on the Mount, Matt. 5–7). To outsiders, the exclusive love of God relegated Christians to an incomprehensible isolation from other divine powers. Yet at the same time, non-Christians were increasingly aware of the astounding service to others, regardless of religion, undertaken by Christians as central to their faith.

Operating under the law of loving one another, rank-and-file Christians gave an impressive witness. Outsiders who paid attention saw the way they took care of each other and even outsiders. The *Letter to Diognetus* (mid–2nd c.) bluntly described Christians as the soul of the world, committed to its well-being, as the soul is to the body (6.1–9). Aristides (writing between 124 and 150) depicted Christians far more in terms of their behavior than of their beliefs, citing a characteristic list that begins in traditional care for orphans and widows. Christians extended this further by opening their homes to needy strangers, nursing the sick, and burying those whose family could not afford it (*Apology* 15–16). Tertullian, writing around 197, pictured Christian service to the needy by sarcastically contrasting how non-Christians attend to their suppliant gods: "So, let Jupiter himself hold out his hand and receive his share, while meantime our pity spends more street by street than your religion does temple by temple."[4] Christian service alleviated physical distress as well as protecting from malevolent powers. Tertullian warned persecutors not to cut the empire off from the Christians' prowess in warding off and expelling evil spirits that threaten disease, invasions, and demon possession (*Apology* 23, 32, 43).

Another selling point of Christianity was the philosophical ideal of self-control actually practiced among many Christians. No pagan philosopher worth his pallium (distinctive cloak worn by philosophers) counseled prodigal eating, drinking, and sex. On the other hand, not many popular philosophers actually practiced what they preached, or even expected second-class humans (such as women, children, lower-class people, and slaves) to attain such ideals. When new Christians adopted a strict moral regimen, especially

To prove this point, many miracles in the genre took place through the hands of the newly converted. John encouraged the newly raised Cleopatra to raise her husband through Christ (*Acts of John* 24). Peter even instructed a former follower of Simon the Magician to ask the Lord Jesus Christ to restore a shattered statue of Caesar in evidence of his recent repentance and the power of faith in the Lord (*Acts of Peter* 11). The powers manipulated by the opponents of Christ's apostles never share their power, while the gracious God of Jesus Christ liberally distributes his gifts. These apocryphal acts draw attention to Jesus as the one power to trust among all the alternatives available, and to trust the authority of his representatives who share in this power.

Both critics and defenders admitted that Christians did amazing things. Origen (d. 251) acknowledged that many anonymously performed healings, exorcisms, and prophecies were still happening through the wisdom of the Son (Logos, or Word) and the power of the Holy Spirit. What is more, Origen had witnessed miraculous conversions of staunch opponents who unexpectedly submitted to the faith, ready to die for it (*Against Celsus* 1.Preface.2; 1.46). Twenty-first-century Westerners should be well aware of the lenses they wear, which filter out the multifaceted reality experienced by the pre-Enlightenment and most of the current non-Western world. For the majority of people now and in the past, reality is not a sterile "What you see is what you get," but rather a cosmos bristling with seen and unseen beings. Early Christians as much as their non-Christian peers knew quite well that supernatural signs pointed to some source of power emanating from the teeming invisible world.

While impressive, miracles were problematic and could not be a stand-alone means of asserting authority or truth. A miracle leaves its viewers uncertain by what power it has been done and even what it might mean. Signs and wonders did indeed provide opportunities to speak the good news, but the audience had to be redirected toward God, who accomplished these deeds, a God who is powerful, is compassionate, and desires physical wholeness.

A Philosopher's Conversion: Justin Martyr

Some seekers found in Christianity the fulfillment of their philosophical pursuit of God. Justin (martyred in Rome ca. 165) left behind a literary version of his journey to God, which shows one way that the story of Jesus could excite Greco-Roman intellectuals (*Dialogue with Trypho* 1–8). Born in Samaria, Justin pursued philosophy, making his way through the Stoics, Aristotelians, and Pythagoreans. Frustrated with the variety and wrangling among those laying claim to ultimate truth, Justin began to hope that the Platonists might lead him to a vision of God. They taught him how to look beyond the world of experience, which is only a shadow of true reality. Justin admitted that "the

perception of immaterial things quite overpowered me, and the contemplation of ideas furnished my mind with wings."[10] At this stage he had a conversation along a quiet beach with a man who gently pointed out some problems
with the Platonic view of the soul, a conversation that left Justin despairing of
ever finding a truth to which he could commit his life. His unnamed conversation partner recommended the divinely inspired prophets of the Jewish God.
Such sages did not waste their time writing impressive treatises about truth,
but rather predicted truth, which has since been fulfilled in Christ, the Son of
the Creator God. So it was that Justin experienced "a flame . . . kindled in my
soul" and entrusted himself to the teaching of the Christians.

At that point the convert became a converter. Justin the Christian philosopher committed himself to encouraging others to make a similar discovery
and thus to achieve the classical goal to "live a happy life." Before Justin,
Aristides similarly declared himself "constrained to declare the truth to such
as care for it and seek the world to come" in a bid to have the emperor give
Christian writings a fair look (*Apology* 16). The New Testament impulse to
"go and tell" upon hearing the good news continued to function even when
the message circulated in the philosophical world of the Gentiles.

COMMUNITY FORMED IN WORSHIP AND RITUAL

Becoming and staying a Christian, whatever the original attractions, involved
the whole person integrated into a new community or nation. Theologized
concepts of time together with the central rituals of baptism and the Lord's
Supper gave an experiential dimension to the story of Jesus, to which a convert had assented. Jesus' story condensed to its most crucial moments, from
his final meal with the disciples to the resurrection, grounded Christian identity in the weekly Lord's Day, the annual Pasch (or Easter), the Lord's Supper, and baptism.

Before the fourth century, we only have snapshots and allusions about
what went on in Christian communities and why. Christians writing to each
other did not have to explain normal practices to their recipients. Writings
directed to non-Christians kept some things a bit vague: holy things belong to
the holy. Worship and ritual involved God's own presence and as such were
not to be described even to Christian-in-training who had not been prepared
to understand the experiences until baptized (*Didache* 9.5). In some cases
communities preferred these rituals to be safeguarded through oral tradition
rather than committed to writing, where outsiders might sneak a peek. On the
other hand, baptism and the holy meals were so central to Christian practice
that, already by Paul's ministry in the 50s, they are assumed and not really

explained. Paul only discussed the Lord's Supper in an attempt to address Corinthian factionalism by appealing to a customary practice that was supposed to enhance their unity rather than destroy it (1 Cor. 11:17–34). ·

Chapter 7 will examine later developments in worship and the sacraments from the broader and more detailed sources available after the second century. What follows, then, is a collage of evidence rather than a template for how all the early Christians worshiped. The practice of worship and the sacraments varied widely, with communities exhibiting different though not mutually exclusive emphases and meanings.

Baptized into the Story

Entry into the community of believers took place in baptism. Methods differed, and images abounded for what baptism meant. The New Testament writings alone talk of life from death, rescue from sins and the power of evil, anointing of the Spirit, union with Christ's death, and subsequent hope to be united in his resurrection. Baptism could take place after instruction or simply in response to hearing the good news. Sometimes the gift of the Spirit preceded water baptism, sometimes the other way around. Sometimes it was in the name of the Lord Jesus or Jesus Christ (Acts), but increasingly in the name of the Father, Son, and Spirit (Matt. 28:19; *Didache* 7). First-century Christians related the saving aspects of baptism with episodes of safety through water, such as Noah's family during the flood (1 Pet. 3:20–21) and the Israelites brought through the Red Sea (1 Cor. 10:1–3). Fellow believers would share the convert's fasting and prayerful preparation for baptism (*Didache* 7; Justin, *1 Apology* 61). By the mid-second century, Justin (*Dialogue with Trypho* 14, 18–19) expounded on how Christian baptism replaced circumcision and provided true, rather than symbolic, repentance, purification, and knowledge of God. Baptism gave life to those who repented, and it delivered unprecedented knowledge of God, which he described as "illumination" (*1 Apology* 61). Baptism brought the individual into relationship with God through Christ, experienced corporately in fellowship with other believers.

Regular Worship

From the first decades of Christianity, worship among the baptized had been important in shaping and strengthening the identity of the Christian community. Of paramount importance were the meetings on Sunday, the day of the Lord's resurrection and thus called the Lord's Day, in contrast to Saturday, the Sabbath and seventh day of creation. Christians, understanding that Christ initiated a new era, sometimes called their day of worship the eighth day, because the resurrection took believers into the era of the new creation. Beyond this, Christians urged each other to assemble often in order to derive strength to live their calling faithfully, a necessity amid the periodic hostility the communities experienced. Gatherings of the faithful were grounded in the experience of Christ's presence in and through the community, punctuated by the presence of Christ and the Spirit through the Lord's Supper, prophets, and written Scripture (see chap. 5). Given the role and unpredictable schedule of traveling prophets, impromptu meetings would supplement the regular Sunday meetings. Some communities met daily. Because the gatherings avoided normal working hours, Christians often met early in the morning.

Easter/ Pasch and Lord's Supper

Easter highlighted the early Christians' year. Because Jesus died during the Passover, Easter coincided with and shared the name of the Jewish Passover, the Pasch (Hebrew *pesakh*; Greek *pascha*). Many communities, especially in Asia Minor, celebrated with the Jewish Passover on Nisan 14. These groups were called Quartodecimans (Party of the Fourteenth). Drawing inspiration from the saving blood of the lamb from the Exodus story of Passover, Christians likewise told the story of the suffering and glorification of the "Lamb of God who takes away the sins of the world!" (John 1:29; cf. 1 Cor. 5:7). The most complete expression of an early Christian paschal celebration survives in Melito of Sardis's poetic, liturgical work, *On the Pasch* (mid–2nd c.).[11] It reflects the way many Christians understood their intimate relationship to Israel's story, now fulfilled in Jesus and interpreted by their prophet-leader Melito. *On the Pasch* shows a Christian Passover that culminated in a meal (stanzas 46–65), where Jesus' salvific death and resurrection bonded believers into the people of God.[12]

The work assumes that the gathered believers have just heard the traditional Passover reading from Exodus 12. Melito carefully marked Christ's fulfillment of God's salvation in the Pasch as *pasch* (Passover) through Jesus' own suffering (*paschein*, "to suffer," stanza 46). The Pasch narrative, for both Christians and Jews, moved from slavery to freedom and culminated in hope for the Christ in sharing and eating the *afikoman* (from the Greek *aphikomenos*, "the Coming One"). The *afikoman* was the middle third of the bread broken during the meal. It was then hidden until the end of the meal. The tradition of eating the *afikoman* that represented the coming Savior helps to explain why the disciples did not leave the Last Supper in utter disgust at Jesus' cannibalistic invitation, "Take, eat; this is my body" (Matt. 26:26).

Christians still firmly rooted in their Jewish heritage continued to celebrate Jesus' stunning revelation of himself in the *afikoman*. Jesus' death after this meal added a sacrificial dimension to the Christian Pasch, transforming the protective blood of the paschal lamb into a saving sacrifice. Believers remembered this saving story by becoming witnesses to Jesus, who has come and will come again. Thus Melito, in the voice of Christ, proclaimed:

> Therefore, come, all families of men, you who have been befouled with sins, and receive forgiveness for your sins. I am your forgiveness, I am the passover of your salvation, I am the lamb which was sacrificed for you, I am your ransom, I am your light, I am your saviour, I am your resurrection, I am your king, I am leading you up to the heights of heaven, I will show you the eternal Father, I will raise you up by my right hand. (103)

In other regions, and as fewer converts came from the Jews, Christians deepened the connection of the Pasch to resurrection. They detached the celebration from its Jewish scheduling and fixed the Christian Pasch to fall always on Sunday, the day of resurrection. By the fourth century the Council of Nicaea declared this to be the church's practice, though not without some dissenters.

The meal derived from the Pasch became the place where believers grounded their identity and hopes, not just once a year but probably as often as they gathered. It was so integral to being the people of God that nonbaptized believers were never allowed to participate or even be present for its celebration until they had been fully inducted into the saving story through baptism. The tradition in the Gospels and in Paul conveys a sense of attentive waiting for when the community will eat and drink with Jesus in the new kingdom. For Paul, these meals were to mold believers into a people freed from the "world's" manner of evaluating value, especially economic and social status. Thus we hear about the ideal Lord's Supper as "sharing" in the blood and body of Christ (1 Cor. 10:16–17) precisely because the meals had disintegrated into the wealthy feasting on their own and leaving the humbler believers out (11:17–34).

Other traditions, such as preserved in the *Didache* and Justin Martyr, emphasized the community's "thanksgiving," or Eucharist (Greek *eucharisteō*, "give thanks") for God's creative and saving work through Jesus, which brought about the believers' unity, rescued them from evil, and revealed God in the real and spiritual food and drink. In the *Didache* (10) the meal reached a climax among the gathered believers with the plea *Maranatha*, "Our Lord, come!" (cf. 1 Cor. 16:22), which retained the ancient Aramaic. In some places, Christians celebrated a love feast (agape, from Greek *agapē*) which may have been the same as the Lord's Supper. In others, the Agape may have been a less ritualized potluck where believers (including those not baptized) ate in fellowship and brought extra supplies for distribution to the needy in the community.

The earliest Christians consistently centered their ritual life on baptism and the Eucharist. They perceived God at work in creating a new people centered on Jesus Christ and grounded in the story of his death and resurrection, even as God had done for Israel in the Pasch. The symbolic acts of baptism and Eucharist were the ritually lived corollary of the core proclamation of the good news.

REFLECTING ON JESUS AND HOPE

Christians of the first three centuries assumed that mission and growth in self-understanding required delving into the One who came and is coming. The story of Jesus did not confine hopes any more than the general story of God's covenant fidelity limited the models of restoration cherished by Jews from the exile onward. A hallmark of those who recognized each other to be in Christ was tolerance, even enthusiasm, for multiple images to express the richness of God's salvation. Here are two early-Christian views of Jesus and the hope that flowed from those views: the Revelation to John, and the letters of Ignatius of Antioch.

The Revelation to John (Late First Century)

Picture this: "a Lamb standing as if it had been slaughtered, having seven horns and seven eyes" (Rev. 5:6); a rider on a white horse, whose "eyes are like a flame of fire, and on his head are many diadems. . . . He is clothed in a robe dipped in blood. . . . From his mouth comes a sharp sword" (19:11–15). Nothing beats apocalyptic writings for vivid imagery and plain befuddlement among readers today. The Revelation to John descends from a revered Jewish genre that dealt symbolically with persecution and covenant hopes.[13] Among the addressees, seven churches in the Roman province of Asia, the hopes of Israel are and will be fulfilled in the person of Jesus. The vision is full of symbols of Israel: hope for the defeat of those who oppose God and his people, the vindication and restoration of the twelve tribes (to which believing Gentiles now belong), and a regathering of the people to live eternally in the presence of God in the new Jerusalem.

Revelation takes up the implications of Jesus as the exalted Messiah, coming to complete his victory. Unlike other Jewish apocalypses, Jesus himself gives the message and is equated with God. He appears initially in the guise of the white-haired Ancient of Days, God himself, from Daniel 7:9. Twenty-

---

APOCALYPTIC LITERATURE

Jewish and Christian apocalypses (revelations) function side by side with the prophetic tradition. Both genres offered warnings to prompt repentance in order to avoid a disastrous future, as well as hopes for a better one. The apocalyptic style uses fantastic images conveyed through a vision. The recipient is guided through the vision by a divine agent for the benefit of the broader belief community. The revelation supports the hopes of a group struggling for survival. It reveals that the current crisis is part of a global and even cosmic struggle, whose outcome God controls for the good of the beleaguered. The group is encouraged to hang tough through the crisis, looking forward to its share of God's ultimate victory. Among Christians, Daniel 7 (with the Ancient of Days and a son of man) proved quite influential, likely stemming from Jesus' usage during his trial (see chap. 2 above).

---

eight times the author uses "The Lamb" for Jesus, underscoring the centrality of his sacrificial yet victorious death. The assembly in the divine throne room acclaims that the Lamb (Jesus) alone is worthy to undertake the final extermination of evil in the world because he was killed as a ransom (Rev. 5:9). Repeatedly, God and the Lamb receive blessing from the assembly of angels and the righteous in the form of hymns, which adapt many acclamations of God from Jewish Scriptures. The vision's intolerance of any worship directed beyond God (as John began toward a later angel guide; 19:10) makes the reverence for Jesus even more stunning.[14] God and the Lamb together form the temple and share a throne in divine Jerusalem (21:22; 22:3).

Staggering in its scope, violence, and power, Revelation allows us to peer into the experience of Christians, whose exalted view of Jesus arose from their experiences of him. The Asian Christians expected worship to be enlivened and directed by the Spirit of God through their in-house prophets, even as John received this vision. The vision is meant to be shared within the worship of the seven churches in Asia as legitimate prophecy (1:3). Thus Jesus through the Spirit played a continuing role among believers, encouraging and exhorting and inspiring them to hymns of praise. In this context the believers call upon Jesus as the true "King of kings" and "Lord of lords" (17:14; 19:16; historically used of the Persian kings, and applied by Jews to God) in defiant, and potentially dangerous, opposition to the claims of Roman emperors.

Paradoxically the Lamb is conqueror, defeating the forces lined up against God by allowing those forces to kill him. In the time line of salvation, Christians already know that the Lamb is enthroned in great glory and power. It is only a matter of time (perhaps very short: 22:6–7) before the whole plan is completed. Hope is based upon what Christ has done in his death and resurrection. Once evil is defeated, God will supervise a final judgment to gather the holy ones (depicted as the new Jerusalem), who are now ready to enjoy their marriage to the Lamb. Life for the holy ones (Rev. 21–22) reprises classical prophetic images of a restored and purified creation, the end of suffering, sorrow, and fear, anchored by God's intimate presence. Marked by God, the saints engage in face-to-face, perpetual worship. Until the completion of all things, each of the seven churches is counseled to "listen to what the Spirit is saying to the churches" by heeding this prophecy and others that Christ may send.

Ignatius of Antioch

Between 110 and 130, Ignatius, bishop of Antioch, urged rather specific teachings about Jesus in order to combat opinions that were causing divisions among believers. To his fellow bishop, Polycarp of Smyrna, Ignatius declared that an "athlete of God" must contend against "strange teachings" by affirming the paradoxical Christ tradition:

> Look for Christ, the Son of God;
> who was before time, yet appeared in time;
> who was invisible by nature, yet visible in the flesh;
> who was impalpable, and could not be touched,
> as being without a body, but for our sakes became such,
>   might be touched and handled in the body;
> who was impassible as God, but became passible for our sakes as man;
>   and who in every kind of way suffered for our sakes.[15]

The idea of Jesus Christ as a human being was at stake. In contrast to the skepticism voiced in the Gospels over Jesus' divine authority, Christians were facing resistance to Christ's humanity. Ignatius made it plain that such duality in Christ (as God and as creature) was not tourism on the Son's part, but done "for our sakes." Having a body with the ability to suffer and die lies at the heart of the hope for salvation (for the struggle to describe divine suffering in Christ, see chap. 10 below). Death in a body is salvation because death makes resurrection of the body possible. Ignatius derived meaning and hope for his looming death from the reality of Christ's own death. He longed to be united with Christ through suffering and death so as to "have fellowship with Him in His death, His resurrection from the dead, and His everlasting life" (*To the Ephesians* 11).[16]

Christ's significance extended far beyond humanity for Ignatius. He shared the cosmic vision of Christ in Colossians 1:15–20, who "is before all things, and in him all things hold together, . . . [and he is] making peace through the blood of his cross." Divisions in the community appeared to Ignatius as direct evidence of the turmoil caused by evil in the universe, which was fighting a losing battle against Christ's work of restoration. Consequently, Christians were responsible for working toward harmony of belief and organization in the church, which reflected the chain of command in God's heavenly court. As attached as Ignatius was to Christ's suffering and death, he acknowledged the magnitude of the incarnation, whereby God enacted his plan of salvation quietly through Jesus' conception within Mary's virginity. Immediately the forces of this world's prince felt their powers weaken at "God Himself being manifested in human form for the renewal of eternal life." Ever since, they have raised "a state of tumult, because He meditated the abolition of death" (*To the Ephesians* 19).

As different as Revelation and Ignatius are, they do show important connections between who Christ is and to what end he would bring his followers. Faith that Jesus, the Lord of lords and Son of God, had entered the world and lives of early Christians became the basis for looking ahead to a glorious future with him, but only if they persevered in a community joined to a nonnegotiable story, passed down and tested within their communities of faith.

CONCLUSIONS: A RECOGNIZABLE PEOPLE

"We are everywhere!" claimed Tertullian at the beginning of the third century: the marketplace, military barracks, sailing crews, aristocratic mansions, merchants' caravans, peasant villages, and philosophical salons (see *Apology* 37, 52). By Tertullian's day, most city dwellers in the Roman Empire would have known of and had personal acquaintance with Christians. The good news spread via numerous named and nameless wandering apostles, prophets, and teachers, not to mention ordinary stay-at-home believers and their families. When Tertullian boasted that Christians were made, not born, he attested to the attraction that Christianity held (*Apology* 18). Many Christians came to the faith after seeing and hearing Christians and their message as adults. Adults had to be convinced by the teachings, the lived examples of the community, and assistance through ordinary and extraordinary means. Christians took for granted that the Spirit inspired and enabled their changed lives and loving service. What non-Christians saw and experienced arose from the bedrock of Jewish ideals of holiness and caring for the vulnerable (sick, poor, widows, orphans, babies, and the unborn) but extended beyond the faith community even as Christ's sacrifice extended to the whole world.

If Christianity had only been a moral code, non-Christians likely would not have persecuted it. What was so disturbing was the worldview and sense of identity shaped by the story of Jesus. Jesus was a stumbling block, but so was exclusive monotheism, which remained the home for Jesus' story. Christians believed in the one Father, Creator of all, who through Israel and Israel's Christ (born, died, and risen) set in motion a cosmic reconciliation of all peoples with God and the forgiveness of sins. This gospel-in-a-nutshell anchored the message and the life of Christians even as it isolated them from the predominant nonexclusive worldviews around them. When confronted, Christians claimed a citizenship and ultimate allegiance to Christ the "Lord," not to Caesar. They treasured a God who manifested divinity by humility, forgiveness, and death, even as they longed for the return of their mighty Savior to put an end to the ambiguity of their existence with the clear establishment of his kingdom. Thus, while Christians might sound or even act like reputable philosophers, the story that underlay their lifestyle and worldview threatened Greek and Roman assumptions about the relationship between the divine and earthly realms, and about the very nature of divinity.

QUESTIONS FOR DISCUSSION

1. What characterized the good news as preached and lived by early Christians? What was tricky about the witness of miracles? How might this be similar to or different from the witness of Christians today?
2. How might Christianity have been attractive to non-Christians? What was odd or alienating?
3. How did experiences of worshiping Christ form community identity and shape believers' hopes in Christ? Is communal and ritual worship necessary to forming and testing beliefs?

SUGGESTED FURTHER READING

Johnson, Luke Timothy. *The Writings of the New Testament: An Interpretation*. Rev. ed. Minneapolis: Fortress Press, 1999.

Kee, Howard Clark. *Miracle in the Early Christian World: A Study in Sociohistorical Method*. New Haven: Yale University Press, 1983.

Neyrey, Jerome H. *Give God the Glory: Ancient Prayer and Worship in Cultural Perspective*. Grand Rapids: Wm. B. Eerdmans Publishing Co., 2007.

Schnabel, Eckhard J. *Early Christian Mission*. 2 vols. Downers Grove, IL: InterVarsity Press, 2004.

Stark, Rodney. *Cities of God: The Real Story of How Christianity Became an Urban Movement and Conquered Rome*. San Francisco: HarperOne, 2006.

4

Christianus/a Sum

I Am a Christian

INTRODUCTION

Despite the many alluring qualities outlined in chapter 3, Christianity would have been an uncomfortable fit for non-Christians on many levels. Within the faith's first few decades, believers had made it to the world stage, but the critics were not giving rave reviews. In examining the ways Christians thought about God, the world, and their relationship with both, the focus will be on conflict, determining boundaries, and creating models of Christian life.

To understand why there was conflict, we must examine how Romans (a general term used here to indicate non-Christians in the Roman Empire), as both enemies and potential converts, perceived Christians. Christians wrestled with how to translate the Christian worldview and lifestyle into terms acceptable to contemptuous non-Christians. At the same time they struggled to define how (or if) they could somehow be Roman and Christian. There were plenty of challenges in daily life; yet during times of violent confrontation, many believers buckled under the pressures of persecution. Communities then struggled to discern how or if such apostates could be reintegrated into the church and how to prepare Christians for the ultimate test of faith. Finally, most Christians, even the backsliders, recognized that those who persevered in their faith through torture and death spoke the truth when they claimed, *"Christianus/a sum"* (I am a Christian). Ideal Christian identity was manifested through the life and death of martyrs, even if some Christians would not or could not attain this ideal.

ROMAN VIEWS OF CHRISTIANS

The Frustrations of a Roman Governor (Paraphrased)

My name is Pliny. You've probably heard of my uncle, the elder Pliny, a naturalist who didn't keep enough distance between himself and the last object of his studies, Mount Vesuvius. I've been sent to Bithynia to straighten up Roman affairs here. I was expecting to find the usual fudged finances and rigged courts, but not Christians. If you ask me, these Christians are just another administrative headache. I was shocked to hear about so many in this province. The emperor has been anxious to keep clubs under control so they don't turn into revolutionary incubators. Upstanding citizens have helpfully submitted names for investigation. I've even had some useful lists of the troublemakers show up anonymously, though I'm a bit concerned about the legitimacy of such submissions. Between you and me and the fly on the wall, I'd prefer that the accused Christians go through the questioning with a wink and a nod. I don't really care about this Christ, but it galls me the way some Christians put on a knowing look and refuse a simple, even meaningless, oath and sprinkling some incense before the gods and the emperor's statue. Then I added a test to see if the accused would also curse Christ. That really parts the oil from the vinegar.

A lot of confused folks we hauled in here had been mixed up with that crazy outfit years ago and now have, thankfully, steered clear. I'm still a bit confused though. The story told by former Christians is not as bad as the scuttlebutt on the street would have it. They meet weekly before dawn to sing a few hymns to this Christ-god. To be a member they had to promise adherence to some basic moral code, no stealing of goods, or having sex with another man's wife, and so on. Then there is some meal gathering later in the day, I think. No, it isn't anything as vile as human flesh, but regular food. I'm stunned that these unsolicited accusations are turning up the names of citizens of the highest classes, men and women, as well as the easily duped lower classes, noncitizens, slaves, and country bumpkins. The fact that they let slaves exert leadership over citizens can only be a sign of madness—oh, you didn't know that? Yes, I tortured a couple of slave women to corroborate the former Christians' story. The slaves served as "deaconesses" or "ministers" with the Christians, but they didn't add anything to what I already knew.

In my concern about how this Christian disease is spreading, I consulted our wise and tolerant emperor, Trajan. He agreed that I'm handling this illegal club well and cautioned against following the anonymous tips. We have nothing like the manpower necessary to search out these creeps, but at least they know that once accused, they have three chances to repent and sacrifice before being sentenced to death. Christians are meeting against the law and have a dangerously stubborn and exclusive allegiance to this Christ; that suggests trouble to public order, even treason. At least greater awareness of this disease has encouraged a return to piety at the temples after a period of disuse. Well, thanks for the chance to vent; I'm off for a meeting at the baths. *Vale!* Be well!

Pliny the Younger's correspondence with the emperor Trajan, paraphrased above, reveals a great deal about Roman attitudes toward nontraditional religions and the basic markers of Christianity (*Letters* 10.96–97; ca. 110). Ancient observers assessed what Christians were doing in order to plot the new religion on the map of known religions. For government officials, like Pliny, that meant evaluating where Christianity stood on the range of approved and unapproved religions. Once mapped, established legal procedures would preserve order and ensure the public good. When the public good was most unstable, Christians found themselves in a vulnerable position.

Scapegoats and Rumors

Despite the colorful image of Christians daily and happily serving themselves to hungry lions over three centuries, both Christian and non-Christian observations from that period deny such a reality. Persecution was not systematic and certainly not a general imperial policy except under certain emperors in the mid to late third century. Instead, persecution broke out sporadically, often in response to adverse conditions. Tertullian mocked the outrage of the townspeople against Christians whenever disasters occurred: "If the Tiber rises as high as the city walls, if the Nile does not send its waters up over the fields, if the heavens give no rain, if there is an earthquake, if there is famine or pestilence, straightway the cry is, 'Away with the Christians to the lion!'"[1] At the mob and imperial levels, the assumption was that Christians represented a potential affront to the gods, who might retaliate against the community unless proper respect was restored.

Pliny's contemporary, the historian Tacitus, deplored the blame that Nero placed on Christians for the devastating fire in Rome (in 64) but agreed that Christians were "hated for depravities" and their "loathing of humanity."[2] Pliny's friend, the historian Suetonius, reiterated Roman distaste for Christians as a "breed of people characterized by an exotic and wicked [*malefica*, code word for black magic] superstition."[3] Many less genteel Romans harbored similar fears. Christians were counted as obviously incestuous because they called each other brother and sister, even between husbands and wives. Romans, who expected sacrifice in a religion, understood rumors about Christian ritual meals comprised of body and blood to be human sacrifice and cannibalism.

The Jewish Connection

Red flags for Pliny (and other officials) were a connection with Judaism, existing bad reputation of Christians, illegal meetings, stubborn resistance to a minimal show of allegiance to the empire (analogous to refusing to stand in honor of a country's flag), flaunting social and gender norms, and reduced participation in traditional worship (and its economic by-products). A further strike against Christians as orderly citizens was their unquestionably close relationship with Jews.

Confusion between Jews and Christians existed on the ground level and was not simply a matter of poorly informed Gentiles muddling the situation. Both used the same set of holy writings, usually the Septuagint translation in Greek. Both worshiped the One God represented in those Scriptures. Both insisted on severing a convert's allegiance to other divine powers upon which the empire's well-being rested, Gentiles assumed. Both took inordinate care of the needy in their communities and unusually—or unwisely, from a Gentile perspective—refused to approve abortion or exposure of infants.

Romans easily accorded Jewish religion approved status, at least for ethnic Jews. They were an identifiable people with a known homeland and an ancient tradition under its national god, attested to by venerable, holy writings. Romans were less tolerant of the Jewish tendency to assert self-rule as the will of God, which resulted in various violent episodes across the empire, including two wars in Palestine itself and the destruction of the temple. Good Romans were disgusted at the mutilation of circumcision and the laziness of taking off one day in seven for the Sabbath. Tacitus's description of Jews holds equally well for Christians, minus circumcision. Jews cultivated "perverted" and "abominable" practices and forced converts "to despise the gods, to renounce their country, and to regard parents, children, and brethren as worthless."[4]

If Christians were just another type of Jew, then Romans reasoned, they were legitimate, but worth watching for signs of revolt or repulsive customs. Gentile converts to Christianity committed the same betrayal of ancestral culture as Gentile converts to Judaism, and so presented a threat. The emperor Septimius Severus launched persecutions to rein in the conversion of Romans to Judaism and Christianity at the end of the second century. By the third century, Roman officials usually distinguished Christianity from Judaism, a move that ruled out any protection for Christianity. The unapproved status of the Christian "club" (in the usage of Pliny and Trajan) meant that its peculiarities could not be overlooked, especially if other alleged crimes were involved.

Questionable Citizenship

Practically all religion in antiquity was defined by what devotees did rather than what they believed. Particular beliefs about the nature of the world and human destiny actually had little to do with honoring the various powers that protected one's household, family, town, ethnic nation, and empire. Intellectual religion was generally the activity of philosophical schools. Gentiles observed that the actions Christians undertook in honor of Christ (ritually and morally) came at the expense of other actions previously owed to the gods. Real Christians, and therefore potentially dangerous ones, held Christ as god so exclusively and narrowly that there was no more room for acknowledging the powers that preserved all levels of community. Romans believed that everyone in the community bore a responsibility to preserve divine benefits through respectful acknowledgment of the gods' role in a community's life. To do otherwise was atheism, an affront to the gods, and a danger to the community. To this end the emperor Decius in 249 invited (i.e., required) citizens to honor Rome's traditional gods and receive certificates that proved their compliance. Since all free inhabitants of the empire were citizens (beginning in 212), insisting on a universal respect of the empire's gods and of the emperor was a logical development.

Overall, Romans prided themselves on tolerance and multiculturalism. Cynically, one might remark that Romans were keen to draw as many gods onto their side as possible to benefit and protect the empire. Different peoples naturally came with their own gods. Romans allowed different peoples to continue to honor their own gods, but they insisted that new "Romans" must also offer worship to the gods of Rome. But what does one do with a people that claims to be a nation, yet has no homeland or tribal lineage, and appeals to a God who supposedly replaces all other divinities? At what other conclusion might Romans arrive concerning converts to Christianity than that they are traitors to their country, culture, and gods?

Many non-Christians pointed to the ways Christians opted out of society, and thus out of the society's protection and benefits. People who stopped attending civic functions (e.g., festivals to the gods, gladiatorial games, and the theater), which expressed and strengthened social ties, really were no longer part of society. Those who refused to protect the empire by serving in the military or taking the customary military oath were playing into the hands of Rome's Germanic or Persian enemies. In a sense Christians had moved themselves outside the law. Romans viewed Christians as a recalcitrant people who could not differentiate particular worship of their own god from polite respect for other gods.

The moral and political stereotype of Christians created a tension whenever personal interactions with Christians suggested a more complex identity. *The Martyrdom of Pionius* (mid–3rd c.) depicts how the leaders of Smyrna were torn between the desire to follow Decius's edict and the respect they had for the Christian teacher Pionius: "Listen to us, Pionius: we love you. There are many reasons why you deserve to live, for your character and righteousness. It is good to live and to see the light."[5] At first the reluctant persecutors sought to satisfy the letter rather than the intent of the law by offering a nibble of sacrificed meat and suggesting that he just walk into the gods' temple rather than actually sacrifice. Even when Pionius refused these options, non-Christians pestered him in prison to come to his senses and save his life. On the one hand, Christians seemed to threaten the stability of the world by insulting the gods; on the other hand, members of this odd "nation" often displayed exemplary character.

ADDRESSING ROMAN FEARS

Some Christians hoped that a systematic, intellectual defense of the faith would build upon the positive day-to-day dealings with Christians that many Romans experienced. An "apology" is what ancient defendants in court would offer to explain what they did and why they should not be found guilty. An apologist was thus a defense attorney. Early in the second century, Christian intellectuals tried to clear the faith in the court of elite public opinion, addressing their treatises to Roman officials and even emperors. Apologists fought on two fronts. First, they had to dispel inflammatory rumors such as incest and cannibalism. Second, they sought to reach common ground with Roman intellectuals by describing the moral values and philosophical worldview that Christians and Romans shared.

Apologists accepted Roman appreciation for good citizenship, support of the emperor, philosophically virtuous lives, belief in one God as source of all, and undisruptive honor for ancient traditions. They trusted that the differences exhibited by the Christian "philosophy" could be tolerated the way other philosophical sects were. What follows will explore how Christians sought to meet Roman culture on its own terms and translate Christian belief into the language of cultured Romans in the areas of virtue, citizenship, and God.

Virtue

Christian apologists demanded to be heard and treated justly on the basis of an exemplary lifestyle. All the gossip about Christians was the slander of the ignorant—which the refined addressees surely were not—who were encouraged by jealous evil spirits. Unlike real criminals, Christians deserved the full protection of Roman law because they shared in and contributed to the very society which all virtue-loving Romans embraced. Tertullian dispelled the aura of hidden immorality around Christian worship by describing their gatherings as virtue clubs (*Apology* 39). Christians assembled in the same manner as non-Christian clubs dedicated to specific deities, and they offered prayers for the peace and well-being of the world. Edifying texts were read and discussed. Members' faults were identified and corrected. Club dues were directed, not toward customary "wine, women, and song," but to simple food and the support of the needy in the group. Christians went home from their meetings not as violent drunks, but "as if we had been at a school of virtue rather than a banquet."[6] Tertullian argued that Christianity was a kind of philosophy, set apart from others only by the way its adherents actually practiced what they preached (*Apology* 46).

Tertullian's contemporary, Clement of Alexandria (ca. 150–ca. 215), offered a philosophical salon where curious non-Christians could see firsthand what Christians taught and how they lived. His textbook for inquirers, *Exhortation to the Greeks*, claimed the philosophical ideal of the wise man ("gnostic") or sage for all Christians. Clement offered a path to truth and wisdom revealed through Christ's new song of salvation (chap. 1). But to know this God, one needed to adhere to the principle that "like perceives like." Humans must clean the windows of the soul (which shares in the divine nature) to look toward and be shaped by the light of truth. In order to know the Divine, one must become like the Divine. Clement put it this way: "If you long to see God truly, take part in purifications meet for Him, not of laurel leaves and fillets embellished with wool and purple, but crown yourself with righteousness, let your wreath be woven from the leaves of self-control, and seek diligently after Christ."[7] Thus the first stage before commitment to Christianity and baptism was to live like a Christian in order to begin to understand the Christian God.

Clement's follow-up volume, *Instructor*, moves from exhortation to instruction. Training in virtue is a practical, initial stage, where Christ the Instructor diagnoses, prescribes, and enables remedies for the "habits, actions, and passions" so candidates may be prepared for baptism and the pursuit of God.[8] After aligning their lives toward God, the baptized may begin to learn about truth and God himself. The whole process intentionally echoes the educational theory shared by non-Christians. Practical training (such as rote memorization) precedes and makes possible theoretical pursuits (such as philosophical inquiry).

Apologists felt that after establishing the easily investigated evidence on Christian virtue, persecutors could then look sympathetically at the group's more peculiar positions on citizenship and God. Certainly Christians stood out starkly when they not only refused to flee the massive outbreaks of measles or smallpox (in 165–180 and 250–266), but instead nursed both Christians and abandoned non-Christians alike. It is uncertain whether the apologists really believed they could break through what they saw to be demon-influenced attitudes against Christians. In time, apologetic works served as in-house resources for Christians to understand and express their faith in a more sophisticated manner.

Citizenship

Apologists enthusiastically listed the concrete results of Christian formation when they defended the quality of Christian citizenship. All apology could be said to rest on the premise that Christians not only shared Roman ideals but also actually practiced them. Virtuous citizens by definition were surely good citizens.

Christians agreed wholeheartedly with tracking down and punishing real criminals to preserve good order. On the other hand, Tertullian observed, non-Christians wanted to find a Christian beneath every tax cheat, insurrectionist, and temple vandal. Not so, Tertullian argued; Christians embraced nonviolence, paid taxes more scrupulously than non-Christians, and honored the emperor "as the human being next to God, who from God has received all his power, and is less than God alone."[9] Christians offered sacrifices for the well-being of the emperor and empire not with dead animals, but with prayer to the One True God. If Rome were truly concerned to preserve good order, Tertullian suggested, then the empire should support Christians, "since, though our numbers are so great—constituting all but the majority in every city—we conduct ourselves so quietly and modestly; I might perhaps say, [we are] known rather as individuals than as organized communities."[10] Early Christians broadly believed that, regardless of demon-instigated persecutions, God had empowered Rome to maintain order at this time in history, referring most often to Paul's advice to pay taxes and honor worldly rulers (Rom. 13:1–7).

Christians tried to answer Roman fears regarding refusal to serve in the military or hold public office. Some soldiers certainly were Christian, but it was a deeply troubling profession for most Christians because of the bloodshed and oaths to the gods and emperor required of soldiers. Public office had similar drawbacks because the accompanying duties could require the officeholder to conduct sacrifices and sentence criminals to death (i.e., bloodshed).

Apologists depicted Christian citizens engaging, through prayer, in warfare against demons (so-called gods) who tortured individuals, drew Rome into civil wars, and enticed enemies to invade. Christians thus fought on the front lines against the destabilizing powers at their sources. Origen of Alexandria (ca. 185–254) ranked Christians as an elite priesthood, whose strict moral life enhanced their prayers before the One God who could actually do something. Romans themselves excluded priests from military duty, so Romans should appreciate Christians as "a special army of piety through our intercessions to God."[11] Origen described how Christian leaders (the clergy) paralleled public officials in conducting correct worship and forming good citizens of God's kingdom, whose virtues benefited the surrounding society.

The conciliatory tone of apologists regarding Christian citizenship carried hints of dissonance. The *Epistle to Diognetus* may have exacerbated confusion about Christian loyalty more than allaying it when the apologist stated that Christians "pass their days on earth, but they are citizens of heaven. They obey the prescribed laws, and at the same time surpass the laws by their lives."[12] So were Christians law-abiding or not? citizens or not? Christians looked for soft spots in the dominant culture of the empire where non-Christian values overlapped with their own. However, there were limits to how Roman the apologists would depict Christianity. Common ground usually disappeared when addressing the topic of God.

DEMONS

In Greek thought *daimones* were neutral spiritual beings, often helpful ones. Socrates claimed his whole life in pursuit of wisdom was directed by a good demon. Christians used the term wholly in the negative to designate evil powers who rebelled against God and dedicated themselves to drawing humans into similar rebellion. The Jewish and Christian counterparts to Gentile good demons were the angels.

God

Christians struggled among themselves as well as with outsiders to find the most accurate way to describe their God. One problem lay in God being somehow both singular and plural. In the second and third centuries, monotheism was prevalent among most of the philosophical schools. Generations of ancient scholars had exerted themselves to reinterpret traditional literature in a way that "cleaned up" the gods' wanton exploits and accommodated the pantheon's origin in a supreme God. Eager to show a common disdain for vulgar and ignorant assumptions about divinity, Christian apologies regularly include chapters mocking episodes like the gods' petty manipulation of the Trojan War and Zeus's philandering.

People today may think that early Christians easily dismissed so-called gods as completely imaginary, given Paul's observation that the gods are no gods (1 Cor. 8:4–5). But at the time it was inconceivable to deny that there were beings beyond visible nature who played a role in their lives, for better or worse. Paul simply meant that the spirits to whom sacrifices were offered were "so-called gods," not truly divine. This was the source of charges of atheism; Christians did not think "gods" were gods, but rather counted them as manipulative demons. Christians were entirely willing to accept at face value the scandalous behavior of the gods, which could not be whitewashed with allegorical interpretations.

Eager to disprove the accusation of atheism, Christians leaped at the chance to show how they too believed in a single divine being. Using terms from Greek philosophy, Aristides of Athens (early 2nd c.) related that the Christian God could be described by the Aristotelian concept of God the unmoved mover (*Apology* 1). This God is without beginning, dependent on nothing, the source of all, and uninfluenced by base emotions; he has no name, no gender, no peers, and no limits. So far, so good.

However, traditional philosophical monotheism remained compatible with polytheism. After investigating Christianity, the pagan Celsus believed Christians still counted as atheists because they focused upon the supreme deity alone. Instead, he argued, "The worship of God becomes more perfect by going through them all [i.e., Zeus, Athena, et al.]."[13] Origen retorted that Christians saw things differently; all praise and worship should go directly to the One God alone, giving credit where credit is really due instead of wasting honor on misanthropic demons, who had no connection with the One God at all.

Early Christians absolutely rejected polytheism, but sometimes they used polytheistic language to position Jesus Christ in relation to the One God. Justin, addressing non-Christians, tried to convey the odd plurality of Christianity's singular God. This God is composed of the "unchangeable and eternal God, the Creator of all"; a Son (Jesus Christ), who is second; and third, the Spirit.[14] In order to connect the material world to an immaterial God, Justin built upon the term used for Jesus Christ in the Gospel of John: Logos (Word/Reason).

Logos resonated with both Stoicism and Platonism. In Greek, *logos* encompassed the role of language, which communicates and organizes thoughts and actions. As a divine concept in Platonism, Logos mediated and revealed the One True God, who could not otherwise be perceived by inhabitants of the material world (similar to John 1:18). Logos, as the cocreator, executed the supreme God's plans for giving order to all that is. Stoics believed Logos to be both the plan of all reality as well as the whole universe organized by the plan.

Justin enthusiastically adapted these views to fit the knowledge of Jesus Christ revealed through Scripture and in worship. Because the Logos created all things (John 1:1–4) and humanity in his image (recalling Genesis), non-

Christian seers and philosophers "spoke well in proportion to the share [each one] had of the spermatic word [*logos*], seeing what was related to it." Christ the Logos (Word-Reason) gave the imprint of rationality on all humanity, which is like a seed (*sperma*) ready to spring to life. As a result, Justin concluded, "whatever things were rightly said among all men, are the property of us Christians."[15]

At the end of the day, though, apologists usually lost their audience in appropriating all divine knowledge to Christianity and in claiming that the divine Son of God, the Logos, became a flesh-and-blood human being while remaining himself the divine organizing principle of all reality.

THE STRUGGLE TO DEFINE WHO IS CHRISTIAN

Drawing Lines in Daily Life

Apologies stressed how well Christians fit in, if only the Romans would appreciate their philosophy and prayerful service to the empire. In-house Christian writings reveal the inner struggles. How do Christians differ from non-Christians, if not in a lifestyle that bears testimony to the real God, who laid out distinct behaviors for his people in Scripture and Christ? While Christian intellectuals were lauding the moral and philosophical qualities of Christianity to non-Christians, they and their less learned brothers and sisters had to make concrete decisions about Christian identity in everyday life. Being brought before a local magistrate to answer the question "Are you a Christian?" was a rare occurrence. Yet the intrinsically religious nature of ancient life meant that Christians had to develop ways of being faithful to the One God of Jesus Christ, ways that allowed them to function with non-Christians on a daily basis.

The foundation of Christian character lay in what believers heard in worship and saw among more senior Christians. But questions still abounded. May I attend a banquet at a Gentile/non-Christian house? How do I complete a business deal or a marriage or a will since contracts and ceremonies might involve the witness of the gods? How can I be educated since the curriculum consists of literature about the gods? Why can't I enjoy the fun of civic festivals since I know that the gods aren't real gods? Whether presented confrontationally or in conciliatory tones, Christian identity made many occupations, habits of speech, and leisure activities off-limits.

Very little counted as religiously neutral for Christians. The world was rife with evil powers, anxious and angry over the humans escaping their grasp on account of Christ. From the late second century, an explosion of Christian literature tried to answer these questions about boundaries, although not to the satisfaction of some believers who thought there was room for greater overlap. Several professions were deemed incompatible with the Christian calling: blatantly immoral jobs such as those dealing with the sale of sex, trades associated with pagan worship (artists, sculptors, incense merchants), schoolteachers and actors whose subject matter consisted in promoting Greco-Roman mythology and religion. Christians were not to swear by the gods, not even in throwaway phrases such as "by Hercules." Tertullian went so far as to insist that Christians should correct non-Christians who swore in their presence, even if that risked divulging one's identity and led to arrest (*On Idolatry* 20).

Hard-liners like Tertullian celebrated examples of believers who did not compromise because such Christians recognized the risk to their eternal fate in seemingly innocuous actions. Tertullian applauded a Roman soldier who refused to wear a celebration wreath handed out to the troops in honor of the emperor and his sons (*The Chaplet*). Citing his allegiance to Christ, the soldier won himself a swift imprisonment and, likely, execution. Many Christians complained that honorary crowns were never forbidden as idolatry in Scripture. Tertullian replied that Christians determine such things through tradition and Scripture; over the years the believing community developed ways of working out the lived implications of Scripture's commands and prohibitions. When Scripture says to worship God alone, this means to avoid all places, objects, and events associated with the gods as determined by earlier generations of the faithful.

Tertullian was not an isolated crank. Personal witness to Christian morality was key to relations with non-Christians, as well as with the God who freed believers from the powers of evil. Christians agreed that officiating at sacrifices, wearing things obviously dedicated to gods, and participating in immoral or criminal behavior were all out of the question. Other situations were disputed. While leaders shuddered at the bloodthirsty games (cf. "You shall not murder"; Exod. 20:13), the immodesty and idolatry of the theater and festivals, many of the faithful asserted these were simply fun and people-oriented diversions rather than service to idols. Tertullian reminded his audience that "Gentiles" would under no circumstances attend a Christian celebration "for they would fear lest they should seem to be Christians. We are not apprehensive lest we seem to be heathens!"[16]

Yet teachers also worked hard to find ways of interacting with non-Christians. Clement of Alexandria helped converts learn how Christians could still go to the baths, exercise, attend dinner parties with non-Christians, and take part in other everyday activities without compromising their faith (*The Instructor*). Tertullian sanctioned Christian participation in domestic ceremonies of life because events like naming ceremonies, betrothals, and marriages focused upon human relations, not on gods (*On Idolatry* 16). He also offered alternative applications of the skills used in off-limits professions; for instance, an idol maker could shift into carpentry.

During the substantial periods without persecution, early Christians shaped their daily life in light of their faith, some more aggressive in their adaptations than others. When identity was put to the test in active persecution, the varied interpretations of how far a Christian could accommodate Roman culture and still be faithful to God created a more pressing dilemma for individual believers and the church.

Weighing the Cost of Fidelity

The Martyrdom of Perpetua and Felicitas preserves a pitiful scene where the distraught father of the young noblewoman Perpetua, a convert to Christianity, pleads for her to consider her unweaned son's life, her father's grief, and the rest of the family's well-being. Later the judge commanded that her father be beaten in front of her in a bid to change her mind. Even non-Christian families of converts stood to lose status, be subjected to torture, and have property confiscated for failing to prevent family members from making an illegal conversion to Christianity. Just what kind of family values did Christians support? Why couldn't Christians also be good mothers or daughters, fathers or sons? What options did Christians have when their identity was challenged?

Persecutions generally put pressure on known leaders (bishops, priests, catechetical teachers, or socially elite converts) in hopes of bringing their followers to their senses and to give notice that the empire would not harbor harmful elements in its midst. When late third-century emperors moved toward universal persecution, and the hoped-for extermination of Christianity, the cost to Christian communities was their church buildings and precious items, such as Scriptures, liturgical books, and other items used for worship. The boundaries set by Roman authorities were simple: Are you a Christian? Will you sacrifice? Will you hand over your religious books? Will you stop holding meetings? The answers to these questions revealed who was dangerously stubborn and who was a reasonable and good citizen.

For Christians, these simple questions (and their consequences) caused enormous individual and communal conflict. The aftermath of each imperial persecution left the Christians scrambling to sort out what to do with those who did not endure according to the pattern of Jesus' suffering and death. Furthermore, dying for the faith seemed to many a very narrow calling. Thus, while many Christians honored the ideal, some had a different idea of how to be a Christian in time of persecution. Could Christians merely go through the motions of a ritual they considered religiously meaningless? Why fault those who committed pro forma acts to protect their loved ones by preserving life, status, reputation, and property? What is the status of those who prudently skipped town entirely, imitating the normal exodus of urban refugees in time of other life-threatening events, such as epidemics or war? What is a book compared to a human life? In fact, during the Great (and last) Persecution (303–312), authorities in the West, who were more accommodating of Christians, often cooperated with church leaders to protect the bulk of the laity by requesting that communities merely hand over (*tradere*) Bibles and liturgical books.

Postpersecution Trauma

With remarkable unity, Christians left picking up the pieces after a persecution came to recognize that all who fudged their identity had betrayed the faith on some level and were to be considered apostates. Those who fled at least did not lie about their membership and often experienced official (and unofficial) confiscation of their assets. With furious rancor, believers split over whether the church could mediate the reintegration of apostates and whether there were any differences in offenses among handing over books (*traditores*, traitors), acquiring a forged certificate of sacrifice (*libellatici*), or offering a sacrifice (*sacrificati*). Imagine the gut-wrenching emotions sparked when an apostate with sound body, untouched material goods, and living family walked back into the Christian assembly following a persecution, into the presence of scarred confessors missing body parts and families reduced to poverty, mourning sons and daughters, mothers and fathers. Consider the dilemma when such an apostate had been a member of the clergy and sought to take up a position of leadership again. Would you want such a priest or bishop to baptize your children? to offer the Eucharist? to teach what he evidently did not think worth standing up for? Finally, visualize not just ten or twenty apostates seeking restoration, but hundreds.

The Decian persecution in 249 took Christians by surprise. Cyprian, bishop of Carthage, regretted the long break from persecution because Christians had grown careless and lazy in the faith. Most Christians were not up to the challenge when it hit. Instead, "immediately at the first words of the threatening foe, the greatest number of the brethren betrayed their faith, and were cast down, not by the onset of persecution, but cast themselves down by voluntary lapse."[17] Magistrates in Rome, Carthage, and Alexandria were overwhelmed with eager Christian sacrificers who desperately dragged along babies and children. Many who sought to get their certificates had to try several days to get through the lines.

One means of restoration increasingly rejected after the institution of empirewide persecutions in the third century, had been for apostates to seek reconciliation through letters of recommendation from heroes, known as confessors, who survived imprisonment and torture during a persecution. This quick recovery caused its own problems within a congregation when neither the apostate nor the faithful had opportunity to heal. Instant reconciliation created awkward tensions between authority based upon suffering and authority of the congregation's chosen bishop. The sheer number of returning apostates could mean easy reintegration for some who had access to the confessors and a long process for others who were not so privileged.

Two alternatives surfaced: to restore or not to restore. Building on earlier developments for reintegrating baptized believers who had committed serious sins after baptism, some Christians opted to provide rehabilitations of apostates. Capitulation to persecution was a symptom of an ill and weak Christian. Cyprian of Carthage recommended, "We ought to give our assistance, our healing art, to those who are wounded; neither let us think them dead, but rather let us regard them as lying half alive, whom we see to have been wounded in the fatal persecution."[18] A single act of allegiance to Rome's gods was certainly a failure more dire than attending the theater, but not to the point of eradicating one's Christian identity entirely. Apostates could enroll in a penitential reorientation process leading to eventual restoration, including reception of the Eucharist (see chap. 8).

Not all Christians thought that mere humans had jurisdiction over the most serious offenses. They drew the line strictly; only God could negotiate such a weighty transgression against himself. Allowing such sinners to return would pollute the church and offend God. Consequently, rigorist believers unconditionally refused to restore fellowship with any apostate from sacrificer, to certificate forger, to book "traitor." Apostates had voluntarily recrossed the boundary between Christian and non-Christian, from which there could be no return. The split over a pure church or healing church persisted within the ancient church. Rigorists who believed there was no hope for any apostate broke fellowship with more permissive Christians. In Rome after Decius's death in 251, Novatian founded a parallel and empirewide set of congregations who believed there to be no forgiveness possible within the church for serious postbaptismal sins such as adultery, murder, and idolatry. Another long-lasting schism was that of the Donatists in Africa, who separated over a bishop deemed illegitimate because one of the bishops who consecrated him allegedly handed over church books during the Great Persecution. Despite imperial enforcement against the Donatists beginning in the fourth century, it took the invasions of the Germanic Vandal tribe in the fifth century to draw the two sides together.

MARTYRS AND THEIR ROLES

Origin of the Term "Martyr"

A martyr (Greek *martys*) in the ancient world was first of all a "witness" in the legal sense: one who has seen an event and can tell what happened, including what it meant. Jesus claimed that all of Jewish Scripture was his witness. After his death and resurrection, followers who experienced the risen Jesus were a special set of witnesses whom Peter claimed were "chosen by God" to take this testimony to others (Acts 10:41–43). The book of Revelation proclaimed "Jesus Christ, the faithful witness [*martys*], the firstborn of the dead, and the ruler of the kings of the earth" (1:5). Jesus was the preeminent witness to the hope to which his followers aspired. Through his death, believers were freed from sins. They could anticipate their own transformation from death to life as a perpetual priestly kingdom through Jesus' blood (1:5–6). Furthermore, believers who persevered in their hope had nothing to fear from mere earthly rulers, who would have to answer to the Christians' Lord.

At some point between Ignatius of Antioch (ca. 110) and Polycarp of Smyrna (d. ca. 155), the term *martyr* developed the full meaning of bearing witness to the good news of Christ's death and resurrection by one's own death in preference to denying Christ.[19] Ignatius morbidly proclaimed that "to be among the wild beasts is to be in the arms of God," but he never called himself a martyr.[20] Yet by 177 the faithful prisoners of Lyons and Vienne in Gaul (France) limited the term *martyr* to those who died due to their confession of Christ. They specifically connected the term with Jesus' title as "martyr/witness" in Revelation 1:5 and 3:14.[21]

Dying at the hands of tyrants rather than abandoning one's principles was an honored tradition among Christians and non-Christians. Socrates regularly showed up in Christian appeals to Roman officials in order to convey why Christians were so stubborn and why they should be respected for their stubbornness. The Roman historian Tacitus was familiar with this among Jews who "believe that the souls of those who die in battle or under execution are immortal."[22] Out of their Jewish treasury, Christians avidly pointed to Daniel and the Maccabees. Jesus' identity as a suffering Messiah echoed the rejection of the true prophets of Israel. True followers were to "take up your cross and follow [Jesus]" because those who denied Christ would in turn find themselves disowned before God and the heavenly court (Matt. 10:32–33; Mark 8:34–38).

Martyrdom offered a privileged opportunity to give public testimony about the message and character of Christians. Great rewards were in store for martyrs in the resurrection and for their fellow believers, who would continue to enjoy the encouragement and patronage of the martyr. Nevertheless, judicial death was not to be sought, for Christians readily observed how dangerous volunteering could be. It often resulted in panicked apostasy of the unprepared believers. The believing community had a responsibility to train members for the potential battle. Only well-trained troops were to engage in direct conflict with evil.

Training

Why did some Christians succumb while others persevered? Much rested upon how individuals opened themselves to Christ and his Spirit. But how? The survivors of the persecution at Lyons and Vienne (France) emphasized the importance of good training, utilizing both athletic and military imagery. Those without proper training would not enjoy victory but would suffer defeat and eternal suffering apart from the "life-giving Name."[23] Ten individuals "appeared unprepared and untrained, weak as yet, and unable to endure so great a conflict."[24] Throughout the account, anxiety over those who might fall away contrasts starkly with the example of those who were well prepared and thus endured. These contests were always team sports; winning and losing impacted the remaining believers. Those who fell away threatened the morale of the other prisoners as well as the rest of the believing community. Additionally, they provided a poor witness to the non-Christians, who treated the apostates with contempt while leaving them imprisoned under charges other than being a Christian.

The newer Christians of Lyons and Vienne were not generally as strong as those who had belonged to the faith longer, in part because they depended upon bodily strength rather than spiritual strength developed through various disciplines. One hope for the weak was exercise in the discipline of repentance, which could take place within prison, where many of the spiritually dead apostates of Lyons were reborn to new life through the ministry and intercession of the confessors (Eusebius, *Church History* 5.1.45–46).

Christians recommended a lifestyle organized around the general principle "Don't get too attached to this life." Persecution increased the pressure for believers to support one another by detaching themselves from excess material goods. During the mid-third-century persecutions, Cyprian of Carthage (*On Works and Alms*) encouraged almsgiving not merely for purifying one's soul, but especially to support those under duress from persecution (such as orphaned children, families who had lost their properties and status). Tertullian understood the Christian regimen to be typified by separation from the world, much as athletes wore themselves out in the gymnasium to hone their skills, and soldiers hardened themselves through arduous drills so that they might dismiss fear and concentrate on victory (*To the Martyrs* 3). Marriage, because it involved Roman ideals of citizenship, family status, and property, was one of those potential encumbrances that Christians might want to avoid. In his treatise against second marriages, *To His Wife*, Tertullian warned against the distraction of marriage because one might be tempted to deny Christ to protect a spouse or children. Furthermore, a lack of Christian upper-class men meant that many upper-class Christian women had pagan husbands who could blackmail their wives with the threat of turning them in as Christians. Tertullian suspected some pagan men of marrying Christian wives precisely to keep the wife's dowry after lodging criminal accusations.

During the Great Persecution (303–312/324), the historian Eusebius described the training that made a recent martyr, Procopius, ready.[25] Procopius organized his life around God and used his professional training for that purpose. As an educated man, he read Scripture during worship and translated Christian works from Greek to Syriac. His avid study of Scripture accompanied by a simple diet, periodic fasting, and prayer kept him strengthened by God. This lifestyle gave him further spiritual tools for fostering the faith of others in conjunction with the liturgical application of his literary skills. Consequently, he was well prepared to oppose the powers of evil.

A life steeped in spiritual and physical labors (*ascesis*; see chap. 8), and oriented toward God and neighbor, shaped Christians' ability to draw the right boundary between themselves and non-Christians. Good training gave "contestants" the ability to make a confession with joy precisely because they were filled by Christ and hardened against the very physical challenges of judicial torture.[26] The hopes that sustained the martyrs and heartened their fellow believers were anchored in beliefs that faithful suffering in the body would lead to resurrection. In death, martyrs assumed an elite position, serving their brothers and sisters left behind.

Imitation of Christ

The community that witnessed Polycarp's last days (ca. 155) did so through the eyes of Christ's passion in the Gospels. Polycarp did not seek death, but when betrayed he, like Christ, asked that God's will be done. He accompanied the arresting soldiers, peacefully riding on a donkey. When questioned by a Roman magistrate, Polycarp offered to discuss the truth, but like Pilate, the magistrate left the outcome to the mob. In effect Christ's passion was replayed before the eyes of the watching believers, who became eyewitnesses not only of the martyrs but also of Christ's victorious suffering.

At Lyons and Vienne, Blandina, though doubly weak according to worldly standards as a slave and a woman, illustrated Christ's passion rather remarkably. After wearing out the torturers, she was fixed to a post for wild beasts to eat her. Believers saw Christ hanging in torture instead of her, assuring them "that every one who suffers for the glory of Christ has fellowship always with the living God."[27] Christ suffered in the martyrs, gave them refreshment and insensibility to pain, and ultimately was the champion who conquered attempts by Satan and his demons to overturn believers' confession of the One True God. When the exceptionally elderly (Bishop Pothinus, age 90) or young (Ponticus, age 15) or weak (slaves and women such as Blandina) held up beyond expectation, the rest of the believers exulted in the power of Christ to transform human weakness into strength.

A related concern about martyrdom derived from contemporary struggles to define Christ himself. The gospel-in-a-nutshell to which Ignatius appealed was not just a handy way to recite Christian beliefs. Ignatius stressed Christ's story against other models of Christ that did away with body, suffering, and death. Apart from the path of humiliation to exaltation, there was no Christianity. There was certainly no reason to bear witness through suffering and death if the body did not matter. Ignatius exclaimed, "But as for me, I do not place my hopes in one who died for me in appearance, but in reality."[28] Hope lived in the body that God would transform from death to even more real life. When martyrs authentically reenacted the gospel, surviving believers praised God in the death of his steadfast followers and were inspired to greater zeal.

Intercessors and Patrons

The communities who recorded martyrdoms firmly believed that God was present in and through the confessors and martyrs. Prisoners for Christ's sake carried special influence with God on behalf of their brothers and sisters in the faith. Where God was close to his martyrs, the martyrs in turn were close to God.

The steadfast confessors of Lyons and Vienne ministered to the wavering Christian captives and the larger Christian community. They engaged in continuous attempts to prompt repentance among backsliders and to intercede with God for them. When many did repent, the confessors declared them forgiven. The newly revived Christians went on to become real martyrs, much to the joy and relief of the whole church community.

Other faithful prisoners exerted prophetic authority in counseling fellow prisoners, believers, and even the clergy. After receiving a vision, Attalus corrected a fellow prisoner, Alcibiades, who refused to relax his customary austere diet in prison. Upon hearing Attalus's message, Alcibiades immediately submitted to the Spirit's counsel and ate the provisions brought to the prisoners by fellow believers. The Carthiginian martyr Perpetua also had a privileged relationship with God. The Spirit's gifts gave her the authority to demand visions, to intercede successfully on behalf of a dead though unbaptized brother, and to arrange reconciliation between a local priest and bishop.

Believers cherished the memory of their homegrown martyrs through texts and celebrations at the martyrs' tombs on their "birthdays" (their birth into new life following their death). By their ritual and textual presence, martyrs continued to teach and lead the congregation. During the Decian persecution, believers in Smyrna retained some of Pionius's own discourses (ca. 250) and filled in the rest of his passion story. They were convinced that their martyred priest "kept many from straying while he dwelt in the world, and when he was finally called to the Lord and bore witness, he left us this writing for our instruction that we might have it even to this day as a memorial of his teaching."[29]

It was a common belief that the martyrs were honored with an immediate resurrection to the Lord's court while all other dead in Christ slept or rested until the general resurrection. The martyr's continued desire to help fellow believers seemed natural. Although torn by persecution, the church family left behind by a martyr stayed in touch. Origen encouraged an imprisoned Christian, Ambrose, to persevere toward martyrdom because it was an opportunity to become a patriarch like Abraham and friend of God.[30] In the capacity of a martyr, Ambrose would "receiv[e] the freedom to benefit" not just his biological family but also any believer who followed his example.[31] Origen further counseled Ambrose that by a faithful death, he could better love and pray for those left behind and thus serve the believers as a father of the faith. The martyrs' blood, when spilled according to the model of Christ, might also redeem and exalt the faithful (*Exhortation to Martyrdom* 50).

Resurrection and the Body

Martyrs and their remaining brothers and sisters gave a deep significance to the role of their bodies. When possible, Christians collected the martyrs' bodily remains because, as explained in Polycarp's passion, they desired "to have fellowship with [the martyrs'] holy flesh."[32] Fellowship consisted of memorial gatherings around the remains of the martyr. The non-Christians in Lyons and Vienne (177) took great pains to destroy the martyrs' bodies in order to deprive the remaining Christians of physical access to their heroes and to thumb their noses at Christians' strange belief in bodily resurrection.

Martyrs' bodies were the location where victory over evil took place and where Christ himself was revealed.[33] In death, believers "read" bodies for marks of the martyr's vindication and resurrection. Looking at Pionius's battered and burned body, the believers of Smyrna declared that his "crown [of victory] was made manifest through his body."[34] They marveled at Pionius's body, which looked like a fit athlete, "so that the Christians were all the more confirmed in the faith and those who had lost the faith returned dismayed and with fearful consciences."

Early Christians did not flinch from connecting martyrdom to sacrifices, drawing on multilayered ritual and scriptural images.[35] Christian observers at Polycarp's burning perceived the odor of sacrificial incense and bread baking (*Martyrdom of Polycarp* 15). This eucharistic image echoed Ignatius's longing to be ground up like wheat by the teeth of beasts in order to become Christ's pure bread (*Epistle to the Romans* 4).[36] The tradition in the Letter to the Hebrews emphasized Christ's dual role as sacrifice and sacrificer (high priest). Underlying the priestly symbol was Israel's tradition (Lev. 21), which required of priests a high level of ritual purity in all aspects of their lives. Origen, who combined these strands, observed how the baptism of blood sealed the martyrs' imitation of Jesus, who set the standard as a pure sacrifice and sacrificer. "Who else," Origen asked, "is the blameless priest [of Lev. 21] offering a blameless sacrifice than the person who holds fast to his confession and fulfills every requirement the account of martyrdom demands?"[37] Believers and nonbelievers alike expressed amazement that Christians endured multiple torture sessions and encounters with wild animals. But the Romans, steeped in a horror of human sacrifice, could not but shrink from a God who accepted these mangled sacrifices.

Conclusion: Martyr as Christian par Excellence

Living with the potential of persecution required attention to the training necessary to produce Christians capable of confessing the faith even to death. Trying to drawing a clear line between Christians and non-Christians made a lot of sense when failure cost not merely one's earthly life, but also eternal life and the community's stability. Martyrs established an ideal for noncompromise built on the hope of dying and living with Christ, who pioneered life after death for humanity. Internal Christian polemic sorted out Christian from non-Christian within their own ranks, using martyrs as the "canon," or measuring stick. In this way martyrs and their abiding reputation bore witness to the struggle to define the center and perimeter of Christian identity in this period.

The canon of the gospel-in-a-nutshell was at stake in all aspects of Christian identity. If Christ's birth, life, death, and resurrection shaped Christians' life in the world, then it also marked what counted as authoritative Scripture and how to interpret that Scripture. The rule/canon of faith determined Christianity's relationship to the story of God in Scripture, both Jewish and new Christian writings. The mainstream Great Church resisted other "gospels" about Jesus which rejected customary Scripture traditions. At the same time Christians enthusiastically developed more sophisticated ways to understand and live according to the rich paradoxes and ambiguities of this diverse collection of holy writings, which would eventually be called the Bible.

QUESTIONS FOR DISCUSSION

1. What was so alarming about Christianity and Christians? Why would these fears lead to persecution?
2. What did Romans hope to accomplish in their persecution of Christians? Did they?
3. How did Christians try to calm non-Christians' fears? How effective was this?
4. To what did martyrs bear witness? Why did martyrs and confessors receive so much honor and authority from their fellow believers?

SUGGESTED FURTHER READING

Acts of the Christian Martyrs. Edited and translated by H. Musurillo. Oxford: Oxford University Press, 1972.

Bowersock, G. W. *Martyrdom and Rome*. New York: Cambridge University Press, 1995.

Clark, Gillian. *Christianity and Roman Society*. New York: Cambridge University Press, 2004.

Wilken, Robert. *Christians as the Romans Saw Them*. 2nd ed. New Haven: Yale University Press, 2003.

5

Scripture

From Jewish to Christian

INTRODUCTION

This chapter continues looking at what it meant to say *"Christianus/a sum,* I am a Christian." To accomplish this, we will explore the oral and written traditions that anchored how Christians thought about God and what it meant to follow him. At the time it was necessary for Christians to define how they would relate both to Gentiles and to Jews. Christian relations with Jews, who also claimed to be God's people, proved the more difficult conundrum. Christians increasingly asked what it meant to depend heavily upon Jewish Scripture and yet claim fundamental differences about God and themselves. In what sense was Jewish Scripture to be authoritative for Christians? How did more recent writings that placed Jesus at the center of the covenant replace or change the authority of Jewish Scripture? What should count for Scripture, and how should believers decide? Even when Christians could describe what constituted Scripture, who had the authority to read and interpret it?

Jews had long considered Torah to be the presence of God in the midst of their scattered communities. Early Christians built on this idea and began to speak of Scripture as an incarnation of God. Jesus was the Son of God revealed (or incarnate) in human flesh. Scripture was the revelation of God in the "body" of a text. Just as the body of Christ pointed to God, so too does Scripture point to God. Christians communed with the Word of God (Christ) through God's Word (Scripture).

Identifying and reading Scripture in this way had important implications. Scripture was heard and interpreted within a community drawn together for the purpose of fellowship with God. Reading God's Word and being the privileged interpreters of it reinforced the community's claim that they were

God's people and heirs to God's continuing story in Christ. This chapter will take up this understanding of Scripture and the Word, an understanding that would determine how Christians came to regard Jewish and specifically Christian writings as one Scripture that was uniquely their own.

WHAT IS SCRIPTURE?

What is Scripture? Etymologically it means sacred "writing," a term applied to the collection of the Jewish (Old Testament, or Covenant) and Christian (New Testament, or Covenant) writings. The Greek term *ta biblia* (scrolls, books) provides our term "Bible." Since the first Christians were Jewish, their references to Scripture meant Jewish Scripture, usually in the Greek Septuagint translation. Christians continued the Jewish belief that Scripture carried the authority of God himself for the continuous formation of his people. The signs that something was considered Scripture were its use in worship and its being invoked with the authoritative phrase "It is written . . ." Christians believed that the Spirit who had inspired earlier Jewish writings continued to reveal and inform new Israel. They assumed that their own experience of God through Jesus, and the written records of that experience, had authority in worship and their lives. Over time it was necessary for later generations of believers to sort out what writings they would call their own.

Written Subset of Tradition

Generations of Jews made difficult choices about what of their family's history with God they ought to pass on to their successors (see chap. 1). Over the centuries, these accounts were preserved in increasingly extensive written compositions. This collecting and bundling of accounts created greater uniformity among them and allowed them to be distributed more widely. The exile proved an invaluable opportunity for Judah's scholars to intensify the process of gathering and editing ancient documents into a recognizable collection, and their work was continued into the Hellenistic period.

When early Christians used Jewish Scripture, they were claiming an identity with Israel and its story. However, these Christians also believed that this story had begun to unfold in new and unanticipated ways. They continued to record the story of God's interaction with his people and share it through writing, proclamation, and worship. Through their preaching, ritual and devotional practices, and sharing of various texts, they imitated the Jewish model of selecting and handing down accounts of God and his people. Eventually, a new body of specifically Christian writings would also be regarded as having the authority of Scripture. The content of this new Scripture would come to be called the "New Testament."

Many believers today might know what it is to be Christian because "the Bible tells me so." However, the Bible today does not look like early Christians' Scripture. Nor was Scripture understood in quite the same way. Protestants will often describe Scripture as their sole and absolute authority. It is difficult for them to grasp how open the early Christians were (and the Roman Catholic and Orthodox traditions are today) to the idea that Christ and the Spirit continued to speak through the community of believers.[1] Scripture was not a sealed collection: it was evolving and malleable.

Tertullian was careful to remind believers that they never justified their practices and beliefs merely by claiming that "it is written": "If . . . you insist upon having positive scripture injunction, you will find none. Tradition will be held forth to you as the originator of them, custom as their strengthener, and faith as their observer."[2] The rituals and meaning of baptism, signing oneself with the cross, and other religious actions depend on Christians learning them from previous Christians ("custom") and testing the practices ("faith as their observer"). In this view, Scripture is a significant but not exclusive authority. It is one aspect of the handing-down process (tradition) whereby Christians know who they are and what God desires for them.

A Contested Family History

Jews drawn to Jesus the Christ had no doubt about the continuing relevance of Israel's story to Christians living in the new covenant. The problem lay with how to invite Gentiles and give them a role in the continuing narrative. Many texts, Christian and Gentile, reveal the tension caused by entering into a relationship with another people's God and history. In one sense the issue was not really whether Gentiles had to become Jews in order to become Christian. The issue was how Jewish the Gentile converts must become. Scripture and identity were interconnected because Scripture effectively rewrote the convert's story. The new believer gained a new past and a new kinship. The old self was washed away, and the new self was now a child of Abraham through faith in the resurrected Christ. Christian leaders took for granted that their audience was (or should be) familiar with foundational narratives of Israel's relationship with God; it was part of a convert's training. The earliest discernible Christian art of the third century depicts just as many, if not more, stories from Israel's past than Christ's story (e.g., Noah and the ark, Jonah, three youths in the furnace). Early Christians took various approaches to distinguish themselves from Judaism while universally retaining the "family history" of Scripture.

Christians appreciated many other edifying texts connected to Israel's Scripture, labeled in modern times as Apocrypha and Pseudepigrapha. The Apocrypha (hidden or obscure) were appended to the Septuagint. The Pseudepigrapha (written under false names) circulated independently of the Septuagint and consisted of works about or attributed to ancient Israelite heroes. These texts arose from the postexilic period; most were written in Aramaic or Greek rather than in Hebrew. Even though these texts survive almost exclusively in Christian collections, most were Jewish compositions ranging from the third century BC into the Christian era. Some may have been Jewish Christian compositions.[3] While Christians often regarded these texts as inspired, they nevertheless afforded them an authority secondary to that of the standard categories of Torah/Prophets/Writings. However, aside from Torah and Prophets, neither Jews nor Christians had compiled a rough list of what counted as Scripture until near the end of the second century AD. Usage, rather than legislation, would settle on a stable set of documents for both communities.

The Christian claim to Jewish Scripture had practical implications for religious and social relations between Jews and Christians. Sharing Scripture suggested to many Christians that they could also share in Jewish worship and practices, much to the consternation of generations of Christian leaders. Consequently, looking at the accepted authority of Jewish Scripture among Christians entails a peek into the complex relations of Jews and Christians in other early Christian texts.

Some early Christian texts are illustrative of the porous boundary between Jew and Christian in the early centuries AD. The *Didache* was a church manual from Syria around AD 100 that incorporated Jewish ethical teaching and prayers. At Rome, the Christian Hermas (*Shepherd of Hermas*, late 1st–mid-2nd c.) received urgent revelations for the church to embody traditional Jewish morality via the Jewish apocalyptic genre, to prepare the church for Christ's return. The *Odes of Solomon* (Syria, 2nd c.) employ biblical psalm conventions to celebrate believers' relationship with Christ. Circulating under the name of Clement of Rome, *Homilies* and the parallel *Recognitions* purported to relate Peter's preaching as witnessed by the young Clement. These curious writings appear in fourth-century versions that were deemed mainstream enough to translate into Latin in the fifth century. Based perhaps on third-century accounts of Peter, the pseudo-Clementine works celebrate the chosenness of the Jewish people and honor Torah ritual purity for food and morality, though not animal sacrifice. They often place the revelation of Moses and Torah on par with Jesus, the True Prophet of the Father. Jesus excels Moses only in being both Prophet and Messiah.[4]

Scholars have recently begun to reassess Jewish-Christian identities and relationships, virtually overturning the long-held assumption that the two

religions actually experienced an abrupt and early "parting of ways." Scholars have progressively abandoned many traditional dates for a definitive
break. One had been the destruction of the temple in AD 70. Another was
the assumed "excommunication" of Christians issued by some Jewish leaders in Jamnia on the Judean coast (ca. 90). Again it was thought that the Bar
Kokhba revolt against Rome (135–137) was the definitive cutoff. Yet such is
the difficulty in distinguishing Christians from Jews until perhaps the third
century AD that no single model suffices for the complex mingling of ethnic
and religious identity. Instead, it appears that Jewish influence and interactions continued to be a treasured, if problematic, heritage for understanding
God's salvation in Jesus and the lifestyle of God's people.

The continued pastoral efforts to keep Christians out of synagogues, even
when Jews were apparently offering refuge during persecutions (*Martyrdom
of Pionius* 13, mid-2nd c.) points instead to persistent mingling that included
keeping Jewish festivals, fasts, and Torah purity requirements. The vehement
denunciation of "Jews" in early Christian literature (2nd–5th c.) actually
exposes the widespread attraction of Jewish worship and practices to Christians, which leaders sought to reverse.[5] These "Judaizing" Christians would
not register quite so clear a boundary between Jew and Christian until the
collapse of ancient Mediterranean urban culture in the Middle Ages.

Explaining why and how Jew differed from Christian depended in great
part upon distinct interpretations of the shared family history, which diverged
at the person of Jesus. Christians understood themselves to be on the receiving end of God's latest update to the covenant, personally delivered and
founded through Jesus and proclaimed in succeeding witnesses through the
Spirit. The initial purpose of spoken and written Christian teaching was to
announce, explain, and safeguard the understanding of Jesus, his life and significance within the context of God's covenant relationship with Israel.

Continuing the Story: New Christian Traditions

In the first century AD, the works that would later form the New Testament were transmitted orally. The texts were meant to be read aloud before a
group. In the second century, the hearers of these texts continued to believe
that the Spirit who had inspired the written messages continued to dwell in
their midst. This same Spirit guided the community's worship, reinforced
its practices, and helped to determine which texts should become normative
for faith and life. Christians began referring to some of their own writings as
Scripture by the end of the first century (Letters of Paul, in 2 Pet. 3:15–16).
Nevertheless, even in the fourth century, Christians were more concerned
with identifying teachings, contemporaneous or written, that accorded with

the story of faith by which they already lived, than with creating a definitive list of canonical texts.

Christians quickly developed a body of writings meant to solve community problems and to shepherd believers in their understanding and living of Jesus' story. They desired to share beliefs and practices to make concrete their fellowship in Christ that exceeded ethnic, geographical, and chronological barriers. As a result, they followed Paul's practice of keeping in touch with each other through letters, often read during worship gatherings. When crises occurred, they wrote letters and treatises to address them. By the late second century, Christians called the writings they deemed sacred by the name of the age: New Covenant, or New Testament. Jewish Scripture, while also revealing Christ, was part of the Old Covenant period and therefore was called the Old Testament. New Testament writings earned their place through widespread use in worship. With a multitude of texts vying for authority and worship space, the same question of discernment that prompted the *Didache* community to test the Spirit of itinerant prophets (see chap. 3 above) required communities to test the Spirit of itinerant texts as well.

The Role of Worship

Although, like most people in antiquity, Christians were not widely literate in the sense of being able to read and write, they were more engaged with listening to and discussing texts than almost any other group besides Jews. Drawing from Jewish veneration of Scripture, Christians too believed that texts were a means that God used to communicate with his people. Worship in the first century was the place where the Spirit of Jesus spoke and taught through inspired believers and texts. Live performances of the Spirit through prophets and communal singing shared worship time with the oral delivery of "recorded" performances in Scripture. Worship was the place where interpretation of Jewish Scripture was created and taught according to the core proclamation of Jesus' story.

As worship developed around texts in the second and third centuries, some communities showed a marked preference for live performances of new revelation in the Spirit over the written ones. Assessing prophecy and revelations of the Holy Spirit could be difficult, as the case of New Prophecy (or Montanism) demonstrated. Around 160, Montanus from Phrygia (west central Turkey) intensified the local brand of charismatic Christianity by claiming authoritative inspiration, even possession, by the Holy Spirit which superseded Scripture (Old Testament) and the teaching of Jesus' apostles (New Testament). Within twenty to thirty years of Montanus's initial prophecy, New Prophecy communities were active in Gaul (France), Rome, Syria, and

North Africa. Adherents to the New Prophecy tended to be exemplary in their morality, if extremely rigorous and unforgiving. Tertullian of Carthage, frustrated with the moral laxity of mainstream Christianity, may have joined the Montanists around 207.

A lot of things bothered mainstream believers about New Prophecy, including intolerance of moral lapses and the authority granted to their female prophets beyond prophetic activity. Yet it was New Prophecy's loose attachment to the apostolic tradition that many Christians saw to be the most disturbing.[6] In line with previous generations, Christian leaders in the second century refused to accept that the Spirit would overturn the special revelation granted to the apostles who first proclaimed the good news. Whatever happened to Montanist prophets during worship, the old rule of discernment still held true. Prophecy in the Spirit of Christ had to clarify and apply the good news preserved in the accepted apostolic teachings (transmitted orally but increasingly written). Despite some requests to leave the Montanists alone, especially because of their heroism during persecution, mainstream Christians rejected the validity of New Prophecy. Privileged revelation belonged to the written forms of apostolic prophecy of the New Testament, which anchored true Christian worship.

According to Justin Martyr (ca. 160), Sunday worship consisted of reading and teaching from apostolic and prophetic (Jewish) writings. This was followed by prayers, which provided opportunity for ad hoc interpretation by congregants beyond the president, who offered the initial instruction after the readings (*1 Apology* 67). Fifty years later, Tertullian was more reticent, content to describe Christian worship in terms of a highly virtuous philosophical club (see chap. 4 above), which attended to the moral application of its sacred texts (*Apology* 39). Worship was the crucial context for regarding a text as Scripture. By the time Christian communities began compiling official lists of Scripture in the fourth and fifth centuries, the lists usually indicated what could be read in worship, while rarely limiting what Christians might read outside worship.

The Contents of Christian Scripture

At first Christians referred to their own authoritative teachings as the gospel or teachings of the Lord, and the apostles. An early apologetic work, *Letter to Diognetus* (ca. 130), expressed the divine revelation of the Son within the believing community at worship:

> Then the fear of the *law* is chanted, and the grace of the *prophets* is known, and the faith of the *gospels* is established, and the *tradition of the Apostles* is preserved, and the grace of the Church exults. . . . For

> whatever things we are moved to utter by the will of the Word com-
> manding us, we communicate to you with pains, and from a love of
> the things that have been revealed to us.[7]

The *Letter to Diognetus* obliquely describes the activities of worship that
strengthen the gathered believers to take the revealed Word to outsiders.
Revelation is an active process experienced by the community through the
Son (Word), who teaches in and through the Law, Prophets, Gospels, and
Apostles, and directs the believers' understanding of these teachings ("by the
will of the Word").

Two categories of new Christian Scripture were already filled with a stable core of books by the early to mid-second century: Gospel (according to
Matthew, Mark, Luke, and John) and Apostles (Letters of Paul to the seven
churches at Corinth, Rome, Ephesus, Thessalonica, Galatia, Philippi, Colossae). Like Jewish Scripture, while the two categories and most of the *contents*
(books) were fixed, the *texts* of individual documents were not entirely set,
as was normal in ancient text production. Only widespread publication over
time ensured an increasingly consistent text base as communities compared
their manuscripts and corrected inevitable variations that accompanied copy-
ing documents by hand.[8]

The gospel regarding Christ traveled in two ways. First there was the
slimmed-down and easily memorized version of Jesus' story, the rule of faith
(or truth), which consisted of (1) Jesus' relationship to the Father; (2) his birth,
life, death, and resurrection; and (3) his exalted role now and in the future. The
details of the rule of faith could be flexible (see chap. 3 above). Second, by the
mid-second century, most Christians knew of the four written Gospels (Matthew, Mark, Luke, John), even if the documents themselves were not always
accessible outside of major Christian centers. Because the gospel was viewed
as a single story about a single person, the tendency was to keep to a singular understanding of Gospel, even when it was transmitted in multiple compositions. Having many versions of Jesus' life and teachings, Christians were
quite aware of the inconsistencies in details and the order of events, especially
between the Synoptics and John. A single narrative option prevailed among
Syrian Christians into the fifth century, where Tatian's *Diatesseron* (late 2nd
c.) was the only gospel book for worship. Tatian harmonized the four Gospels
into a continuous narrative that did away with distracting differences.

Some writings were regarded as marginal in some regions, while central in
others. For instance, though considered Scripture by Clement of Rome at the
turn of the first century, the Letter to the Hebrews did not gain as wide appeal
in the West as it did in the East. Revelation enjoyed an early popularity but,
after the second century, when its view of end times and apostolic authorship
was challenged, Christians in the East tended to marginalize it. Much more

important for Christians of the second and third centuries were the *Shepherd of Hermas*, *1 Clement* and *Letter of Pseudo-Barnabas*. These texts played roles in teaching and preaching that far exceeded works accorded scriptural status in the fourth and fifth centuries, such as Hebrews, 2 Peter, James, 2 and 3 John.[9]

Evaluating Christian Writings

Following Paul's counsel, Christians understood all writings not dismissed as heretical to be inspired: "No one speaking by the Spirit of God ever says 'Let Jesus be cursed!' and no one can say 'Jesus is Lord' except by the Holy Spirit" (1 Cor. 12:3). So while many writings conveyed the Spirit's insights, only a few were recognized to overcome their original specificity, such as the Letters of Paul, and to have relevance for the whole church over time.

Early Christians had a great appetite for stories about Jesus, his disciples, and the martyrs. Devotional compositions flourished from the second century that embellished and dramatized the sober accounts read in worship. Many explored Jesus' divine presence in the world, filling in the blanks left by the four Gospels. The *Infancy Gospel of Thomas* recounts the adventures of the boy wonder Jesus, who could use his power against playmates or to get out of trouble. The *Gospel of Peter* heightens the spectacle of Jesus' resurrection with giant angels accompanying him to heaven, followed by a talking cross. Other texts claimed to replace or purify the clunky Gospels with pure spiritual accounts of Jesus. They skipped or downplayed Jesus' earthly life and conveyed nonnarrative expositions of the Savior's spiritual teachings (see chap. 6 below). By the end of the second century, Christians asked, "Just how many writings are appropriate for grounding faith in Jesus?"

This led Irenaeus of Lyons (ca. 180) to undertake a theological strategy to recommend four Gospels: no more, no less. He did so by appealing to the singular nature of the Gospels' inspiration and the multiple necessary facets of their witness to Christ. Irenaeus warned that communities knowing of other Gospels but stubbornly refusing to collect and use all four risked a narrowness that could lead to risky misunderstandings of Christ himself (*Against Heresies* 3.11). Matthew by itself could be taken too "Jewishly" in its honor of Torah. Luke read by itself (as Marcion did, see pp. 105, 127–28) or John could be used to reject everything Jewish. John was proving the darling of gnostic interpreters, to the exclusion of the Synoptic Gospels. Some used Mark's austere Gospel to separate the human Jesus from the divine Christ.

Irenaeus wove a complex metaphor likening the four Gospels to the heavenly pillars on which God's throne and the church rest. The four Gospels illustrate and balance the rich reality of Christ and his work (*Against Heresies* 3.11). Using the image of the four living creatures at God's throne (man, lion, ox, and eagle in Ezek. 1:10; Rev. 4:7), Irenaeus explained that John's portrait reveals the creative lordship of the Word, who was "in the beginning" (royal lion). Second, Luke's presentation emphasizes Christ's priestly work (sacrificial calf). The human figure applies to Matthew because that Gospel's genealogy directs attention to Jesus' humanity as descended from Adam, the first human. Finally, drawing from an image of the Spirit's winged spread of the good news, Irenaeus aligned Mark's Gospel with the eagle.

Irenaeus theorized that the four creatures were emblematic of Christ's saving work: through his work in creation (royal lion); through God's initial relationship with Israel through the sacrificial system (calf), which was fulfilled in Christ's own incarnation (man); and finally through Christ bearing humanity to heaven on his saving wings (eagle). Perhaps the metaphor is less convincing to Christians today, but the basic argument remains. For Irenaeus, a multidimensional image of Christ safeguarded authentic faith better than a single, exclusive perspective. The argument for a fourfold Gospel depended upon a specific story of salvation in Christ, the underlying "gospel," which Irenaeus called the rule/canon of truth (see p. 101).

Not every Christian community was as rigid as Irenaeus about the number of Gospels. They instead tested documents against the received faith in consultation with church leaders. For instance, Bishop Serapion in Antioch (ca. 200) addressed a dispute among believers in the rural town of Rhossos regarding their use of the *Gospel of Peter*. Some liked it, others didn't. Serapion told them, "If this is the only thing that occasions dispute among you, let it be read." Later, however, Serapion felt compelled to break his own general rule in the case of this particular Gospel. During the initial dispute, he had not yet had personal contact with the work, even though he resided in cosmopolitan Antioch. However, he later learned that those who advocated for its use were interpreting it in ways that did not accord "with the true doctrine of the Saviour" and were suggesting that Christ was not really human.[10] This break from apostolic teaching compelled Serapion to recant his earlier approval.

Canon is the Greek word for a ruler in carpentry that can test when materials are straight. By extension, a canon is a rule or standard against which things can be tested, whether physically or intellectually. Its usage as an authoritative list derives from the eighteenth century, not the early church.

Three things emerge from this account. First, church leaders were not surprised that different congregations consulted different texts about Jesus. Second, these variations were not of themselves alarming. Indeed Serapion encouraged a broad tolerance of texts among the Rhossos Christians. Third, alarm bells went off only when a text of itself or in the way it was being used contradicted the accepted understanding of Jesus' story. The parallels with the *Didache*'s instruction regarding prophets is striking. The Spirit may communicate with and edify believers in many formats, yet believers remain responsible for testing these messages.

People today looking for a decisive list of what early Christians understood to be Scripture can be frustrated by the approach early Christians took. Until the fourth and fifth centuries, the idea of a fixed "canon" or list of what is Scripture was foreign to early Christians, who thought much more in terms of how writings accorded with the faith they had received, that is, the rule/canon of faith/truth.[11] Early in the second century, Ignatius of Antioch recommended that believers use such summaries of the faith to distinguish between reliable teachers and so-called Christians who followed another story. A different story, or interpretive principle, exposed teachers who were not in accord with the traditions passed down from Jesus to the apostles, from the apostles to their successors, and so forth. By the end of the second century, Irenaeus of Lyons called this the "apostolic tradition" conveyed through "apostolic succession" (*Against the Heresies* 3.2.2). The rule of faith summarized the apostolic tradition. Generations of legitimate leaders handed down the same good news that they had received. As an example, Irenaeus traced the lineage of apostolic teaching in the church of Rome from Peter and Paul to his contemporary Eleutherius (bishop of Rome, ca. 174–189). Irenaeus emphasized his own reception of the tradition as heir to John through John's disciple, Polycarp of Smyrna.

The testing process among less apostolically connected communities involved a bishop composing a statement of faith, which the closest apostolic communities would approve, so as to confirm apostolic fellowship among congregations. When testing a text rather than a teacher, communities measured a document's fidelity to the rule: the story of Jesus' life, death, and resurrection and its transmission by direct heirs to the original witnesses.

INTERPRETING SCRIPTURE: CHRISTIANS AND THE JEWISH HERITAGE

The fundamental dispute between Jews and Christians was the implications of the gospel for interpreting Jewish Scripture. Beginning with the witnesses to Jesus' death and resurrection, Christians shifted from Scripture to Jesus as the locus for knowing God. Jesus was recognized to be Christ through a careful rereading of what God had been hinting through Israel's story in Scripture. Jesus was the interpretive key for rereading Jewish Scripture. This rereading involved the search for representative texts (*testimonia*) and symbols (types).

TESTIMONIA

Qumran scrolls include a text called *Testimonia,* or Testimonies/Proofs (mid–1st c. BC). It lists scriptural passages outlining characteristics of their hoped-for messiah(s). This document shows a format that second-century Christians may have used in collecting scriptural passages to illustrate their understanding of Jesus as the Messiah. Christian collections were often grouped by themes such as the resurrection, suffering, and death of the Messiah. *Testimonia* explain why Christian authors cite the same passages in the same order and sometimes with the same adaptive translations (favoring more messianic tones than the original wording suggested). One common source was the citation of Jewish Scripture in Paul's Letters.

Second-century approaches to Jewish Scripture appear to consist of nothing more than proof-texting: convincing others by stacking up more supporting passages than one's opponents. Christians, with their new interpretive story, decoded Scripture by locating Christ's story in Israel's story, from the overall pattern of salvation to the particulars of Christ's life, death, and resurrection. Like a dot-to-dot picture, Christians developed lists of thematic passages that, when connected, established the contours of Jesus' story in Scripture.[12] *Testimonia* did not really try to win by quoting the most passages in one's favor. Instead, they were the footnotes that illustrated rather than proved the governing hypothesis (rule of faith) of God's plan, the pattern for establishing the entire faith. Highly skilled and dedicated scholars of Jewish Scripture engaged in exhaustive study to tease out passages that often had not been associated with covenant fulfillment in a Christ. And they did it without access to indices or computer-aided textual searches.

Testimonia operated by drawing together passages where specific details reflected, even if dimly, Christ's life and mission. Typology, on the other hand, made adaptive reuse of familiar images in new ways. Interpreters, working backward from the given of Christ's saving crucifixion, might take references to "wood" or "tree" throughout Scripture as pointers to the cross. Christians found this practice already at work in Scripture when psalms or prophets refer to details in the exodus to describe their own situations. Paul reinterpreted symbols and events to offer a specifically Christian meaning. Jews and Christians were "reemploying images to understand and explain the present in terms of the past, and so being anticipated by the past."[13] This method sought to understand events, phrases, and people (as types) in the ancient Scripture by means of parallels to Jesus' life, death, and resurrection (as antitypes). These types, in turn, broadened the material for further understanding of Jesus himself. As the prototype, Christ was simultaneously the source and fulfillment of these types.

However, not all Christians agreed on the basic premise of searching for Christ "beginning with Moses and all the prophets" (Luke 24:27). The *Letter of Pseudo-Barnabas* and Justin, for example, use both *testimonia* collections and typology. Marcion, on the other hand, jettisoned Moses and the Prophets entirely. Each author's interpretation of Scripture reveals specific attitudes toward Christianity's Jewish heritage.

Letter of Pseudo-Barnabas (ca. 130):
Jewish Scripture Belongs Only to Christians

This popular text was attributed to Barnabas, who introduced Paul to the Jerusalem Christians in Acts. The author was worried about how Christians in his circle commonly accepted that Jews and Christians shared the covenant of Abraham and Moses. He believed that the covenant is about and for believers in Jesus alone. As an ethnic nation, Israel lost the covenant when it worshiped the golden calf and Moses destroyed the stone tablets written by God (14). As the true heirs of the covenant, Christians properly receive the Scripture and understand how it should be applied.

The letter reveals a community that believed each member was the renewed temple (16). Because the Lord lives within Christians, they are able to understand past, present, and future events (5). They are inspired to discern the true covenant through words, objects, events, and people in Torah and the Prophets which the Jews had long misunderstood. Torah, temple, and promised land are respectively signs or types of God's true communication in Christ. God's presence consists of his indwelling within Christ-believers (not a building). Salvation involves Christ's second coming, where a reshaped humanity will rule creation as intended in the beginning. Torah and Prophets remain in force for Pseudo-Barnabas; they are quoted or alluded to over eighty times in this work, and not merely to correct "Jewish" misunderstandings. The letter quotes a Christian text only once. Pseudo-Barnabas urgently encouraged righteousness, keeping the commandments, and preserving purity because, just as Israel lost out on the covenant, so might Christians (4).

Justin on the Logos: Jesus in Jewish Scripture

A couple decades after Pseudo-Barnabas, Justin Martyr honed and expanded this approach to assert that Christ himself dwelled within Scripture. To recover Christ's prehistory in Jewish Scripture, Justin elaborated the Platonically shaped Stoic concept of the Logos (Word) that the Gospel of John uses for Jesus (see chap. 4 above). Christians understood God's Logos to be the premier divine message/messenger, the cocreator of the universe and all meaning.

The inspired prophets of Israel spoke only what the Logos gave them. Likewise, the indwelling of the Logos and his Spirit in Jesus' followers enabled them to understand the real meaning of the Jewish Scriptures. The ramification of this Logos theology meant that Christ himself was the primary message and actor of all Jewish Scripture. Only those open to Christ the Logos can discern the true meaning of Scripture: Christians, not Jews.

With the help of Logos theology, Justin identified instances where Christ himself appeared in the Jewish Scripture. Whenever God is said to have appeared to a figure, Justin understands "God" to be Christ the Logos, since God "[the Maker and Father of all things] remains ever in the super-celestial places, invisible to all men, holding personal intercourse with none."[14] When God appeared to Moses in the burning bush, or to old Abraham and Sarah to announce the future birth of their son Isaac, Justin believed that "God" could only be the mediating Logos.

For Justin, the Logos was hidden throughout Jewish Scripture, just as the new covenant in Christ was foreshadowed there too. History is important enough for Justin to acknowledge the legitimacy of the first covenant and its requirements for the Jews. It remained important to Christians because the details of Israel's law, history, and prophets provide the types that point toward and are fulfilled in Christ himself. Thus, like Pseudo-Barnabas, Justin labored to uncover the Christ-oriented reality behind literal Jewish observances such as circumcision (a spiritual separation from the world and idolatry) and the Passover lamb (Christ, whose blood saves from death). Justin employed existing *testimonia* from the Prophets that testified to a Jesus-type messiah and salvation. This detailed accuracy and truthfulness of the prophets' messages were enough to convince Justin to adopt Christianity as his sole philosophy. For Justin, where truth is, so is God as its sole source. The testimonies of prophets demonstrated that their message came directly from God through the Logos. He contrasted this to the best efforts of philosophers, who attempt to glean truth on their own (*Dialogue with Trypho* 7).

Marcion: Making a Clean Break

Christians today still wince at God's hardening Pharaoh's heart, thereby forcing innocent Egyptians to suffer plagues, or Joshua being instructed to destroy both people and animals when the Israelites conquered Canaan. It should therefore be easy to understand why those not already sympathetic to Israel's God in antiquity would have doubts about his goodness and divinity. Scholarly non-Christians already uncomfortable with the immoral behavior of their own gods had composed detailed allegorical interpretations of Homer's *Iliad* and *Odyssey* in attempts to rehabilitate the stories as models of timeless virtues. Philo of Alexandria engaged in a similar program for Jewish Scripture, and Christians were dabbling in it as well. A few Christians found these methods of interpretation to be convoluted. One Christian from Sinope (on the Black Sea in Turkey) decided to take the apostle Paul very seriously.

Whatever Marcion's murky past (perhaps excommunicated by his bishop father), he argued for radical grace and the absolute novelty of Jesus. His version of Christianity found refuge in an utterly alien and transcendent God, who took pity on the beleaguered creatures of this world's limited god, the Jewish Creator YHWH. Marcion struck a popular chord when he refused to undertake awkward interpretations of Jewish Scripture that would somehow excuse YHWH's embarrassing violence and harsh legislation.

MARCION AND THOMAS JEFFERSON

Enlightenment thinkers (18th c.) were committed to purifying Christianity from irrational, supernatural, and dogmatic elements. Thomas Jefferson, like Marcion, removed unseemly elements so that his "Bible" consisted of a condensation of the four Gospels into one narrative. Jesus was a Deist teacher whose true message was characterized by rational morality, not miracles, incarnation, or resurrection.

Marcion's version of Christian Scripture did away with all Jewish Scripture as well as any apostolic writings that seemed tainted by Jewish concepts, including parts of Jesus' teachings in the Gospels. Jewish writings were still inspired, but by the Spirit of YHWH, not the Savior God. In Marcion's view, Torah demonstrates the harshness of YHWH (e.g., "eye for an eye" justice). YHWH is just but not good. YHWH's prophets pointed to a coming Jewish Messiah along the political lines that Jesus' contemporaries expected. The Jews are correct; Jesus is not YHWH's messiah. Marcion retained the Gospel of Luke and ten Letters of Paul. He edited all these documents, primarily by removing material that could connect YHWH to Jesus.[15] Marcion's theory prompted immediate outcry from Syria to France to North Africa. The church in Rome returned his sizable donations and excommunicated him in 144. Marcion remains important, however, because he forced Christians to think seriously about whether there was any room for the Jewish Scripture in the Christian story.

Ultimately contemporary leaders were not worried that Christians would abandon the Scripture, old and new, that anchored their worship. Marcion's endeavor did not change what most other Christians continued to hear in worship or quote in their writings. His threat lay in his attempts to revise basic understandings about Jesus and salvation. If Jesus were not part of Israel or Israel's God, then who was he, and what other saving story was at work? These same issues fed believers' opposition to gnostic versions of Christianity. Like Marcion, gnostic Christians also demoted YHWH from transcendent status (see chap. 6 below) and severely limited what counted as authoritative texts and teachings, in contrast to the breadth of Scripture held by mainstream Christians.

ORIGEN: ENCOUNTERING CHRIST IN THE WHOLE SCRIPTURE

Meet Origen

Pastoral concerns and a genuine thirst for Christ in the Scriptures motivated Origen of Alexandria (ca. 186–255) to undertake an unprecedented program of interpreting the entire Bible. Origen the teacher and preacher did things in a big way. His fervor for the faith, so the stories go, led to a reputation for excess in his youth. The son of a martyr, Origen tried to turn himself in during a persecution, only to be stymied when his mother hid his clothes (probably). Another story suggested that he castrated himself out of concerns for purity (probably not). His passion for Scripture led him to create an enormous textual tool called the *Hexapla*, a "six-columned," side-by-side presentation of Jewish Scripture in Hebrew (actual and transliterated into Greek) and four different Greek translations. In addition to its utility in conversations with Jews, the *Hexapla* provided a means to develop a more accurate text of Scripture through comparing variant readings, similar to what scholars today call a critical edition. His literary output numbered nearly one thousand works, most of which were homilies and commentaries on the Bible. Regrettably, most of these works have been lost due to fifth-century condemnations of his speculative theology. What remains fills some thirteen sizable volumes, not to mention the countless Eastern and Western theological works that, knowingly or not, incorporated Origen's labors up to the Reformation.

Convinced that understanding Scripture required not only Christ, but also knowledge of Jewish traditions, Origen learned Hebrew from Jewish scholars and continually consulted rabbis on Jewish texts and interpretive traditions. Origen can also be credited with producing the first systematic and speculative treatise on the whole of Christian belief, *On First Principles*. He was so prized by Roman authorities that they drew out his tortures over two years in hopes that his apostasy would break the will of other Christians in Palestine and beyond. Released after the death of Decius, Origen died in 252, a free man inhabiting a body permanently stretched, broken, and seared by numerous torture devices. Though a confessor, he did not attain the martyrdom he had sought.

Scripture: A Field of Buried Treasure

In his *Commentary on Matthew*, Origen extensively developed a theme that Irenaeus of Lyons had used to discuss Jesus' parable of Treasure Hidden in a Field (Matt. 13:44). Both writers considered Jesus himself to be the treasure who is and reveals Scripture. Irenaeus insisted that true Christian teaching preserves the divine record of Jewish Scripture, not "blaspheming God, nor dishonouring the patriarchs, nor despising the prophets."[16] Origen agreed that the field of Scripture provides benefits for non-Christian inquirers, who may then perceive the treasure and proceed to full instruction in the faith.

Book 4 of *On First Principles* focuses on how to dig for treasure buried within Scripture. Scripture is divine; its source and power is God. Origen retained an oral, performative, and relational sense of God speaking and acting through Scripture in the same way that prophets were inspired. He pointed to the amazing impact of relatively unlearned preachers and of a Scripture that lacks literary pizzazz as proof that only a message empowered by God could reach and persuade so many people to follow Christ despite threats of persecution (4.1.1–2). Like Irenaeus, Origen concluded that Christ's incarnation, his revelation of God in the flesh, made it possible to see the divine nature of Jewish Scripture. Only Jesus makes clear Scripture's universal applicability and meaning.

The first thing to understand in Origen's concept of Scripture (a concept shared by many early Christians) is how active and dynamic, even magical, Scripture is. As God's own outreach to humanity through Christ the Logos, Scripture functions very personally, according to an individual's needs and ability to comprehend. Believers' engagement with Scripture unfolds together with their maturation in the faith as they progress in likeness to God. Interpretation of Scripture was relational and an integral component of the believing community's overall seeking of God. It was not impersonal puzzle-solving, or an archaeological dig for curious artifacts of bygone beliefs. Mysteries concealed in difficult passages required a disciplined lifestyle devoted to

> the utmost purity and sobriety and through nights of watching, by which means perchance [the Christian] might be able to trace out the deeply hidden meaning of the Spirit of God, concealed under the language of an ordinary narrative which points in a different direction, and that so [the Christian] might become a sharer of the Spirit's knowledge and a partaker of his divine counsel.[17]

A right orientation toward God assumed openness to God's formative and revelatory influence (see chap. 8 below). The process of understanding repeats the original inspiration: interpreters and teachers must be like the prophets who beheld God "not with the eyes of the body, but with a pure heart" in accord with Jesus' promise that the pure of heart will see God (Matt. 5:8).[18] Prayer and studying Scripture were interdependent vehicles for God's formation of the pray-er and interpreter in a manner similar to the sacraments. When believers fed on Scripture, they encountered and became transformed by Christ the Logos himself.

Because Scripture's divine author is still alive and in a sense writing his message on believers' hearts through their prayerful reading, Scripture is eternally relevant to believers. Even the hard passages that make hearers balk somehow convey God. Origen believed that the hard parts are actually marks of Scripture's divine origins; the Spirit planted obstacles in the plain narrative in order to nudge readers to contemplate the spiritual jewels that lie beneath the surface of troublesome passages (*On First Principles* 4.15). Origen assumed that his students would be familiar with this way of proceeding from their literary or philosophical studies. Ancient scholars regularly examined the symbolic meaning of letters and numbers, and the etymologies of individual words, thus to glean insights into a text's purpose and meaning. Eager students knew to dig deeper when Plato's meaning was not immediately clear. Similarly, ardent disciples of Christ knew God's Word would yield higher truths through diligent effort.

Less ardent believers usually found that paying attention to Christ in Scripture was neither easy nor attractive. Origen grew frustrated by parishioners telling stories, setting up business deals in a back corner of the church, or skipping out after the readings. He feared negligent Christians' wild misunderstandings of Scripture and their self-chosen detachment from God himself by ignoring his Word.[19] Further, Origen warned that interpreting Scripture without attentiveness to how it conveys the Spirit through a literary vehicle leads to understandings that do not accord either with apostolic teaching or with common sense. Sometimes the literal or narrative meaning of a passage is itself metaphorical or symbolic, such as the promise that the predators will dwell peacefully with former prey in the age of the Messiah (*On First Principles* 4.2.1 on Isa. 11:6–9). Sometimes Scripture speaks of God as dangerously emotional, erratic, and the instigator of evil, but these must be taken as God using baby talk to the immature in faith, who cannot understand God except in terms of human behavior (*Commentary on Jeremiah* 18.6). These two paths could lead to rejecting Jesus as Messiah or rejecting the Creator as the One God of all.

Relation of Literal to Nonliteral Meanings

Some scholars past and present have maintained two inaccurate points about Origen's method of interpreting Scripture, views that have diminished his importance as a seminal thinker. The first point is that Origen's method of interpreting Scripture depended primarily on his pioneering notion of three levels of meaning in Scripture. Indeed, he discussed the body (what the narrative is about), soul (moral instruction), and spirit (divine realities like the nature of God and heaven) of Scripture in *On First Principles* (4.2.4–6). However, he rarely followed this format when commenting upon Scripture, either in his homilies or in his theological treatises. When describing his method to hostile outsiders, Origen was more prone to note that Christians distinguished between literal and figurative (spiritual) meanings in Scripture.[20]

The second point is that Origen disdained the plain, narrative sense of Scripture. However, by looking at the role Origen assigned to "literal" level, we can catch a better idea of Origen's rich range of tools employed to discover meaning within Scripture. Origen gladly defended the generally useful and certainly divine nature of the plain narrative sense. The accounts of creation, God's people, Jesus' life and teachings, the apostles' lives and teachings—all provide moral examples and reveal enough to bring people to a saving encounter with God. He vociferously denounced those who flung a slippery-slope argument against him; just because he recognized some places where the "literal" passage did not carry the Spirit's meaning, this did not mean that he abandoned the plain sense entirely (*On First Principles* 4.2.8).

Moreover, we must be careful not to impose our contemporary meaning of "literal" on a figure who wrote over 1,700 years ago. According to ancient literary methods, the literal or "letter" task of analysis prepared a reader/speaker to use a text.[21] Literal analysis included everything from determining where words ended and punctuation should go (neither of these were marked in ancient manuscripts) to clarifying what words meant, especially if the word or concept was no longer used regularly (such as the vocabulary of Homer or ancient Hebrew). The literal level also identified what a story or book is about (e.g., plot, moral, or didactic purpose) and provided something of an abstract or thesis statement (called the hypothesis). Ancient literal analysis did not mean recovering the cultural and historic meaning intended by the author, as Bible scholars today mean by the literal and historical. Figuring out the "letter" was as much engaged in uncovering symbols as was "figurative" or nonliteral analysis; literal analysis simply had letters and words as its primary object rather than more complex "figures" of speech. Examining the letter began the task of entering into a continuum of meaning.

For Origen, all other levels of nonliteral meaning come from the basic truthfulness of the plain story ("the outer covering"), except in a few cases where the plain meaning had to be taken figuratively. For instance, Origen pointed out that in the temptation, Jesus obviously could not have physically seen all the world's kingdoms from a mountaintop (yes, the ancient world knew that the earth was round), or that in colder climes it is not expedient to have only one coat and no shoes, as Jesus commands his disciples in Matt. 10:10 (*On First Principles* 4.3.1, 3). Origen's dismissal of the surface meaning was not arbitrary. Together with passages that at face value appeared impossible or illogical, Origen excluded things that were wrong to say or think about God (e.g., that God acted evilly or inconsistently).

Nonliteral interpretations, sometimes given the blanket term "allegory," abound because Origen believed the Spirit meets humans where they are. In replying to snide non-Christian remarks about the blue-collar reputation of Christians, Origen proudly pointed out that all the finely polished sentences or lofty truths of Plato did little for actual public good beyond the leisured elite, and certainly never really prompted readers "toward a pure religion at all." In contrast "the mean style of the divine scriptures has made honest readers inspired by it."[22] Christ the Word prepared nourishment proper to the condition of the believer, be it milk for the young in faith, bland foods for the sick, or spicy and hearty fare for the strong (*Against Celsus* 4.18). Origen recognized from experience that believers function with varying levels of personal commitment to the faith and with different capabilities for understanding it. Unlike what some varieties of Christianity were touting (spiritual or moral elitism), Origen was in the mainstream, strenuously defending the potential for the most simple believer to be saved, even while chafing at the indifference many Christians showed.

In addition to the differing needs of Christians in their faith walk, multiple levels of meaning can occur simply by the common practice of interpreting Scripture through Scripture, as ancient scholars had long done for Homer and Plato. Ancient scholars tried to understand how an author used terms or images by examining related terms and images throughout his work. What joined these correspondences and gave them meaning was locating the key purpose of the text (its *skopos*) and its unitive plot (or *hypothesis*).[23] For early Christians, the *hypothesis* that held together the unwieldy bulk of Scripture was the rule of faith, while Scripture's *skopos* was to convey Christ. When Christians used this rationale, it was because they believed that Scripture ultimately derived from a single author, God the Father, through his Son (the Logos) and the Spirit.

The exodus episode of the Israelites leaving Egypt and crossing the Red Sea provides an informative example of the multiform interpretation born in study, prayer, and pastoral concerns that animated Origen's scriptural tasks.[24] Whatever may have happened with real Egyptians chasing real Israelites, Origen preferred to focus on the immediate significance for Christians, following Paul's observation (see 1 Cor. 10:11) that Scripture "has been written for our [Christian] instruction and admonition" (*Homily 1 on Exodus* 5). Christians, assured of God's saving intent by the "history," need insight into how these patterns reveal spiritual struggles and God's assistance among believers, "not only in this world, which is figuratively called Egypt, but in each of us also" (*Homily 2 on Exodus* 1).

Paul laid the foundation for considering the escape from Egpyt as an image of baptism (1 Cor. 10:1–2). Pondering the relationship between the moral life and the mystery of baptism, Origen considered the pursuing Egyptians as evil habits and desires that seek to draw the convert away from God and back to the old life of sin. Intertextual echoes (interpreting Scripture by Scripture) are brought to bear on baptism. Baptism "drowns" the evil spirits: an image that draws on the drowning of Pharaoh's army and Jesus' expelling the demons Legion into a herd of pigs, which then drowned (Mark 5). Furthermore, Origen discerned that the passage deals with the struggle against opponents (heretics and persecutors) of the Christian faith. The Red Sea depicts the "flood" of flesh-and-blood adversaries whom Christians can expect to assail their faith. Moses' staff, which beat down the waters to make a path through the sea, becomes a symbol for the power of Scripture to strike down the threatening waves launched by foes. Scripture works not only to destroy the arguments that oppose the truth (by its message and its formative influence on individuals' lives), but also to convince opponents and win them over to the truth. The Egyptians are "all sordid and impure thoughts," which must be cast out of the heart and destroyed in order to preserve the freed slave, who now lives under the lordship of God in Jesus Christ. Clearly, there are no separate literal, moral, and spiritual meanings at work in Origen's forays; they are intertwined and build upon each other.

CONCLUSIONS

Christians grappled with the transformation of Israel's story wrought by accepting Jesus as Christ. Worship offered opportunities for Christians to extrapolate what Scripture really meant and, in doing so, created a distinctive new corpus of Scripture that still depended upon and conversed with the old. Such textual interaction took place in parallel with Jewish-Christian social relations, where believers variously butted heads and mingled with the people of YHWH who did not see Jesus as messiah. Most Christians claimed

Scripture as truly belonging to Christians, who alone knew what it meant. Yet most did not deny that Scripture had an initial meaning and purpose for the Jews before Christ. Marcion's challenge mirrored that of gnostics and had less to do with a body of Scripture than with underlying ideas about God. Mainstream Christians had to think and articulate why they had "always" done and believed in particular ways.

When early Christians encountered Scripture, they drank a robust and abundant flow of meaning that rarely fell into neat categories of "literal" or "figurative" despite the way modern scholars have tried to characterize patristic interpretation.[25] All symbols in Scripture invited the church to enter into relationship with a variety of meanings offered dynamically through the presence of God in his Word/word. From individual letters and words to the enormous range of literary figures of speech and complex symbolism of whole narratives, believers trusted God to speak through Scripture. To this end they borrowed the full range of literary, rhetorical, and philosophical tools already in the scholarly toolbox of classical learning and added them to the Christian tools of prayer, contemplation, and the liturgy.

Grounding interpretation in the encounter with God, Origen proved to be the master who dedicated himself to making the whole of Scripture applicable to the journey of the soul to God through Christ. However, various approaches—eventually regarded as heretical—arose from those who believed themselves to be devoted to the same task, motivated by the same yearning to experience and unite with God as the orthodox. The questions of gnostic Christians would move mainstream Christians adamantly to embrace the Jewish insistence upon the goodness of YHWH, his creation, and his Scripture. The next chapter will examine the gnostic struggle, which arose in great part from the different levels of personal commitment and understanding among believers. Some Christians explored the blanks between the lines and at the fringes of the rule of faith that others thought went too far.

QUESTIONS FOR DISCUSSION

1. How is Scripture more than a set of writings?
2. How did the story of Jesus contained in the rule of faith help to "measure" or determine what counted as Scripture?
3. Why is it useful to think of Scripture resulting from a group effort?
4. What are some social as well as theological implications of the choice to retain Jewish Scripture?
5. What are the advantages of assuming that Scripture has multiple meanings? Disadvantages? How do the advantages compare to the disadvantages?

SUGGESTED FURTHER READING

Becker, Adam H., and Annette Yoshiko Reed, eds. *The Ways That Never Parted: Jews and Christians in Late Antiquity and the Early Middle Ages.* Texts and Studies in Ancient Judaism 95. Tübingen: Mohr Siebeck, 2003.

Gamble, Harry Y. *Books and Readers in the Early Church: A History of Early Chrisitan Texts.* New Haven: Yale University Press, 1995.

Wilken, Robert L. *John Chrysostom and the Jews: Rhetoric and Reality in the Late Fourth Century.* Los Angeles: University of California Press, 1983.

Young, Frances M. *Biblical Exegesis and the Formation of Christian Culture.* Peabody, MA: Hendrickson Publishers, 2002.

6

Heresy

Congregational Dynamics and Theological Method

INTRODUCTION

Christian communities were no strangers to debate and diversity. The story of heresy in the second and third centuries coincided with and spurred Christian thought about Scripture and tradition. On the ground, the term *heresy* applied when another story supplanted the rule of faith and resulted in separation among the faithful, both conceptually and socially. Heresy is at heart a matter of broken fellowship more than simply wrong beliefs.

This chapter analyzes heresy through the catchall category of *gnosticism* (Greek *gnōsis*, knowledge). As seen in the previous chapter, early Christians preferred multiplicity over single interpretations (Origen's multilayered approach) or texts (four Gospels instead of one). Yet believers balked at some systems, at some messages and messengers, at some texts and teachers that challenged the diversity of models and insisted upon one perspective while casting out the rest. A particular community might show the interloper the door. But what were Christians to do when divisive ideas took hold across many communities? What perceived needs did the exclusive views meet? How did Christians shape their responses to potentially dangerous teachings while seeking to address the real yearnings that so often prompted the extracurricular speculations in the first place?

Our investigation begins with the troubling inconsistencies among believers. Out of the ranks of ordinary or apathetic Christians, particularly zealous and educated believers struggled to explore and make sense of the faith they had adopted. An examination of gnostic variations on the Christian story reveals some attractive yet problematic attempts to channel the faith into a rational system.

PROTO-ORTHODOX

A recent term coined to designate what was developing into mainstream Christianity before the fourth century. Pagans like Celsus in the second century recognized a universal mainstream and called it "the Great Church." Believers described it as "orthodox" (correct belief) or "catholic" (universal).

Proto-orthodox[1] believers of the Great Church assessed some of these variants to be a completely different story, a different God, and a different community—rather than helpful perspectives on the central tradition. The chapter concludes with the positive theology produced by the Great Church in response to gnostic renderings of the faith. Building a system in accord with the rule of faith, the church insisted upon connecting Jesus to YHWH the Creator, who offers salvation to all. Christian leaders recognized the legitimate yearning among believers for a deeper relationship with God by developing practices and systems for knowing God within the rule of faith.

CHOICES AND DIVISIONS

Among the Greeks, heresy (the action of choosing) amounted to a school of thought chosen by each adherent. In this sense, Jewish "heresies" included the doctrines of Sadducees and Pharisees. However, salvation for Christians depended upon abiding within the right school of thought. Outside of the true story of salvation through Christ, there could be no return to God. It was ultimately a matter of idolatry. Adopting a flawed and distorted understanding of God and reality was tantamount to creating an idol and worshiping a false god.

The choices pursued by gnostics challenged mainstream Christians to evaluate what they had taken for granted. Up for grabs were the identity of God; the content, interpretation, and authority of Scripture; and the valuation of material/physical existence. At stake was the very notion of Christ as both historical and beyond history, a Christ at once Jewish and cosmic. At the same time when the Great Church was seeking ways to offer second chances to lapsed believers after persecutions, it also faced the claims (as perceived by a number of believers) that only the spiritually enlightened gnostics would achieve salvation.

Pastoral Crisis

Heresy in this period highlights the perennial tension among believers with differing levels of maturity, understanding, and commitment. Pastors faced challenges from both ends of the spectrum: those who hungered for a rich spiritual banquet, and those who struggled to conform to basic beliefs and behavior expected of Christians. During persecution the differences could result in apostasy. Some Christians welcomed active persecution simply to weed out less committed members. By falling away, they proved that they had never really been part of God's people. In contrast were the Christians who strove to expand penitential disciplines to rehabilitate the weak in faith. Similarly, earnest pastors defended those with simple faith whose anthropomorphic conceptions of God offended more "sophisticated" believers.

Pastoral concerns motivated proto-orthodox objections to divisive systems and behavior. The unfortunate by-product of some "sophisticated" seeking was callous bigotry against unsophisticated or apathetic believers, and theological systems that grew increasingly distant from the mainstream. Around 180, Irenaeus, bishop of Lyons, wrote *Exposé and Overthrow of What Is Falsely Called Knowledge* (better known as *Against Heresies*) to other Christian leaders to warn them about several schools of thought that threatened their flocks.[2] He worried about the way "simple" and "inexperienced" believers were being drawn away by alternative versions of Christianity. Ironically, these "simple" believers (who thought themselves sophisticated) were all too easily swept away in the desire to be "in the know." False teachers offered so-called knowledge (gnosis) that seemed "more excellent and sublime." Irenaeus hoped other pastors would be on the lookout for wolves in sheep's clothing, whose "language resembles ours, while their sentiment is very different." In North Africa Tertullian scorned Valentinians' smug refusals to talk about their views to ordinary believers: "If you propose to them inquiries sincere and honest, they answer you with stern look and contracted brow, and say, 'The subject is profound.'"[3] After taking the risk to become a Christian, second- and third-century believers were profoundly disturbed over which communities and teachers assured saving knowledge in Christ.

The disparities revealed a desperate spiritual hunger experienced by many believers then and now. Recall that, before his conversion, Justin Martyr was one of many philosophers intent upon encountering God. Justin ultimately found rest in Christian philosophy. However, other Christians who yearned for transcendence could feel impelled to seek knowledge of God beyond the Prophets (Jewish Scripture) and "friends of Christ" (apostolic tradition), with whom Justin was content to practice his philosophy (*Dialogue with Trypho* 7). Adherents labeled heretical by proto-orthodox Christian leaders were often considered by themselves, and others, to be the most genuine followers of Christ. Around 200, Tertullian observed the anxiety sparked when seeming pillars of the church defected to heresies. The remaining believers asked, "Why did this woman or this man change sides, [who were] the most faithful and

most insightful, and most closely associated to the church?"[4] Unsatisfied with
the faith at face value and feeling pressured to park their brains at the baptismal font, many seekers took "Search, and you will find" (cf. Matt. 7:7) as their
motto. The attitude of educated converts in the early church is not unlike that
of believers throughout history who consider themselves sufficiently mature
in the faith to explore advanced beliefs outside the mainstream.

Divisive elitism among Christians came in different guises; for example,
only martyrs are real Christians or only celibate believers are real Christians.
Nothing was new about some people being (or considering themselves to be)
better than others at some things. However, when the belief system that in-
the-know Christians endorsed overturned key elements of the rule of faith,
pastors felt responsible to point out that these resulted in something other
than Christianity.

Defining Gnostic Choices

As a brand of intellectual and spiritual elitism, gnostic Christianity sought
to improve knowledge of God through Christ. Much like Montanus's New
Prophecy (see chap. 5), gnostic heresies show the attraction of religion
detached from communal sources of revelation. Traditionally, these communal sources were clergy, martyrs/confessors, tradition, and Scripture. Gnostic
Christians told stories with the same characters and used the same patterns
of salvation that ordinary Christians cherished. Most gnostics continued to
worship together with less "knowledgeable" believers. They could hear Scripture, pray, and sing the same hymns at worship, yet believe it all to mean
something different from what most of the faithful believed. What provoked
pastors were the many places where beliefs almost coincided. Polemic is often
at its most virulent when the paths are closest; those far apart in opinion rarely
have much to say to each other in the first place.[5]

SCRIPTURE AND VALENTINIANISM

Valentinus took his school of thought from Egypt to Rome in the 130s. He and his students (especially Ptolemy and Heracleon in the mid to late 2nd c.) were among the first
Christians to compose works dedicated to scriptural interpretation. Taking seriously how
jarring Israel's story and God were, Valentinians developed systems for discerning Christ's
relationship to the Scripture and God of Israel. Dismissing allegorical efforts to conjure
Christ from Jewish Scripture (as Justin was doing at the time), they took it as their job to
distinguish the incomplete revelation to the Jews from the complete revelation in Christ.
Incomplete revelation pointed toward the inadequacy of its inspiration: YHWH and human
traditions in Moses.

According to gnostic elitism, traditional Christianity was of use only to the majority of dull believers. Gnostic movements, such as that led by Valentinus, attracted believers who were longing to draw near to God through the more "enlightened" and "spiritual" teachings of Jesus. Ptolemy, a disciple of Valentinus, wrote to Flora, an orthodox Christian he regarded as worthy to advance to the next stage of enlightenment. Through Ptolemy's alternative tradition, he tempted her with a direct link to the truth that the "blind" Great Church "completely missed."[6]

The terms *gnostic* and *gnosticism* are used here to describe positions that many early Christians found to be incompatible with their understanding of the faith, rather than to indicate a single religion or heresy. Today many scholars recommend jettisoning the term entirely.[7] Recent discoveries of ancient gnostic texts, such as the Nag Hammadi library, promote different systems, with distinct values and no singular origin.[8] Gnostic texts rarely use that title to identify their own adherents, instead preferring "perfect" or even the biblical terms "brothers" and "children."

NAG HAMMADI (EGYPT)

Twelve codices (books) were discovered here in 1945 in which one can now read texts related to what the Christian polemicists were attacking. The mid-fourth-century codices contain Coptic (Egyptian language written with a modified Greek alphabet) translations of originally Greek texts. There are apocalypses (revelations) to apostles, treatises, hymns, gospels, acts of apostles, and prayers, most of which could not have been understood apart from Christianity. It is possible that the texts in their mid-fourth-century versions were related to a nearby orthodox monastery (just three miles away) and perhaps functioned as devotional texts for some circles of orthodox Christians.

Gnosticism emerges as a meaningful category created by the Christian leaders of the second and third centuries who most vociferously and systematically responded to several religious trends. Pastors responding to gnosticism selectively represented their opponents. What motivated and unified the proto-orthodox Christian attack was the reality that many ordinary believers cringed at the alien Christ depicted by gnostics and feared themselves to be cut off from salvation. Irenaeus used the term *gnostic* to deride the religious leaders who attracted followers by promising access to privileged gnosis (knowledge) by means of their learned versions of Christianity. For proto-orthodox Christians in the second and third centuries, "gnostic" was roughly equivalent to the term "heretical."

Attitudes served to unite the gnostic heresies far more than particular beliefs. Gnostics were seekers in the positive sense of yearning to know and understand more about themselves and the divine. Yet there was also a negative side: restlessness, instability of belief systems, shifting revelation and community, and readiness to create new myths and paradigms when dissatisfied with old ones. Privileging individual over communal revelation, gnostics rejected both the Scripture, which blamed humans for alienation from God, and the notion of God as a Creator, who was disturbingly involved with his human creatures. Gnostic Christians rejected being bound to reading Jesus in continuity with Scripture and the larger believing community. In gnostic usage, Scripture according to the rule of faith became antiscripture, against which gnostics composed contrasting myths that sought to solve the dilemma of the origins of suffering and evil.

SIMILAR PATTERNS, DIFFERENT STORY

Descent and Return

Imagine that you wake up one morning and find yourself working as a slave, with no idea who you are or how you came to be here. At first it doesn't seem so strange; everyone else takes you and your situation for granted. Yet you cannot escape a desire to discover your past. When you begin to ask questions, your fellow slaves mock you while your master threatens you. It is so much easier to go with the flow and leave the questions behind: live for the day.

One evening under cover of darkness, someone whispers at the door of your hovel. "This must be some scam," you think as you listen anxiously. But wait—things begin to make sense, as does your identity and your restlessness. The covert messenger reveals that you are the son of a great king, whose mission in a foreign land has been thwarted. The locals discovered and captured you, ultimately so scarring your psyche that you forgot who you were. Rejoicing at this revelation of your true identity and destiny, you pick up the map and royal robe left by the messenger and begin your difficult but joyous journey home.

> The Hymn of the Pearl is found in some manuscripts of the widely read Acts of Thomas (Syria, mid–3rd c.). Scholars note that, depending on its interpretation in various communities, this hymn could have been understood as orthodox, gnostic, or Manichean.

The foregoing summary of the Hymn of the Pearl captures themes central to many gnostic texts circulating from the second and third centuries.[9] At the same time, it echoes Plato's allegory of the cave and Jesus' parable of the Prodigal Son. All three depict the human condition as lost. Salvation is to be found by remembering who you are and returning home. This return must be facilitated by some gracious intermediary from the divine realm.

The Great Church already embraced this pattern of salvation in the Philippians' Christ hymn (2:5b–11), which celebrates Jesus' mission as a saving descent from and reascent to heaven. Christ humbly descended from the Father to become human. After suffering death, Christ reascended to the Father, who exalted him above all creation and powers. Gnostic Christians would have understood the hymn in their own spiritualized way. For example, a gnostic could believe that Christ left his spiritual domain behind and deigned to descend to the world of physical beings (taking the *form* of a human slave, but not the reality). Christ delivered saving knowledge that could release poor, enslaved humans and enable them to return to their rightful spiritual nature and relationship with the supreme Deity. Gnostics believed that this thick, dense world of material existence resisted the appearance of divinity. Materially befogged people and the evil powers of this world saw Christ and his message as a threat. These powers killed Jesus, meaning Christ's human body, while Christ returned triumphantly to the divine spiritual reality, knowing that his message would continue to release the prisoners from their material chains.

Even today, this framework for understanding oneself in the world is appealing. Existence in bodies leaves humans inextricably bound to pain, suffering, and relationships that bring anxiety and grief. After all, Christians sing "I'll Fly Away" for "Heaven Is My Home." Many Christians believe that our present reality threatens or submerges our true identity. Like the heretics they condemned, proto-orthodox believers understood this world to be less good than God desires and knew that our bodies often challenge our commitment to what is best for us spiritually and physically. Just look at North Americans today: we love junk food even though we know it is bad for us; we know we ought to exercise, but instead we lounge in front of the television.

The Gnostic Fall and the Origins of Evil

For gnostics, the thorniest question was why the world is not as good as one would expect from a good God. As we saw in Marcion, the Creator in Genesis did not seem to offer sufficient explanation. Gnostics blamed the Jewish creator god (and his mother) for wrecking things. The varied gnostic accounts disclose the origins of the spiritual (rather than the material) cosmos that preceded biblical Genesis.

Among those desperate to experience God and feel the intimacy that Christ seemed to offer, gnostics took seriously how distant and different humanity is from God. They created diagrams of the universe and treatises that charted their painful awareness of the moral and cosmic distance humans must overcome to reach their longed-for reunion with the divine. Celsus included one such diagram in his attack of Christianity. Origen described and deconstructed this diagram when wrote against Celsus in the third century (*Against Celsus* 6.24–38).

Gnostic models of reality begin with the supreme deity, whose life overflows (emanates) like a fountain and spills out to form increasingly distant pools. These pools were at the same time distinct spiritual beings (aeons) ruling their own spheres within a divine expanse known as the *plērōma*, or Fullness. This was somewhat analogous to "heaven" and had astrological connections with the planets. The aeons were named according to scriptural names for God and divine qualities: for example, Son, Christ, Spirit, Will, Grace, Truth, and Wisdom. Increasing distance from the supreme deity resulted in attenuated likeness to it. Finally, some sort of "fall" occurred, even though gnostics did not blame humans for this catastrophic event.

For example the *Apocryphon of John* (2nd or 3rd c.) describes a secret revelation from Jesus Christ to the apostle John, whose faith falters after Christ's return to the Father.[10] Jesus appears to John and proceeds to reveal the real prehistory and meaning of Genesis. This description shares many characteristics of the gnostic myths most worrisome to Christian authors like Irenaeus and Tertullian. The Jesus in the *Apocryphon* describes the Father as perfection, the origin of all, yet utterly transcendent, beyond human words or concepts. In the beginning, the Father produced Thought (personified), which in turn brought forth another divine being, the virgin Spirit. With the Father's permission (this is important to the story of the fall), the divine beings took up the creative impulse and brought forth more aeons. This included a Trinity of Father-Spirit-Son/Christ. At last one aeon, Sophia (Wisdom), accidentally breached the Pleroma and initiated the fall when she created without the Father's permission. She immediately cast out her creation, Yaltabaoth (the Jewish god), into a dimension outside the divine Pleroma. There, Yaltabaoth remained ignorant of any divinity superior to himself.[11] His creative activity unknowingly reflected the organization of the Pleroma, where his archons (angels) paralleled the aeons in the Pleroma.

At this point the *Apocryphon* touches on the Genesis creation accounts. Sophia restlessly moved about in anxiety over her mistaken offspring's actions (the spirit of God hovering over the waters; Gen. 1:2). By the Father's intervention, Yaltabaoth unsuspectingly created humanity in the image of the divine aeon, Adam. Furthermore, humanity covertly received divine breath (spirit) from the aeon Christ. Yaltabaoth's archons became eternally jealous of humanity, for they recognized that humans possess qualities from the Pleroma that Yaltabaoth himself lacked and could never bestow upon the archons. In retaliation the archons trapped humanity in material bodies.

So it happened that material Adam (and all subsequent humanity), though harboring a divine origin and image, is generally ignorant of his divine image. The *Apocryphon* portrays eating the forbidden fruit and expulsion from the garden of Eden as good developments. Surprisingly, Christ encourages Adam to eat from the tree forbidden by Yaltabaoth, since that act will enlighten humanity. When Adam eats of the tree of knowledge of good and evil, he has taken an important step toward recalling his true identity. Adam and Eve were forced to leave "paradise" because they knew the truth. Yaltabaoth dogged their steps through curses, foremost of which is sexual desire, which binds them to his lower creation through the creation of and care for further generations of materially trapped beings.

There follows an unfortunate interlude featuring the fiasco of Cain and Abel, children begotten through Yaltabaoth's seduction of Eve. After murdering Abel, Cain passes on Yaltabaoth's counterfeit, material spirit to his descendants. Then Adam and Eve give birth to Seth in the image of the divine aeon Seth. The descendants of Seth are called the "immovable race," whose eventual elevation to the Pleroma is guaranteed. Other humans, the descendants of Cain, are under Yaltabaoth's control. Simple Christians are to be counted among these descendants. They may still escape and return to the Pleroma, but not without the help of a person who already has the Spirit of Life (one of the perfected humans).

Gnostic Salvation and Orthodox Ignorance

Gnostic texts leave no doubt that Christ is the key figure in human salvation and that Jesus of Nazareth had some connection to Christ in delivering saving wisdom. This is one of the reasons why it is unwise to dismiss gnosticism as entirely foreign to Christianity. Salvation was a process of revelation. Christ opened a path to ultimate reality by charting the cosmos in his teachings and in his pioneering descent/ascent. In the *Wisdom [Sophia] of Jesus Christ*, Jesus asks his disciples, "'What are you searching for?' Philip said: 'For the underlying reality of the universe and the plan.'" The disciples are seekers, and Christ is the privileged messenger who has seen true reality.[12] Gnostics marveled at Christ's daring journey from the Pleroma to the world of matter to bring wisdom, knowledge, and a map or passwords for returning to their divine home.

When describing human distance from God, gnostics tended to call it "ignorance" while proto-orthodox believers grounded ignorance in the biblical notion of "sin." Ignorance does not entail the same level of personal guilt and responsibility as sin. Recall the paradigm in the *Apocryphon of John*. If our world and material existence resulted from disobedience (Sophia's creation of

Yaltabaoth without permission) and ignorance (Yaltabaoth ignorantly thinks he is the top god) and jealousy (archons trapping humans in physical bodies), then it makes sense to distrust things of this world, especially the authority of Jewish Scripture.

This scenario lets humanity off the hook. The body and sin are not our fault. Evil is built into this limited world by its limited creator. Moral evil and the suffering it causes, as well as impersonal evils such as illness and natural disasters—all are the fault of the creator god. Resistance to all that comes from this world's god (such as procreation and the Great Church) is appropriate for those oriented to a divine and spiritual existence. Salvation from suffering and evil will come when one's spirit is reunited to the Pleroma, no longer harassed by the evil powers of this world.

Gnostics looked with great disdain on the Great Church's association of salvation with the divine messenger's death. Gnostic treatises reveal how laughable they found the proto-orthodox rule of faith that emphasized Christ's human life and death. The Coptic *Apocalypse of Peter* shows Jesus warning Peter about those closed-minded believers (including bishops and deacons).[13] In the later vision, Peter sees Jesus being nailed to the cross. The "blind and deaf" (56) think that the Savior is being crucified. Instead, Jesus tells Peter, "He whom you saw on the tree, glad and laughing, this is the living Jesus. But this one into whose hands and feet they drive the nails is his fleshly part, which is the substitute" (81). The proto-orthodox leaders and their flocks are lambasted as "dry canals," following a dead man rather than the real Savior, who is pure spirit. Likewise, in the *Second Treatise of the Great Seth*, Christ takes possession of a human in order to visit the earth.[14] Christ laughs at the ignorance of those who thought he was nailed to the cross, wearing the crown of thorns. The proto-orthodox "think that they are advancing the name of Christ," but are "like dumb animals" who persecute real Christians and their true gnosis of Christ (59). The gnostic Jesus Christ regrets that believers of the Great Church sadly follow the "doctrine of a dead man" (60).

True Christians are gnostics, so the gnostics say. Many proto-orthodox believers were frightened by the threefold categories of humanity (material, ensouled, and spiritual) described by Valentinians and other gnostic writers. The popular reception raised fears that material humans had absolutely no hope of acquiring the knowledge necessary for salvation. Ordinary Christians feared and resented being cast as ignorant, earthly, even beastlike people, with no link to the Pleroma. They were entirely products of the limited, material creator of this world. A second higher class, sometimes called the ensouled or those progressing, had some seed or spark of divine spirit hidden within them. With ascetic discipline and access to the gnostic teachings to nurture the sparks, the ensouled might return to the Pleroma. Last, there were the

spirituals or the perfect, who are assured of their return. Sometimes proto-
orthodox Christian leaders were angered more by the fear these categories
introduced into their flocks than by what they said about Jesus. Genuine concern for their flock's welfare, in tandem with a concern for right belief, led
many to challenge gnostic views.

These categories reflect what many believers regularly observe to this day.
It is roughly analogous to a current set of categories: sinners (unconverted),
backsliders, and born-again believers. Some people call themselves Christian
but rarely show up at church except for baptisms, marriages, and funerals.
Others might attend worship as a social duty, with absolutely no impact on
their lives outside of the church walls. Across the centuries, Christians have
labored to understand how to handle differing levels of commitment to the
faith, what election to salvation might mean, and whether salvation is in some
sense universal.

Gnostics, too, observed disparities in the church and surmised that the
potential for salvation was predetermined for some, yet a matter of choice for
others. There is a great deal of ambiguity in gnostic texts about the determinism so abhorrent to Irenaeus and other orthodox. Gnostic texts, and even
some descriptions of gnostics in Irenaeus, leave open the possibility of growth
rather than strict determinism. The gnostic believer is challenged, in Christ's
words, to "search, and you will find" (cf. Matt. 7:7).[15] Those who never "seek
and find" have freely chosen never to progress spiritually and will be destroyed
when the rest of the material realm is destroyed.

Wild as such accounts may seem to readers today, consider what the gnostic Christians accomplished. In detaching the Creator (YHWH) from the
One True God, gnostics preserved a transcendent divinity who could not
and would not ever have direct dealings with the pollution, decay, and death
that is inherent in material existence. The ungodlike behavior of the Creator
then no longer required awkward explanations and intricate allegorical inven-
tions; Scripture was correct about YHWH's character. Human yearning and
restlessness revealed that the believers most sensitive to the One True God
had good reason not to feel at home since their home was with God, not in
the mess YHWH had created. Christ saved through revealing and leading
trapped spirits back to God. The return is arduous. YHWH and his archons
offer temptations of physicality (food, sex, luxury) and social conventions
(familial ties, civic expectations, and orthodox Christian standards) to prevent
any human spirits from escaping.

Day-to-day life among the faithful laid the foundation for gnostic separatism. Believers who thought the faith utterly clear, who saw everything in black
and white, who had no imagination for the grandeur of the One True God
or human potential, who made no effort to mature beyond rote childhood

beliefs: surely these simple or apathetic believers had nothing in common with the Christ who offers peace, love, and reunion with God, did they? Against this separatism stood pastors forming the heart of proto-orthodoxy. While exasperated by the laissez-faire attitude of some in their flock, they nonetheless insisted that the faith of the simple differed from that of mature believers only in depth, not in content. Salvation, they argued, was open to believers at all levels of understanding, with hope even for those only loosely committed to the faith.

ORTHODOX METHODOLOGY
THROUGH THE RULE OF FAITH

Proto-orthodox Christianity claimed that no one, not even the most sophisticated believer, could abandon a certain earthiness to God and his actions. Every spiritual understanding had to be grounded, sometimes quite literally, in the material world. The Son of God became a real human being. The person and history of Jesus Christ comprised the heart of the rule of faith. This insistence on the nondisposability of the basic story of Jesus had many implications. It shaped the Great Church's designation of legitimate authority and legitimate "seeking" within the faith. It was the foundation for asserting that God, the Jewish Creator, was the good and transcendent Father of Jesus Christ. Finally, the rule of faith clearly connected bodies to salvation through the incarnation, death, and resurrection of Jesus. Proto-orthodox leaders enunciated their own cosmic plan of salvation in Christ that filtered philosophical assumptions and scriptural authority through this rule.

Rule of Faith as Filter

Christians remained faithful to their belief in the ongoing activity of the Holy Spirit, and this prevented them from completely denying the possibility of new revelation. However, proto-orthodox Christians emphasized an identity rooted in real events and people who handed down stories of those events across generations.[16] For mainstream Christianity, truth resided in history and community more than in individuals. Thus, they tended to regard groups who claimed privileged access to new revelation as dishonoring the experience of past believers and their written traditions.

Gnostic texts sometimes anticipate this complaint by introducing new revelation through an apostle or Jesus. While introducing new revelation outside of, and even contrary to, the great tradition, they do so in the guise of a secret apostolic tradition that conveys a hidden rule or interpretive key for returning to God. Gnostic Christians thereby use (however creatively) both Jewish Scripture (most often to highlight problematic passages) and some of the new Christian Scriptures (New Testament). This made it difficult to appeal to a written tradition as a definitive authority and led to consternation among Christians and their leaders. Tertullian went so far as to counsel Christians to avoid using Scripture in debates with heretics since both sides claimed to possess the true interpretation (*Prescription against the Heretics* 18–19).

Proto-orthodox leaders solved this difficulty by appealing to a community of belief marked by the rule of faith, rather than to individual inspiration. Tertullian asked, "What then if a bishop, a deacon, a widow, a virgin, a teacher, [or] even a martyr has fallen from the rule?"[17] If so, they too were heretics; the rule trumps individuals, or at least tests the validity of individual inspiration, even for those considered the most respected believers.

The rule or standard (canon) was the means for determining whether beliefs, ways of life (on martyrs, see chap. 4), and texts (on Scripture, see chap. 5) were in line with the one gospel handed down by the apostles. The rule of faith was the governing hypothesis whereby Christians understood the entire religion. It was the operating system for Christianity: it organized the data of reality (worldview) and made it both accessible to and functional in the church. The rule provided the interpretive lens for making sense of Scripture through Christ and of Christ through the Scripture. Thus the rule filtered out what was incongruent in seeing and knowing Christ and the Christian faith. Like a 3-D movie, one needs the right glasses in order to see the picture as it is meant to be seen.

In practice the rule of faith followed the basic doctrinal instruction for new Christians and resulted in statements of faith made at baptism. In *Proof of the Apostolic Preaching*, Irenaeus reminded his audience of the threefold God in whom they were baptized:

> God, the Father, uncreated, beyond grasp, invisible, one God the maker of all; this is the first and foremost article of our faith. But the second article is the Word of God, the Son of God, Christ Jesus our Lord, who was shown forth by the prophets according to the design of their prophecy and according to the manner in which the Father disposed; and through Him were made all things whatsoever. He also, *in the end of times*, for the recapitulation of all things, is become a man among men, visible and tangible, in order to abolish death and bring to light life, and bring about communion of God and man. And the third article is the Holy Spirit, through whom the prophets prophesied and the patriarchs were taught about God and the just were led in the path of justice, and who *in the end of times*, has been poured forth in a new manner upon humanity over all the earth, renewing man to God.[18]

The rule of faith specifically filtered out heretical tangents from the shared foundation of faith. God is the Creator, not some God above the ignorant Creator. Jesus Christ is the Son of God the Creator, and he plays a key role in creation himself. Jesus Christ was born, suffered, and died. His human living and dying was real and important to salvation. Rather than assuming that a good God would not mete out punishments (such as Marcion alleged), Jesus as the final judge shared both the mercy and the justice of God manifested in Jewish Scripture. In contrast to the tendency of gnostics to abstract Christ from the events of the Gospels and the Jewish tradition, the rule rooted the universal claims of Christianity within concrete events centered on Jesus Christ.

Importantly, proto-orthodox theologians insisted that their tradition of saving knowledge was not withheld from common believers by some spiritual elite. For those baptized into Christianity, the central story of God's saving acts had been revealed during catechetical training. While the rule was, to a certain extent, kept secret from the unconverted and unbaptized, it lay open to all baptized believers. All baptismal candidates not only agreed with the story but entered the story when they, too, died and rose again with Christ in baptism. Thus, Irenaeus found it impossible for any secret teaching to be apostolic. "For if the apostles had known hidden mysteries, which they were in the habit of imparting to 'the perfect' apart and privily from the rest, they would have delivered them especially to those to whom they were also committing the Churches themselves."[19] Church leaders had the same foundation as other Christians.

Rule of Faith as Launch Pad for Orthodox "Gnostics"

Tertullian identified "Seek, and you shall find" to be the dangerous guiding spirit of gnosticism. Extant gnostic texts do challenge adherents to engage in spiritual growth through seeking and finding. Some gnostic texts hint that even the spiritual or perfect must maintain vigilance in their pursuit of self-understanding so as to avoid degenerating to the bestial or earthly level.[20] At face value, proto-orthodox leaders had no quarrel with this except when orthodox Christians were labeled as irredeemable beasts. What Tertullian and others opposed about seeking was not seeking as such, but where the seeking occurred and why it was done.

Two problems loomed in unorthodox seeking. One involved perpetual sampling, which revealed a lack of commitment or arrogant refusal to submit to any worldview. Proto-orthodox apologists argued that real Christians (or real philosophers for that matter!) must eventually settle on a system around which to build their whole lives. Second, yet equally disturbing, was the extent to which perpetual sampling of philosophies infected how seekers interpreted Christianity. When seekers let philosophical sampling dominate the rule of faith, the result was no longer Christian. In the oft-quoted passage where he rejected any relationship between Athens (philosophy) and Jerusalem (Christianity), Tertullian states, "No one seeks, except the one who either never had [it] or lost [it]."[21] Christians are those who have indeed sought and then found (i.e., believed in) Christ in the rule of faith.

Despite the unyielding tone that Tertullian adopted against seeking, he clearly embraced analysis of the faith in common with other leaders of the Great Church. Such inquiries had to be conducted among fellow believers (especially those known to be wise and experienced) who submitted the fruit of their explorations to the rule of faith. Under such conditions, Tertullian counseled, "You may seek and discuss as much as you please, and give full rein to your curiosity, in whatever seems to you to hang in doubt, or to be shrouded in obscurity."[22]

This attitude has much in common with Origen's notoriously speculative approach to the faith. Origen agreed that Christians have given up seeking for the sake of seeking and instead have chosen to learn exclusively from Christ.[23] While granting the necessity that speculation must be measured by the rule of faith, Origen equally understood that the rule only covered the most basic and necessary principles for conveying salvation in Christ. The apostles and the Holy Spirit left large swaths of theological geography to be explored by those with divinely given and humanly trained talents. In addition to Christian disciplines of prayer, worship, and service, Origen assumed that rigorous training in many non-Christian disciplines—including linguistics, logic, natural sciences, and philosophy—would aid seeking within the faith. Origen eagerly followed the traditional interpretation of the Israelites' plundering the goods of the Egyptians (Exod. 12:35–36). Here was God's approval for Christians to appropriate all truth wherever it might be found. Non-Christian insights could be useful in believers' yearning to draw near and be transformed by ultimate Truth, Christ himself.

In place of feckless seekers, the Great Church daringly encouraged its own brand of gnostics and spirituals (see Clement of Alexandria's wise man, in chap. 4 above). Irenaeus countered the gnostic, predetermined, spiritual elite with his own portrait of the true "spiritual disciple" (*Against Heresies* 4.33.1–7, 15) who was by no means a blind-faith follower. With the help of the Spirit, a spiritual disciple must test and question religious assumptions, whether prevailing Greco-Roman philosophies and religions, Judaism, or alternative interpretations of Christianity. The spiritual disciple's assessment is based upon discerning which ideas are inconsistent with true knowledge passed down through the apostles and safeguarded by the believers in the church.

This served both to protect the believer and, potentially, to convert those who had wandered away (*Against Heresies* Preface.1–2).

ORTHODOX "GNOSIS" OF GOD AND SALVATION

Christian debates about the definition of God and his goodness took place in the midst of, and were a subcategory of, contemporary debates within non-Christian philosophical circles. Non-Christian philosophers disagreed over whether the supreme God cared about the rest of reality, and how he could do something if he did care.[24] Both Scripture and the rule of faith depicted matter and divinity connected in ways that raised questions common to the era. How does one understand God as good and as Creator? How is divinity related to humanity? Certainly no divinity, assuming Christ partook of this status, could die, but some (Christians and non-Christians) argued that divinity could be aware of undivine sensations such as change and negative emotions (fear or sadness) without these having power over the divine (see more in chap. 10).

The proto-orthodox account of God and reality, like that of the gnostics, began with beginnings. Their first task was to affirm that God is good, even in his creative activity. From there they tracked the origins of evil within creatures who, through God's goodness in Christ, rewove goodness into all creation by becoming, living, dying, and rising again as a human being.

God, Evil, and Creation

Just about everybody agreed that the material world, as humans were experiencing it, did not exhibit the perfection of having been created by an ultimate, transcendent divinity. The question of God's goodness and the origin of evil perplexed those who stayed within Christianity as well as those who left it. Tertullian observed that many set out from the faith "morbidly brooding over the question of the origin of evil."[25] The failure of humans and the rest of creation to reflect God properly was a symptom of evil.

In this period, the concept of evil had more to do with disorder throughout the whole system of lived reality than with individual malicious actions. For example, things constantly change from summer to winter, from health to illness, from birth to death, from being to nonbeing. Thus, some argued that material creation manifested evil, that is, change or mutability. This condition made material creation utterly unlike the good, immutable God. To those heretics who separated the True God from creation, and thereby rendered God unknowable except through exclusive revelation, Christians insisted that the world does does truly bear witness to the One, Highest, Good God. Stoics could argue from observable patterns of existence in the world that there is a divinely rational organization (Logos) of the universe. Likewise, Christians argued that the world, history, and the community of believers bear witness to the One True God through the Logos Christ.

Both gnostics and Marcionites sought to protect the majesty and perfection of transcendent divinity by visualizing a nearly insurmountable distance between our reality and that of the Divine. From the human perspective, this resulted in the practical impossibility of knowing God. The proto-orthodox brought creation and human instinct to the witness stand on behalf of a known God. Surely, Tertullian argued, human ignorance is not more powerful than the transcendent God: "God neither could have been nor ought to have been unknown. *Could* not have been, because of His greatness; *ought* not to have been, because of His goodness."[26] Even befuddled by ignorance, humanity has been inspired to worship glorious aspects of the creation as gods. Tertullian noted that while mistaken in their object of worship, people have always recognized the glory of the true Creator through his creation. He pointed out how even the small, humble elements of creation can manifest the greatness of the Creator. Citing the proverb "Greatness has its proof in lowliness," Tertullian drew attention to the intricacy of a single flower or shellfish; the products of bees, spiders, and ants; even ingenious irritants like bedbugs (*Against Marcion* 1.13–14). If God's goodness, in the sense of power, order, and planning, is so evident even in small things, then the wonder of humanity becomes an even more astonishing affirmation of God's goodness. Pressing further, Tertullian asked, "What superior god is this, of whom it has not been possible to find any work so great as *the man* of the lesser god [i.e., the Jewish creator in Marcion's system]!"[27]

Christians had much in common with the pagan philosopher Plotinus (mid-3rd c.), who directed a treatise against gnostics for similar reasons.[28] How could there be any power along the whole spiritual hierarchy that opposed rather than witnessed to the goodness of the One God and source of all? The goodness of this world simply points to the possibility of even greater goodness as one returned to God. Plotinus was flabbergasted that gnostics could value their own spiritual nature, yet demean the grandeur of the visible universe.

Although it was perhaps of little use in convincing their opponents, proto-orthodox authors carefully analyzed the New Testament to demonstrate how the rule of faith establishes continuity between God the Creator's actions in the Jewish tradition and the saving activity of Jesus (see book 3 of Irenaeus's *Against Heresies*). As to the source of evil, Christians across the board placed the responsibility of fallenness on humans. Humans were not tragically flawed creatures (thus God's fault), but perfectly free reflections of

God who suffer the consequences of choosing badly. Salvation arises from the same gracious Creator who intends for the end to reflect the beginning. Christians anticipated the once and future glory of creation in the "new heaven and new earth" (Isa. 65:17; Rev. 21:1), where the "wolf shall live with the lamb" (Isa. 11:6; 65:25) and humanity is resurrected into "changed" bodies (1 Cor. 15:50–52) in the "new Jerusalem" (Isa. 65:17–25; Rev. 21:1–4). Proto-orthodox views concerning future reality were rooted in the stories of beginnings and intimately tied to the God of Israel. The proto-orthodox Christians cherished the good Creator in Genesis, who carefully planned and accomplished his goals, in contrast to the accidental or botched creation in the gnostic myths.

Believers of the Great Church, governed by a model of the Creator God of mercy and love, were not utterly opposed to philosophical models of God. The models that allowed for appreciating creation and for divine care of it were natural intellectual allies for the Great Church. Christians opposed other models that insisted upon an emotionless divinity so transcendent as to be severed from material reality. Care for even the smallest of details in creation demonstrated true divinity for Christians. Christ's life and teachings suggested a far more hands-on God than that of the gnostics. Jesus Christ himself was deemed the very Word and Image of God, bursting into the world to save what he helped to create.

Salvation Open to All

Jesus Christ is the Savior. Here gnostics and other Christians were on the same page. However, details of the gnostic Christ provided an opportunity for proto-orthodox Christians to think about what most had simply assumed regarding Jesus and salvation. Both perspectives agreed that it is an enormous event for divinity to enter into our world. The proto-orthodox position centered upon an earthy and yet divine Jesus Christ, who inexplicably was born, died, and rose again. For these mainstream Christians, as for Jews before them, it was not so much a plan or messages they wanted to know as much as God. Christ was more than his teachings. Indeed, *Christ himself* was the good news and not merely the bearer of the news. Nevertheless, both sides recognized that not all the baptized committed themselves to the faith fully or with sophisticated understanding, and that most people were not Christian at all. Were some humans by nature irredeemable?

Many gnostic texts do not directly cut off large swaths of believers from salvation. However, there was a panic among many proto-orthodox believers about their potentially predetermined inability to receive salvation. Practically speaking, the "knowing" smugness of many gnostics implied the futility of hope for those who did not want to abandon or embellish the faith into which they had been baptized. Rank-and-file believers naturally rankled at being called simple or bestial.

Irenaeus emphasized the opportunity and responsibility shared by all humans to use God-given freedom for salvation (*Against Heresies* 4.37). Being good, after God's initial gifts in baptism and in his constantly inviting presence, is left in the power of the individual to choose freely. The individual chooses whether or not to receive the good and act upon it. Irenaeus objected that there is no work or zeal or love (or reward, for that matter) involved in being good for those who are good by nature and not by choice. Predeterminism also resulted in a pastoral nightmare that left some believers overly assured of their perfection and salvation, while others despaired or had little incentive to dedicate themselves more fully to spiritual growth.

The gnostics' reputation for limiting who might be saved served to temper orthodox tendencies toward a narrow view of salvation. Irenaeus countered the perceived elitism of gnostic systems by proclaiming: "The fact that some know more by virtue of their intelligence, and some less, does not come about by their changing the doctrine (of Christianity) itself."[29] Both the long-winded and those of few words, those of great understanding and those with little, belong to the same religion and ultimately share in the same hope of salvation. In the third century, Origen boldly clarified the Valentinian categories (the simple, the progressing, the complete) to describe levels of spiritual maturity, rather than categories of saved and unsaved.

Salvation in Jesus Christ

The Great Church refused to explain away Christ's death as peripheral to the faith. Tertullian asserted that "the whole weight and fruit of the Christian name" depends upon Christ's death, especially the hope for a bodily resurrection.[30] Reprising Paul in 1 Corinthians 15, Tertullian derided any claim to the Christian hope for resurrection if Christ himself did not really die and was not really raised again. Further, Tertullian raised the question of how anyone could trust a god who concocted a lie in sending Christ if he was not really what he appeared to be: a human being. Believers convinced of the impossibility of divinity and matter intersecting beheld with horror the assertion that divinity could, or would, undergo something so unbefitting as birth and death. It was utterly ungodlike for divinity to make itself vulnerable. Tertullian saw these paradoxes as evidence of the magnitude of God's power. Reveling in the squalor of both birth and death, Tertullian suggested

that a Christ detached from full humanity was the product of heretics' squea-
mishness rather than a supposed protection of divine dignity (*Against Marcion* 3.11). After all, Tertullian asked, is it not a greater show of power to do
something in reality rather than to pretend to do it in a phantom humanity
of Christ?

But to what end does God's salvation in a born-died-raised Christ tend?
Irenaeus took gnostic cosmology head-on by developing the New Testament
concept of recapitulation. Images from the Gospel of John and the Letters
of Paul link Christ the Creator to Christ the Savior, and show the fallen first
Adam as restored and perfected in Christ, the second Adam. Recapitulation
makes use of the term in Ephesians 1:10 of God's plan to "*gather up* all things
in him [Christ], things in heaven and things on earth." Recapitulation was a
specific literary-rhetorical term referring to the summation of an argument.[31]
The author-speaker would list the main points to remind the audience what
was most important about the foregoing speech. At the same time, the speaker
placed these points in conjunction to each other so as to see them in a new
light, which corresponded with the author's interpretation or plan. In this
way, "recapitulation" functions like the closing arguments at the end of a trial.
Any educated reader/listener back then would have recognized Paul's and
Irenaeus's use of the word in that sense.

If Jesus Christ is God's closing argument, then typology (see chap. 5, on
the Bible) as a means of accommodating the Old Testament to Christianity
was far more than a tool. Irenaeus believed the correspondences to be crucial
to Christianity precisely because Christ has revealed, and is himself, the true
meaning of God's activity. Typology links the Old Testament with the New
Testament by listing the main points of the Old through the organization
provided in the New: the apostolic tradition about Christ. Christ "sums up"
human history, especially as witnessed through the Jewish Scripture. That is
why the developing orthodox perception of reality depended upon the rule of
faith, which demonstrated the unity of Christ the Word in Scripture, Old and
New (Irenaeus, *Proof of the Apostolic Preaching* 3).

Consequently, Irenaeus was inexorably drawn to Christ's role as Savior,
who recapitulated (or summed up) the whole of creation through the incarnation. Drawing on Paul's analogy of first Adam and second Adam (Christ),
Irenaeus emphasized the divinely planned correspondence of creation and
salvation.[32] Christ's incarnation, "born of a virgin by the Will and Wisdom
of God," corresponds to Adam's creation "from God's Will and Wisdom,
and from virgin earth" (*Proof* 32). God the Father incarnated both Adam and
Christ (*Against Heresies* 3.21.10). Eve's disobedience is healed in Mary's obedience (*Proof* 33). Sin occasioned by the tree of the knowledge of good and
evil is destroyed by Christ's death on the "tree" of the cross (*Proof* 34). These

connections were not suddenly discovered by Irenaeus, but rather were examples developed through the rule of faith by earlier generations.

In Irenaeus's schema, the incarnation is a conclusion in the sense of restoring humanity to its created capacity and completing human development. Christ completes the maturation intended for humanity from the beginning. Irenaeus described humanity as still a "little one," a "child," in the garden of Eden.[33] The fall, while deservedly entailing severe consequences, also reflected the immature decision-making skills of youthful humanity. For Irenaeus, the incarnation was not an emergency plan, but part of God's good creation from the start.

Unfortunately human disobedience required a restorative dimension to the incarnation in addition to the completion of humanity, which Irenaeus located in the image of God.

> When [the Son of God] became incarnate, and was made man, He commenced afresh [summed up] the long line of human beings, and furnished us, in a brief, comprehensive manner, with salvation; so that what we had lost in Adam—namely, to be according to the image and likeness of God—that we might recover in Christ Jesus.[34]

Since recapitulation required an exact correspondence, Irenaeus hammered home the necessity of Christ fully joining himself to his own creation. Alone, crippled human nature could not save itself.[35] Humanity needed rescue from sin and death, both of which required "that [the Son of God] should Himself be made that very same thing which he was, that is, man." Irenaeus insisted that the incarnation encompassed all aspects of human existence: "He passed through every stage of life, restoring communion with God." Through the Logos undertaking a complete human life and death, the hidden and damaged image of God was thus restored and perfected.

The incarnation is a double revelation of Christ the Word, in whose image humanity was created and through whom that image was restored within humanity itself:

> When, however, the Word of God became flesh, He confirmed both these: for He both showed forth the image truly, since He became Himself what was His image; and He re-established the similitude after a sure manner, by assimilating man to the invisible Father through means of the visible Word.[36]

God's plan of salvation is comprehensive and involves a sense of history repeating itself in a way that heals the past. There is a linear history from Adam to Christ to the End, but a circular shape to the salvation accomplished in Christ.

CONCLUSIONS: IMPLICATIONS OF STANCES AND OUTSTANDING QUESTIONS

The tumults of heresy raised legitimate questions about what mainstream Christians assumed, even as it prompted them to examine the meaning of traditional beliefs and to state them more clearly. The Great Church discovered the importance of formalizing the often-unwritten customs and beliefs held by most believers. Buoyed by the bodily suffering and death of Jesus Christ, believers gloried in the heroism of martyrs and in a common hope of a bodily resurrection. Challenged by less incarnational versions of Christ, the Great Church developed more systematic accounts of salvation through a divine-human Christ.

God, as both Creator and Father of Jesus Christ, had for the most part been unquestioned and perhaps underappreciated until disputed. Ever afterward, Christian insistence upon the goodness of creation served to limit overspiritualization of the faith into extremes of ascetic discipline or abstract thought. It also contributed to early considerations about Christ's humanity, his role as cocreator, and his transformative presence through the sacraments. Such explorations gave material for meditations on the nature of Christ himself, first in relation to the Father and then with respect to his existence as somehow both divine and human—reflection that took place over the following centuries (see chap. 10). The orthodox slogan "God became man that man might become God" actually had its origins in Irenaeus's claim that "the Word of God, our Lord Jesus Christ, . . . did, through His transcendent love, become what we are, that He might bring us to be even what He is Himself."[37]

The impetus for perfection, spiritual growth, and encounters with God did not disappear; they continued both to trouble and to nourish orthodox theology and lifestyles. With the end of persecution at the beginning of the fourth century, disparities among believers intensified, occupying Christians with turning the promises of baptism into lived realities (see chaps. 7 and 8). Material bodies received much attention as the locus for serving Christ as well as the source of dangerous distractions from God. Christian energies unleashed in the fourth century embraced diverse opportunities to enrich spiritual and intellectual yearning for the new generations of orthodox gnostics. Those hungering for spiritual and intellectual "meat" elaborated upon the existing menus (the rule of faith) and venues (the church) for feasting, yet without rejecting from salvation those still nourished on "milk."

QUESTIONS FOR DISCUSSION

1. How was heresy related to disparities among believers in the church? How was it as much a pastoral as a doctrinal struggle?

2. How did gnostics seek to improve Christianity? What problems did they seek to solve with their alternative versions of the faith?
3. How did concepts of God, Christ, and salvation in orthodox gnosticism compare to that of the heretical gnostic systems?
4. Why would leaders of the Great Church continue to use and even solidify the concept of gnosis (knowledge) within orthodox Christianity?
5. Why was the rule of faith so important in addressing and correcting gnostic claims to being "real" Christianity?

SUGGESTED FURTHER READING

Behr, John. *The Way to Nicaea*. Vol. 1 of *The Formation of Christian Theology*. Crestwood, NY: St. Vladimir's Seminary Press, 2001.

Hurtado, Larry W. *Lord Jesus Christ: Devotion to Jesus in Earliest Christianity*. Grand Rapids: Wm. B. Eerdmans Publishing Co., 2003.

King, Karen L. *What Is Gnosticism?* Cambridge, MA: Belknap Press of Harvard University Press, 2003.

Robinson, James M., ed. *The Nag Hammadi Library in English*. 4th, rev. ed. Leiden and New York: E. J. Brill, 1996.

Williams, Michael Allen. *Rethinking "Gnosticism": An Argument for Dismantling a Dubious Category*. Princeton, NJ: Princeton University Press, 1996.

Part III

A Dynamic Golden Age
(Fourth and Fifth Centuries)

ISSUES

An astounding turn of events in the early fourth century nearly rivaled the incarnation of God. By 312 in the Western Roman Empire and 324 in the East, the Great Persecution ended by the fiat of an emperor devoted to Christ. Before he died in 337, Constantine I (the Great) moved the imperial capital eastward from old Rome to the New Rome of Constantine's City, Constantinople. The fourth and fifth centuries are commonly called the "golden age" of Christianity: freed from general persecution, Christians wrote, taught, built, and lived their faith in utterly new circumstances, which offered new challenges.

Setting the stage for the discussion of this, chapter 7 explores the corporate identity of Christians as the people of God in the church: what being "church" meant, how one joined the family, and how worship and sacraments brought them together in Christ despite broad differences in commitment and motives for conversion. Within this family, zealous members and "parents" offered the fruits of their own interior lives for the formation of fellow members and children of God. Chapter 8 takes up the formative experiences available within the church, from the basics in catechism, worship, and sacraments to intense ascesis and contemplative prayer. By these means, the faithful sought to become more aware of God and more open to his transforming presence. Created in the image of God, Christ re-created humans in that image to restore fellowship among God and humans. Chapter 9 looks at some directions early Christians took to realize these insights about human nature in concrete relationships with others: in families and in society at large. Finally it became clear that all Christians, professionals (ascetics and church leaders) and ordinary believers, faced the ongoing task of clarifying beliefs that had been taken for granted. Chapter 10 shows that nowhere was the need for clarification more pressing than in the issue of Christ himself. Humans only know themselves fully within Christ, who is exact image of God. So the issues of chapters 8 and 9, the inner life and its manifestation in the world, depended upon who believers understood Christ to be and how they hoped to be saved.

HISTORICAL CONTEXT (312–500)

Constantine styled himself as a bishop to the empire, analogous to the bishops of the church. In good Roman fashion, he anxiously sought unity through safeguarding right worship, this time through the God of Jesus Christ. Having established himself as sole emperor in 324, Constantine immediately invited bishops from all over the Roman world to convene at Nicaea in 325. The church had a great opportunity to enjoy even more unity by addressing disciplinary and theological irregularities through this ecumenical (universal) council.

Newfound stability and imperial favor changed the face of Christianity. Constantine insisted that all the confiscated church property be returned. He further allocated immense funds to replace liturgical books and to rebuild churches. Granted the status of legal corporations, Christian congregations could receive bequests and gifts; they expanded their own service institutions, such as orphanages and hospitals. From Constantine; his mother, Helena; and his sons Constantine, Constantius, and Constans, many churches received the royal treatment in building and beautification. Throughout the empire, the traditional drive of the elite to enhance their communities and gain prestige themselves through building programs shifted from pagan temples to churches.

Not only was the artistic and architectural face of Christianity affected, but also the human face. Already at the end of the third century, sizable congregations in cities had experienced cycles of abandonment during the persecution, only to "burst at the seams" after the persecution. Now with persecution apparently gone for good, attending Christian worship became popular. The large-scale basilica (lawcourt style) churches reflected the reality that huge numbers had to be accommodated, if not every Sunday, at least on high feasts such as Easter. Non-Christians found many reasons to attend the liturgy. Some were curious. Some, like Augustine at the end of the fourth century, came for the entertainment provided by some of the finest orators in the empire. Some thought it expedient to their careers and marriage prospects to be seen as sympathetic to the empire's favored religion.

Through immunities from taxes and civic duties equal to those granted priests of traditional cults, Constantine and his successors made a career in the church more attractive. Traditional pagan priests held office for a limited time, but Christian clergy were for life. Bishops increasingly hailed from the elite ranks of Roman society, equipped by class to undertake leadership, at home with the best of classical language and thought, and still dedicated to using their family's wealth to build up their communities. This combination resulted in many leaders who could navigate theological waters with unprecedented facility, using the tools of traditional non-Christian literary and philosophical analysis. It also meant that creative bishops could dream and try to shape their cities into Christian polities, where urban spaces, civic festivities, social welfare, and even marriage could be marked by Christ. Sometimes, though, clerical immunities made for unfit clergy. Joining the clergy seemed to be a good way for the elite to keep from going bankrupt from providing public entertainment, maintaining public buildings, paying taxes, and so forth. Imperial legislation tried to limit this loophole, which allowed the elite to shelter their property and avoid financially painful civic responsibilities. Church law tightened its procedures for excluding morally unqualified candidates.

Not everyone retained the excitement that marked Christian acclamations of Constantine. For a brief but sobering period, Christians faced an imperially driven pagan revival. After surviving a purge of Constantinian family members when Constantius II became emperor in 337, Julian, a nephew of Constantine, eventually rejected Christianity. During his short reign (361–363) Julian attempted to revive traditional Greco-Roman religion, though modified by charitable, ascetic, and philosophical ideals. Rome itself, abandoned as a political capital, still harbored powerful, pagan traditionalists who argued vehemently, but futilely, against legislation enacted by the emperors Theodosius I (East) and Gratian (West) that made Christianity the official religion of the Roman Empire at the end of the fourth century.

Christians learned that having the emperor on their side had its drawbacks, not to mention the potential of losing the emperor's approval. The same tools that emperors had used to encourage religious and political unity before Constantine remained in the toolbox of Christian emperors. When the emperor adopted a theological position at odds with other views, opposing bishops risked removal from office and exile. Ecumenical councils suffered from ordinary political maneuvering, even violence, magnified by the high-profile assemblies made possible by imperial resources. Wrangling among church leaders had previously been conducted long-distance through the insulation of time and the written word. Now with the imperial purse paying for transportation, room, and board, the confrontations grew more acrimonious. Strong personalities used to ruling their home territories met and argued in person, with bodyguards in tow.

After Constantine created his capital, Constantinople, in 330, competition was fierce to become the emperor's choice for bishop (or patriarch) of the imperial capital. Ecumenical councils (Constantinople, 381; Chalcedon, 451) accorded New Rome (Constantinople) honor in the church second only in the church to Old Rome. The Roman patriarchs resented any suggestion that their honor derived from the political position of Rome within the empire rather than the primacy of Peter among the apostles. Attempts by Roman bishops to implement a jurisdictional authority over other patriarchs took hold in this era. Both powerhouse churches of Syria (Antioch) and Egypt (Alexandria) resented the implied demotion behind the two Romes. Antioch and Alexandria vied for appointments made from their clergy in order to promote their personal influence and that of their native theologies. Political prestige and theological clout were at stake as each city claimed distinct theological emphases that would collide throughout the fifth century. When the Council of Chalcedon (451) rejected an extreme form of Alexandrian Christology, Egypt and other eastern Christian communities lobbied influential people at court to convince emperors to tolerate the non-Chalcedonian bishops in these areas.

The empire itself experienced several crises that signaled its eventual disintegration, especially in Europe and Africa. Since the third century, various Germanic groups had alternated between being refugees, invaders, and even troops employed by the empire. Goths, most of whom had been converted to Arian Christianity, wrought a horrendous defeat of Roman forces in the East (378) and during the next century set up their own kingdoms in Spain, parts of Gaul (France), the Balkans, and Italy. Before this disaster, the Goths, fleeing the Hun invasion of present-day Ukraine, were welcomed as allied troops by the emperor Valens in 376. A local famine in the settlement area, soured by the callous Roman response to the settlers' hunger, resulted in a revolt that killed both Valens and nearly two-thirds of his forces at the disastrous Battle of Adrianople in 378.

The terms for peace negotiated by the next emperor, Theodosius I, in 379 involved the mass induction of Goth troops into the Roman army to replace the troops whom the Goths had killed. Another Gothic group sacked Rome itself in 410, marking a blow as psychologically powerful as the military victory at Adrianople. By compromised settlement and eventually outright conquest, Roman provinces from Hungary to the Balkan Peninsula became home to many tribes. However, after the death of the puppet emperor Romulus Augustulus in 476, emperors in Constantinople refused to grant imperial status to the barbarian kings who now ruled across the former western provinces.

Instead, emperors accorded the rank of patrician (imperial senatorial class) or consul (highest Roman magistracy, honorary only) as if dealing with client kings rather than utterly independent rulers. From 493 to 526 Theodoric, the able and Romanized king of the Ostrogoths, ruled Italy as emperor of the West in everything but title. The Franks ultimately became ascendant in chaotic Gaul, and under their king, Clovis, they converted to Catholic Christianity (ca. 500). North Africa fell to the Vandal tribe that lay siege to Augustine's city of Hippo in the same year he died, 430.

The inability of the empire either to absorb migrants peacefully or to prevent tribal incursions exacerbated existing theological and cultural divisions between the eastern (Greek) and western (Latin) sides of the empire. In the East two fundamental ecumenical councils (Ephesus, 431; Chalcedon, 451) struggled to say enough, but not too much, about how Christ is both divine and human. Leo the Great, bishop of Rome from 440 to 461, kept track of the controversies by letter and personal representatives. Yet Leo's job as bishop in the old capital, so bereft of imperial power, involved safeguarding the city itself, even to negotiating with Huns and Vandals to save Rome from further sacks. By the end of the fifth century, little remained of the Roman Empire in Europe and Africa except for the remaining Roman nobles and the ideal of being Roman. The ancient grandeur of Rome would inspire later generations of Germanic rulers to reestablish empire in the West. It also contributed to the prestige of the church where the vestiges of Roman organization and leadership survived.

7

Ekklēsia

The People of God

INTRODUCTION

When the emperor Constantine recognized the God of Christians to be his patron, he insisted upon legal toleration of Christianity, first in 312 as emperor of the West, and later in 324 as emperor of the East too. It soon became fashionable for pagans, whom Tertullian a century earlier had claimed would not be caught dead in a church, to attend worship, to hear well-crafted homilies, and to enjoy the splendor of churches built and decorated with the help of imperial funds. The arrival of so many inquirers once more raised the usual postpersecution reflection about the communal identity of the people of God: What did it mean to be "church"? Belonging to the church had never been so easy.

This chapter delves into the character and experiences associated with the community called *ekklēsia* (assembly) in the two centuries following the empire's landmark toleration of Christianity. As in the previous era, being a Christian and thinking as one depended upon the corporate experience of worship and life among fellow believers. This chapter begins by considering how early Christians encountered the church as the gathered people of God, including members well beyond those immediately visible in time or place. A newcomer to this "family" traveled a well-worn path of learning how to think and live as a Christian, culminating in the elaborate liturgy of baptism. Anchoring and sustaining the community were the concrete experiences of tangible and incarnated worship, whereby communion with God in the Eucharist created and strengthened communion with fellow believers.

A PEOPLE NOT A PLACE

Ekklēsia

English speakers perhaps suffer from their Germanic ancestors' choice of the term *church*, which derived from the *place* Christians gathered (German *kirche*, from the Greek term for a place "belonging to the Lord," *kyriake*, or *kyriakon*). *Church* for the first Christians meant the *people* (Greek *ekklēsia*; Latin *ecclesia*: "assembly"), who always remain in some sense assembled. *Church* communicated a living and dynamic relationship among the members and with God himself. Gentile converts might associate *church* with town assemblies (*ekklēsiai*), where citizens gathered for political and juridical deliberation. Greek-speaking Jews across the Mediterranean world knew that *ekklēsia* in the Septuagint translation of Scripture regularly referred to the visible "assembly" of the covenant people. These were solemn gatherings of the whole people of God, men and women, young and old, to worship God, to be taught by God, and to affirm their fidelity to God.

Early Christians took for granted the ancient assumption that communal membership governs individual identity. People without a community had no identity and functioned on the margins of society—proverbial fish out of water. Individuals exercised an identity based upon the situation of their birth: nationality, hometown, and family. Christians, as noted in chapter 4, daringly switched their nationality, theoretically leaving behind, or at least devaluing, their former Roman identity or other ethnopolitical membership. Today it is hard to grasp that religious people (Christian or otherwise) before the modern period rarely conceived of their identity, much less a relationship with the divine, apart from the fellowship of cobelievers. Ancient elitists occasionally fancied themselves above institutional religion and claimed that they had simply adopted the philosophy of Christianity. Marius Victorinus (d. after 362) was such a pagan who, after defending traditional Roman religion, came to appreciate Christian truth intellectually. Truth for Victorinus did not seem to require going through rituals, but rather living in accord with abstract, disembodied truth. Mistaking the place for the people, he would jokingly ask his Christian friend, Simplicianus, "Do walls make Christians?"[1] However, after delving more deeply into Christian Scriptures and tradition, he sensed the need to shed his pride and publicly commit to an embodied community and the incarnate Truth, Jesus Christ. He assented to the necessity not of walls but of entry into relationships. Being part of the church meant entering into a community-based relationship with the God who founded and sustained the church.

Images for Being Church

Early Christians busily constructed multilayered images to explore their place within the church and their ultimate homeland. In tune with the importance that Christians placed on the continuity of God's covenant activity through Jesus, biblical terms and images for the initial covenant people were understood to be types and images of the church. The examples that follow proved to be long-lasting resources for Christians as they contemplated the church in its diversity of gifts, levels of zeal, and unity with Christ: God's temple, the body of Christ, the Good Samaritan, Noah's ark, and the family of God.

Israel's relationship with God through his temple loomed large in the Letter to the Ephesians. Ezekiel 37:15–28 provides an interesting parallel with the imagery of Ephesians 2:11–22. To understand how early Christians thought, one must continually attend to echoes of Israel's Scriptures in the new Scriptures, written from a deep trust that the past actions and promises of Israel's God gave insight into his present work through Jesus. In Ezekiel 37 God instructed the prophet to demonstrate the hopes for reunification of the kingdoms of Israel and Judah by joining two sticks held in one hand. God forgives human rebellion and establishes a new covenant unity, a "covenant of peace." God promises to dwell among them in his sanctuary as one people (not two) after he removes their apostasies and cleanses their sins. In Ezekiel this anticipates the rebuilt temple, as seen by the prophet in its heavenly perfection (Ezek. 40–43); the promised temple is God's pledge for future unity. In Ephesians, Jesus is the one who makes peace in his own body between two peoples, Israel and the Gentiles, who now comprise God's dwelling place.[2] The people of God have become the temple of God. The Pauline adaptation of the eschatological "covenant of peace" emphasizes that Jesus' blood-flesh-body, which suffered death, is the visible guarantee of God's promise to humanity, much like the rainbow cemented God's covenant with creation after the flood in Genesis.

The suffering and dying Messiah refounds humanity. As the "cornerstone," he regathers the human family, thus building a community that can be called "a holy temple in the Lord; in whom you also are built together spiritually into a dwelling place for God" (Eph. 2:21–22). Recalling the accusation against Jesus about raising up a temple "not made with hands" (Mark 14:58), Ephesians also reaches back to imagery of the temple plan revealed to Moses in Exodus 25 for the tent-temple (tabernacle) and seen in a vision by Ezekiel (40–43). Israel's hope for regathering is fulfilled in all humanity among those gathered to God by Christ, who makes God present among them.

Early Christians reflected upon this phrase "not made with hands" to talk about how God was or would be fully present, without need of the geographically and ethnically limited temple and its traditions. Stephen, before being stoned, accused temple leaders of having chosen the temple made with hands over Jesus (Acts 7:44–53). Elaborating on the body as tabernacle or tent, Paul described Christian resurrection hope in these terms as well (2 Cor. 5:1). Just as the tabernacle had a limited purpose, the earthly "tent" of the body will die. God then will supply a "house not made by hands" for our eternal dwelling with him. Hebrews 9 takes the imagery to another level by depicting Jesus' suffering and death as qualifications for perfect priestly mediation on behalf of all people. Hebrews contrasts the finite tabernacle with the "greater and perfect tent (not made with hands, that is, not of this creation)" (9:11; see also 9:24), where Jesus offers the true, once-for-all sacrifice (9:26) that purifies humanity and ratifies the new covenant of the heart promised in Jeremiah 31:31–34 (Heb. 8:7–13).

Paul adapted body-politic language to unite the factious energies of the Corinthian Christians within the "body of Christ," the church (e.g., 1 Cor. 12:12–31). Believers are distinct body parts ("members") united in a variety of gifts and functions. They are mutually connected to each other and led by Christ, the "head," who unites them in the eucharistic meal of his own body and blood. Christians quickly embraced the image and applied it to a variety of uses. The second-century apologetic *Letter to Diognetus* translated the image to illustrate the role of the church in the world. Just as Paul understood Jesus to animate all the parts of his church body, the *Letter* (6) suggested that Christians were the unifying and life-giving soul of the world. By the fifth century, leaders across the Christian world appealed to the body of Christ in two ways: sacramentally and morally. Consuming the consecrated bread and wine as Christ's body and blood created a union with Christ, and consequently, a communion with one's table mates: near and far, past, present, and future. Without abandoning the community-creating action, Eastern Christians during the Christological controversies (see chap. 10 below) often focused on the divinizing effect of the Eucharist within believers. Conversely, without rejecting the divine gifts received by individual participants in the Eucharist, Western Christians preferred to highlight the church-making quality of receiving the body and blood of Christ. Western Christians typically had reservations about their Eastern siblings' "becoming-godlike" language.

The purity of Christ's eucharistically constituted body provided a platform for encouraging Christians to lead holy lives that would not sully Christ. In North Africa, Augustine of Hippo (354–430) railed against members who had no qualms about polluting Christ's body. He was frustrated at believers who attended immoral pagan entertainment, mixed blithely with pagans and prostitutes, participated in pagan rituals, or retained idols in their homes to avoid upsetting pagan friends and powerful patrons.[3] Such behavior dishonors Christ's body additionally because new, simple, or weak members, as well as non-Christians, see a deformed image of Christ through the behavior of lax members. Augustine, together with his contemporary pastors, targeted believers whose weekday lifestyle differed little from that of the pagans.

Other useful images developed around the healing and saving activities offered through the church. Jesus' parable of the Good Samaritan (Luke 10:25–37) recounts how a battered victim of robbery received lifesaving aid from an unlikely rescuer. Interpreters saw here the story of salvation in a nutshell (Irenaeus, Origen, John Chrysostom, and Augustine, to name a few).[4] Jesus, the despised Samaritan, rescued humanity by placing it on his pack animal. The beast of burden then shifts to refer to Christ's compassionate incarnation since he carried wounded human nature to a haven for healing: the inn (church). Under the direction of the innkeeper (teachers and clergy), the church shares in Christ's task of healing bodies and souls stricken by the fall. The church's role in the here and now is that of a hospital looking forward to being a community of the healthy, at which point it will no longer be a temporary inn, but an eternal home in the kingdom of heaven.

Another instance where early Christians discerned that church and Christ overlapped was in the account of Noah's ark, first linked to baptism in 1 Peter 3:20–21. Augustine noted that all interpretations he had encountered related the ark to the pilgrim church (or "city of God"). The church/ark weathers the storms of this world and saves the lives of those inside through the wooden vehicle of Christ's cross.[5] In Augustine's reckoning, the ark shares the proportions of the human body and thus represents Christ's body, even to the spear wound (the ark's door). From the wound come lifesaving sacraments that allow entrance into the ark/church. At the same time, Christian leaders admitted that not everyone who entered the single door is a "clean animal" who will remain in God's household.

Beginning with the earliest Christian household organization, Christians saw themselves as an extended family adopted, transformed, or grafted into God. Christ's nativity (Christmas) gave Leo I of Rome (mid-5th c.) the opportunity to reflect upon the noble nativity of the church family born through Christ:

> For the birth of Christ is the source of life for Christian folk, and the birthday of the Head is the birthday of the body. Although every individual that is called has his own order, and all the sons of the Church are separated from one another by intervals of time, yet as the entire body of the faithful being born in the font of baptism is crucified with Christ in His passion, raised again in His resurrection, and placed at the Father's right hand in His ascension, so with Him are they born in this nativity. For any believer in whatever part of the world that is

re-born in Christ, quits the old paths of his original nature and passes
into a new man by being re-born; and no longer is he reckoned of
his earthly father's stock but among the seed of the Saviour, Who
became the Son of man in order that we might have the power to be
the sons of God (John 1:12).[6]

Baptism created a precious mystery "that God should call man son, and man
should name God Father." The story of salvation and the liturgical entry into
the church were at heart a change from one family to another.

MEMBERS OF THE FAMILY

Complementing the big-picture reflections on the nature and purpose of the
church was the cultivation of family language at the level of local congregations. Like other families in the ancient world, while Christians cherished
affectionate relationships, members did not expect equality with each other.
Under the local father's (bishop's) ideally benevolent and wise direction of the
household, family members (the laity, or people) contributed to the household's well-being in their own spheres of activity. So it was that the horizontal
insistence upon all believers as children of God in baptism, and thus brothers
and sisters, existed in perpetual tension with the vertically arrayed realities of
church offices, moral and spiritual maturity, and worldly social distinctions.

The Parental Bishop

In his role as overseer (Greek *episkopos*; Latin *episcopus*) and chief priest in a
locale, the bishop bore primary parental responsibility. Just as a few families
are wealthy, many humble, some highly educated, some skilled, some not
so much—so also with local church families. Whatever population had been
granted official "city" status under Roman civil organization generally had
its own bishop, even if it was a small or isolated city. Consequently, although
many bishops were drawn from biological families who already held local
leadership roles, such bishops might be quite humble in means and education.
In a time before any seminaries, becoming a member of the clergy involved a
lot of on-the-job training built upon whatever education candidates brought
with them.

Scripturally and practically, being a bishop was a multiform task. The
Syriac *Didascalia Apostolorum*, a compilation of moral and ritual instructions
widely used from at least the fourth century, situated the enormity of the
episcopal office in the context of both Old and New Testaments. The bishop,
personally and through his staff, was expected to be a steward of God's pos-

---

KINDS OF BISHOPS

Church organization in the fourth and fifth centuries generally mirrored Roman civic jurisdictions. The most important bishops were those set over imperial capitals (Rome, Milan, Ravenna, Constantinople) or chief cities in the empire (Alexandria, Antioch, Carthage) or traditionally honored Christian sites (Caesarea in Palestine, Ephesus, Jerusalem). By the mid-fifth century, the bishops of Alexandria, Antioch, Constantinople, Jerusalem, and Rome were called *patriarchs*, whose authority extended over several provinces. These chief-fathers often received the title "papa" or pope. Within each patriarchate, *metropolitans* (overseers of a "mother" church) managed their own provinces from their seat ("see") in an imperial provincial capital. Ordinary bishops served in the lesser provincial cities. They in turn directed the ministry of *chorbishops* (rural bishops), who circulated among neighboring estates and villages as ministers and missionaries for the peasantry.

---

sessions on behalf of the needy, priest, and Levite to the Christian children of Israel; a shepherd pursuing the lost sheep; a father guiding and disciplining his children; and a physician to the ailing body and soul.[7] Should the bishop fail in compassion and mercy toward those who depended upon him, his own hope for mercy from God was at risk.

The *Didascalia* also relayed instructions to the lay members. They must honor the bishop, who is both father (in running the community) and mother (in presiding over their "birth" at baptism and providing nourishment in teaching and the Eucharist). Furthermore, the laity was encouraged to think about the clergy in terms of the inner "family" of God, which extended to the apostles: bishop as the Father; deacon as Christ; deaconess as the Spirit (the word *spirit* is feminine in Syriac); priests as apostles. The "family" altar consisted of the needy faithful who received the community's offerings and alms and in turn offered prayers on behalf of the community.[8]

A father-bishop could also be called to risk his life on behalf of individuals and entire cities. For instance, a mob in Antioch rashly knocked over the official imperial statues in anger over a tax raise in 387. Since this meant the same as an actual attempt to "overthrow" the emperor, the entire city feared Theodosius I's reprisal. Repeatedly calling the bishop "father," John Chrysostom (a priest at the time) characterized Flavian's intercession before Theodosius as the pinnacle of a father's care for his children. Pondering the bishop's empty throne behind him, Chrysostom reflected on their father's Christlike shepherding, being willing to "lay down his life for his sheep" (John 10:11).[9] Torn with anxiety over his children's fate back home, Flavian wept, prayed, and offered himself to Theodosius as a sacrifice for the children's indefensible crime.[10] He succeeded. With great rejoicing, Antioch welcomed home father Flavian in time for the Pasch (Easter), a doubly joyful celebration of new life arising from death.

Brothers and Sisters

With respect to bishops or priests, lay Christians were to be obedient and respectful sons and daughters, ready to be corrected and faithful in attendance at family gatherings. Yet, as in any closely bound group, familiarity can breed contempt. Father-bishops frequently addressed quarrels within local church families. Polarities tugged at idealized relationships: clergy versus laity, ascetics versus worldly Christians, upper-class versus lower-class Christians. Consequently, bishops had to inculcate the brother-and-sister bond among their children through exhorting mutual care. Cyril of Jerusalem (mid-4th c.) counseled his newly enrolled candidates for baptism on their new relationship with each other and the church:

> Now that you have been enrolled you have become sons and daughters of the same mother. When you enter the Church before the time of the exorcisms, you should only talk about things that are conducive to devotion. If one of you is missing, go to look for him. If you had been invited to a dinner party, wouldn't you wait for your fellow guest? If you had a brother, wouldn't you look for what was good for him?[11]

Here even before baptism, Cyril considered catechumens to be children of God through mother church, and already they were to act upon that relationship by caring for each other.

As baptized members, the responsibility was even greater, though not pursued zealously by all. Instead of praising the meager few who showed up for worship on a regular Sunday, John Chrysostom lambasted their indifference to the well-being of fellow Christians who did not come to the assembly, particularly those whom worshipers had left at home. Chrysostom held ordinary believers accountable for "giv(ing) a helping hand to the salvation of your brethren": husbands, wives, children, friends, sisters, brothers, slaves, and even enemies. He shuddered how on most Sundays "the greater part of the body of the Church is like a dead and motionless carcass." Real members of Christ's body, the church, should not come to worship without the best offering of all: brothers and sisters.[12]

On the other hand, some brothers and sisters meddled actively with their lackluster siblings to the point that bishops had to intervene. Tensions similar to those that gave rise to gnostic variations in the second and third centuries led to puritanical elitism, leaving ordinary, worldly Christians anxious about their salvation. This could happen within a bishop's own staff. Asterius of Amaseia (early 5th c., Asia Minor) publicly upbraided some self-proclaimed super-Christians during a regular liturgy (including some of his own priests sitting behind him). Calling them self-righteous Pharisees and comparing them to the intolerant older brother of the Prodigal Son, Asterius accused them of excommunicating believers who sought out the sacrament of repentance, "tak[ing] away the hope for God's benevolence and block up, as they believe, the bounteous fount of compassion, . . . bar[ring] the entrance of the kingdom to those who have wandered astray."[13] Bishops tried to redirect zealous Christians into becoming examples for and servants to less motivated brothers and sisters, but with uneven success.

The Dead

No account of early Christians' thoughts about being the church would be complete without discussing the membership of the dead. Normal non-Christians kept the stately, static ancestors safely outside city limits, where family members might annually enjoy a feast at their tombs. In marked contrast, Christians included the dead as active members. From a non-Christian perspective, Christians polluted the spaces meant for the living by housing the dead, both relics of the saints and ordinary burials, on church grounds and within city limits. Even more horrifying, they touched, kissed, and caressed the bones and dust around the tombs and shrines of the saints. It was enough to nauseate a sensible pagan. Christians responded that since the baptized dead are not truly dead, then there is no pollution associated with their remains; rather, there is holiness and hope in the coming resurrection

There were two kinds of Christian dead: those already resurrected, and those waiting or sleeping until the universal resurrection. The already-resurrected martyrs and saints could grant favors through Christ to brothers and sisters left behind, while the less holy dead in Christ could receive favors from God through the intercession of brothers and sisters still living (see chap. 4). None of the dead in Christ were completely severed from the earthly church, as was regularly made clear during the liturgy. It was at worship and other liturgical celebrations that the "assembly" of the church was mystically gathered as a whole. Within the anaphora prayer preceding the Eucharist, the bishop first commemorated and sought intercessions from the resurrected dead on behalf of the faithful. These petitions were followed by prayers of the faithful on behalf of the "waiting" dead in conjunction with Christ's sacrifice in the Eucharist. Knowing that this would a difficult concept for the newly baptized, Cyril of Jerusalem explained that just as political exiles can be reconciled to the emperor in response to petitions from the exile's friends, so do "we offer to [God] our supplications for those who have fallen asleep, though they be sinners, . . . but offer up Christ sacrificed for our sins, propitiating our merciful God both for them and for ourselves."[14] Augustine too felt the need to clarify the relationship of the sleeping dead to their brothers and sisters still enjoying bodily life.[15] Alms, works of mercy, and the compassionate prayer of the church could be offered for the dead whose lives fell between the obvious sanctity of saints, and the equally obvious wickedness of obstinately unrepentant yet baptized members. Augustine believed that the dead still belong to this time-bound dimension while waiting for resurrection and judgment (at the end of time). For this reason some dead might still experience their deserved punishments, but ultimately be spared eternal punishment through God's gracious acquittal in response to living Christians' prayers.

JOINING THE FAMILY

Catechesis

Rituals and content varied considerably across the empire, but by the fifth century several catechetical materials illuminate central features and meanings behind Christian initiation. Catechesis referred to learning by "listening" to formal teaching about the faith and worship, but included moral formation and ritual purification as well. The only exceptions to this process were those who could not listen with understanding (babies and young children) or the dying.

CATECHETICAL GUIDES

The *Catechetical and Mystagogical Lectures* by Cyril of Jerusalem are the earliest extant curriculum for baptismal candidates and the newly baptized (ca. 349). Gregory of Nyssa composed the *Great Catechism* (ca. 385) to instruct catechetical teachers (fellow bishops); it is a volume of systematic theology that would go right over the heads of normal catechumens, and perhaps even bishops. Imbued with Greek Christian teachings, Ambrose of Milan lectured the newly baptized *On the Mysteries* and *On the Sacraments* (ca. 380–390). In the fifth century Theodore of Mopsuestia, John Chrysostom, Augustine, and others composed catechetical texts to guide their congregations.

Although joining the church was now legal, most people did not immediately sign up for baptism. Numerous Christians were actually members of the catechumenate or "hearers," sometimes for decades. Once catechumens enrolled for baptism, they would be called Those-Being-Illumined or the Competent or the Elect. Those enrolled underwent intensive prebaptismal preparation during the penitential season of Forty Days or Fasting (ancient names for Lent) prior to Easter. Well after Theodosius I proclaimed Christianity to be the empire's sole official religion (380), bishops were still fretting about catechumens who preferred to delay baptism. Many catechumens believed that full membership would necessitate too many lifestyle changes in order to avoid serious sins and the long-term penitential disciplines that would follow. Around 406 Augustine had the unenviable job as a guest homilist to remind the congregation that a recently deceased catechumen could not be buried with the faithful. Death had surprised the man in his prime, and now he was forever dead.[16] Augustine spoke from his own tardy experience: he had been a catechumen for years, including a stint as a heretic among the Manicheans, before his baptism at age thirty-two. Merely signing up as a catechumen and attending worship did not save a person.

Those who did take the "plunge" often had mixed motives. The open-door policy of the church prompted catechetical teachers to resort to dire warnings about the consequences of seeking baptism for reasons other than seeking God. Cyril of Jerusalem challenged the Elect in their first class (the *Procatechesis*) to put aside any improper motives for seeking baptism: everything from juvenile curiosity about what goes on behind closed doors, to pressure from future in-laws, to calculated attempts to network with the burgeoning Christian elite.[17] Instead, they should be aware that receiving instruction and baptism under false pretenses will have two results: first, Christ will throw party-crashers out of his wedding banquet with no second chances to enter; second, baptism would not be effective since the Spirit will refuse to enter such people. Cyril warned that entering into divine things bestowed awesome responsibility to keep the secrets of the faith. Even general catechumens must not hear about the mysteries because they did not yet have the Spirit speaking within them, nor the protective blessings and exorcisms which the Elect enjoyed.

Baptismal candidates gradually switched allegiance from the power of Satan and the world to Jesus Christ in their ways of thinking and living.[18] Similar to many Christian traditions today, instructors led candidates through core beliefs (the ancient rule of faith) by means of a creed that the candidates would recite or acknowledge at baptism. Cyril wanted his candidates to know what Christians believed and why, so they could engage in the inevitable battles with outsiders: Christians offering variant teachings and non-Christian family and friends. Cyril urged catechumens to take off the dirty clothing of sin and commit themselves to "cleaning up their acts" during the forty days of final training and repentance before baptism. Still, his lectures are rooted less in moral instruction than in teachings about God through the creed (14 of the 18 lectures before baptism).

New Christians increasingly experienced catechesis geared toward making them intellectually informed citizens of God's kingdom, but not necessarily formed in the lifestyle of the kingdom.[19] The teachings of the church were emphasized both to facilitate catechizing greater numbers efficiently and to safeguard hotly disputed beliefs about Christ. Augustine worried that this kind of catechesis wrongly distanced "faith" (belief in doctrinal teaching) from "works" (Christian habits of heart and action) so that most neophytes had not been formed into a Christian character before baptism.[20] After the persecutions, new members did not find themselves forced to cut ties with their former life in the same way as Christians had before, even though bishops continually told them to do so. The old life tended to cling to new members through unchanged colleagues, occupation, and habits.

Baptism

Before surveying the more common experience of adult baptism, it is important to consider the less common practice of infant baptism (children up to age seven, too young to speak for themselves).[21] Baptism of infants appears in late second-century sources to be already an accepted, though exceptional, option within the church. Sometimes the baptism of infants took place because parents recognized how swiftly and unexpectedly death could strike down their children and wanted to guarantee the little ones membership in God's people. Only in later centuries did the practice prompt theological explanation. In the third century Origen tried to explain the practice by observing that simply being in a material body implied a stain of decay, a condition of falling from an original spiritual existence. He did not envision the stain as a guilty sentence for individually committed sins, nor for what human ancestors had done. Augustine took the novel route of attributing guilt for the first humans' disobedience to all successive humanity from the moment of conception. In contrast, most early Christians operated under an understanding that infants and children benefited greatly from the sanctification of the sacraments even if such young ones had no sins that needed cleansing. Teaching the faith was the family's responsibility as the baptized child grew. By the fourth century, the main rationale for delaying baptism, for children and adults alike, was the fear that they would commit serious sins and find themselves burdened with lengthy penance.

Despite widespread conversion in the fourth and fifth centuries, adult baptism remained an exciting and exalting experience, culminating a long process of detachment from Satan and attachment to Christ. Initiates, accompanied by their sponsors, went through intense preparation in the last week before Easter, which culminated in the Easter Vigil, lasting from Saturday night to Sunday morning. Daily exorcisms purified the candidates from any remaining evil spirits. Teachers laid hands on the candidates and quizzed witnesses about the candidates' moral conduct, which could result in withholding baptism until a later date. Candidates fasted and prayed and, in some communities, stopped bathing until The Bath of baptism. Committed to the whole person's salvation, clergy marked candidates' foreheads, ears, and nose with some combination of a breath and the sign of the cross, to seal their purity in preparation for receiving the Holy Spirit in baptism.

Cyril of Jerusalem, concerned to keep holy things from the unbaptized, did not go over the significance of the liturgical rituals until after the catechumens had been baptized and participated in their first Eucharist. The church at large agreed that only then were believers appropriately equipped with the Holy Spirit to understand what had just happened to them. Postbaptismal *mystagogy* "led" (*agōg-*) the new "initiates" (*mystai*) through a commentary of the actions and words comprising baptism and the Eucharist. For the sake of convenience, what follows focuses upon Cyril's reflections. Keep in mind that while most Christians of this period experienced a similar pattern of instruction, purification, renunciation, and threefold baptism (always "in the name of the Father and the Son and the Holy Spirit"), there were widely accepted variations in wording and order and meaning.

RENUNCIATION AND ALLEGIANCE

I renounce you Satan . . . and all your works . . . and all [your] pomp . . . and all your service. . . . I believe in the Father, and in the Son, and in the Holy Ghost, and in one Baptism of repentance.

CREED OF JERUSALEM (CA. 350)

We believe in one God, the Father, Almighty, Maker of heaven and earth, of all things visible and invisible;

And in one Lord Jesus Christ, the only begotten Son of God, begotten true God of the Father before all ages, through whom all things were made. Who rose on the third day, and ascended to heaven, and sat down at the right of the Father, and is to come in glory to judge living and dead, of whose reign there will be no end;

And in one Holy Spirit, the Paraclete who spoke in the prophets, and in one baptism of repentance unto the remission of sins, and in one holy catholic church, and in the resurrection of the flesh, and in life everlasting.

Before entering the baptistery (a special building or room just for baptisms), Cyril's candidates faced the symbolically dark west to renounce Satan and all associations with him, including unholy behavior: magic and horoscopes, popular entertainment like the theater, and gladiatorial and animal contests, which involved idolatry and immoral bloodshed. Turning to the symbolically light east, they committed themselves to the Father, Son, and Holy Spirit as understood from the previous weeks' instructions on a creed.[22] Upon entering the baptistery, candidates stripped (men and women were baptized in separate groups). Leaving the clothes of the old life behind corresponded to the verbal renunciation of Satan's kingdom as well as experiencing Christ's nakedness on the cross. Once candidates received their final exorcism, they one by one affirmed their new allegiance to the Christian God. The bishop immersed the candidates three times in the pool, reflecting Christ's three days in the tomb. Personal declarations to Christ and to the new community could be even more public than what Cyril depicted. While he assumed a semiprivate gathering of the candidates, sponsors, bishop, and assisting ministers, Augustine recounted how in late fourth-century Rome candidates (clothed!) had to confess their faith in the triune God while on a platform in front of the whole congregation (*Confessions* 8.5). Pandemonium could break out among the faithful when influential pagans confessed the faith, as Augustine recounted in the case of Marius Victorinus.

Arising from the water, the once-dead person entered the fellowship of Christ and the living. The formerly dirty person left the cleansing waters, where all evil powers were drowned in Christ's real sufferings, and joined the holy ones (saints) in new white robes. Anointing with holy oil (chrism) on the forehead, ears, nose, and chest after baptism completed the process, which made not simply new Christians, but also new "Christs," who were "anointed" body and soul with the Holy Spirit.

Early Christians saw entry into the faith to be composed of concrete actions that paralleled and completed the spiritual effects. This followed the same logic that considered Christians to be apostates when they engaged in non-Christian rituals even though most of the lapsed did not believe in the pagan rituals. What happened next for the newly baptized was a holy consumption of the body and blood of Christ in the Eucharist, which cemented their new identity. Until Christ's return, this sacred act of participation and union would continue to nourish the body of Christ whenever it assembled for worship.

CARRY-OUT MEAL?

Many Christians did not need convincing that God was in the bread and wine after their ritual transformation. They were regularly reminded that this is Christ, the Bread from heaven for eternal life (John 6:51), and they considered it to have divinizing, protective, and medicinal powers. From at least the third century, Christians shared portions of the consecrated bread with sister churches, as a sign of fellowship, with homebound members, or with the communing faithful, to sustain the family during the week. By the fourth century, church leaders frowned upon the privatization of the Eucharist. Leaders feared believers were trying to manipulate Christ magically and had lost sight of how the liturgy is directed toward communion. Setting up a home communion alone or with select friends broke communion with one's local church assembly and appeared to be setting up an alternative church.

ON EARTH AS IN HEAVEN:
THE MYSTERY OF WORSHIP

Liturgy was the general term for the regular worship service that included the Eucharist and was the climax of baptism. Liturgy literally means the people's labor or service, a communal activity of seeking, praising, and being in God's presence, which is also a duty. By the fifth century the liturgies used in centers like Alexandria, Antioch, Cappadocia, Constantinople, Jerusalem, and Rome became the foundation for the primary liturgies still in use today: St. Basil, St. John Chrysostom, St. James, and the Roman rite. In addition to the attention given to Scripture readings and interpretation (homilies), all the major liturgies are full of Scripture, by way of either direct quotation or allusions. Just as the word of Scripture carried the divine Word of God, early Christians believed that other earthly things could communicate really-real divine things. Ambrose of Milan instructed the newly baptized in the late fourth century, "You must not trust, then, wholly to your bodily eyes; that which is not seen is more really seen, for the object of sight is temporal, but that other [is] eternal, which is not apprehended by the eye, but is discerned by the mind and spirit."[23] Early Christians understood God to transform believers through many means: all aspects of worship and the material objects by which God comes. As they contemplated Christ's incarnation more carefully in this period, Christians fleshed out an approach to worship that appreciated how the human body might cooperate in knowing and growing in God.

Christians believed that the whole of creation had sacramental potential because it was created by and reflected God. Depending on one's spiritual insight, sacraments were everywhere. Two of the most powerful ritual encounters with God occurred in baptism and the Eucharist. Greek-speaking Christians appropriated the New Testament use of "mysteries" for God's plan of salvation in Jesus Christ, adapting a term for non-Christian initiations into privileged relationships with gods and goddesses. The West generally, but not exclusively, used the term "sacrament," which commonly referred to the Roman military oath of allegiance. Westerners tended to think of sacraments as means of humans dedicating themselves to God, who in turn accepted them and granted them the gifts appropriate to their new status among his people. Although characteristic, these approaches were not mutually exclusive, nor completely a matter of culture and geography. To understand the significance of baptism and the Eucharist for early Christians, one must recall that these rituals were utterly dependent upon the context of worship, which prepared for and presented fellowship with the divine.

Thinking about Ritual Encounters with God

Worship broke barriers and blurred boundaries, allowing communal contact between heaven and earth, spiritual and material dimensions, eternity and time-bound existence. Most liturgies from the fourth century, East and West, highlight that those about to commune in the Eucharist do so in the company of all the heavenly creatures, resurrected biblical heroes, and saints. At that point, the people join the heavenly chorus with the "Holy, Holy, Holy" canticle derived from the divine throne scenes in Isaiah 6 and Revelation 4. Worship followed the saving paradigm of the incarnation: the God who became human makes the invisible God visible and brings humanity into fellowship with the Divine. Because of this intimate link of God to humanity, the church could proclaim *lex orandi, lex credendi* (the law of worship is the law of belief): the way Christians worship shapes how and what they believe.[24]

As with Scripture itself, believers interpreted their worship experiences. Two themes predominated: memorials of God's saving activity and actual participation in divinity. Put another way, Christians could relive patterns of Christ's life, death, and resurrection as well as look ahead to the contours of resurrected life with and in God. These were not mutually exclusive perspectives. Some Christians associated with Antioch gave preference to remembering and reliving biblical events ritually so as to reinforce communal identity as Jews did with the Pasch/Passover. Cyril of Jerusalem's instructions on baptism depict the candidates following the pattern of the Red Sea crossing as well as Jesus' suffering, death, and resurrection. The latter was quite powerful since the candidates took part in instructions and worship at the traditional sites of Christ's passion and resurrection. Theodore of Mopsuestia (d. 428) described the Eucharist in terms of Christ's journey (procession of the bread and wine) to the cross (altar), where he died a sacrificial death.[25]

The mystical (God-encountering) approach emphasized how worship is a conduit for divinization (*theōsis*) and communion with the divine realities, which humans do not usually perceive. Pseudo-Dionysius the Areopagite extended this idea in his commentary on the liturgy and other basic rituals, *The Ecclesiastical Hierarchy*. Every participant, gesture, and movement led worshipers from the outlines of reality experienced by the body to the inner realities detected by spiritual senses. Taken as a whole and culminating with communion in the Eucharist, worship (*synaxis*, gathering) "draws our fragmented lives together into a one—like divinization. It forges a divine unity out of the divisions within us. It grants us communion and union with the One [God]."[26] God is One, but out of love he extends himself through multiple rich images of word and deed in order to create unity within individual believers and among the company of the church assembled in worship (*Ecclesiastical*

Hierarchy 3.3). For Pseudo-Dionysius the broken fragments of Christ's body consumed in the Eucharist completed in a very concrete way the liturgy's role in God's transforming outflow and return.

PSEUDO-DIONYSIUS THE AREOPAGITE

This unknown author borrowed a pen name from one of Paul's converts in Acts 17:34. Perhaps from Syria, he wrote toward the end of the fifth century. His writings suggest that he had intellectual ties to the philosophical schools in Athens, where Christians and non-Christians studied the highly religious possibilities in Plato's writings. He was fascinated with the way God allows earthly, material things to convey divine things, not merely as symbols (signs that point to something else), but also as entry points for meeting and communion. Later medieval theologians in the West were intrigued with the Dionysian writings, penning commentaries and incorporating his ideas into their own.

Fifth-century christological debates sharpened and divided the two views of worship and sacraments arising from Antioch and Alexandria (see chap. 10 below). Antiochenes, such as Theodore of Mopsuestia, cherished how sacraments conveyed spiritual gifts for a reform of life, for entry into and solidarity with the actual body of Christ, but not with the Logos. Theodore believed it to be impossible for a human, even Christ, to experience union with the pure divinity of the Son of God, the Logos.[27] Taking Theodore's assumptions too far could result in merely symbolic acts denuded of actual encounters with God (which was not his purpose). Conversely, too much emphasis on the divine and heavenly realities could sap and denigrate embodied worship and life here below (which was not Pseudo-Dionysius's purpose).

Incarnate Experiences of the Divine

Nobody disputed that humans rightfully use their bodies to relate to God in worship. They agreed that in worship and the sacraments humanity and divinity came into closest and most fruitful fellowship. In this light, let us take a pilgrimage through early Christians' sensual experience of worship: hearing, smelling, seeing, and tasting/touching.

Hearing words is the most obvious activity of the liturgy: chanting the liturgy, singing psalms, offering prayers, preaching the homily. In the late fourth century, a stalwart Western pilgrim to Jerusalem, Sister Egeria, remarked how long the dismissal was delayed for the Lord's Day (Sunday) liturgy because of the many homilies presented by a succession of priests, followed by the bishop. A five- to six-hour liturgy tested even her enthusiasm.[28] Yet words drew people, including many of the elite and educated, whether Christian or not. Contemptuous of Christianity itself, Augustine's initial attraction to Christian worship lay entirely in the fine rhetoric performed by Bishop Ambrose of Milan (*Confessions* 5.23–24). Christian homilies offered a daring and creative outlet for classical rhetoric. In late antiquity, rhetoric remained a vital skill for knitting together educated peers across the empire, managing social relations, and personalizing unwieldy government workings.[29] Yet in the church, speechmaking recovered its object to teach and move to action large communities composed of every conceivable level of education, status, and spiritual zeal. The homily was the instrument whereby most Christians learned to interpret and apply Scripture. It was not a particularly passive experience—much to the frustration of preachers! Worshipers interrupted with skeptical questions, cheers, or boos. Like Augustine, people could appreciate pleasing rhythms, plays on words, rhymes, surprising imagery, emotional descriptions, and other tools of rhetoric. Controversial moral critiques or theological positions could prompt unrest in the audience, with the potential to spill out into the streets.

Sung words had their own unique power to touch hearts. Unison chanting provided a bodily approach to internalizing Scripture, which could direct believers toward God while aurally uniting worshipers. The liturgy proceeded by means of chanted prayers, readings, and psalms. Augustine was amazed at the way music allowed truths about God to enter his inmost being: "How I wept during your hymns and songs! . . . The sounds flowed into my ears and the truth was distilled into my heart." As a pastor, Augustine had some reservations about the potential for beautiful music to distract worshipers from the words it carried, but he conceded "that through the delights of the ear the weaker mind may rise up towards the devotion of worship."[30] The danger of distracting melodies was related to an even greater danger associated with instrumental music. In the culture of this period, instrumental music created a confusing environment, which called to mind wild wedding parties, immoral public entertainment, and pagan ceremonies. For this reason most early Christians excluded instrumental music from worship and celebrated the divine instrument of the human voice. This practice continues among most Eastern Orthodox traditions to this day.

Ready to use her ears at a Sunday morning prayer in Jerusalem, Sister Egeria experienced an additional sensory surprise. Right before the bishop read the Gospel, she gasped as incense surrounded the worshipers, imbuing them and the whole church with its fragrance (*Diary* 49–50). By the fifth century, incense in the liturgy was not unusual, and believers inhaled its rich symbolism. Pseudo-Dionysius commented on the role of censing, which the bishop performed just before dismissing those unqualified for the Eucharist (catechumens and penitents).[31] The bishop's circuit from the altar and around the church encompassed believers regardless of the different levels of initiation or recovery from sin, making them one holy fragrance. Similarly, holy chrism (*myron*, ointment) used in a variety of rituals, took advantage of the strong, pleasing odor to attract the faithful by making them aware of the proximity of holiness. This scent of heaven clung to worshipers as they dispersed back into the world, bringing a whiff of the kingdom to those with functioning noses.

The eyes certainly had more to feast upon with imperial toleration and favor. Large churches opened new sight lines for art and more complex liturgical parades. Basilicas were popular in communities that could afford them. The interior presented a long hallway (nave), divided into smaller hallways by the lines of supporting pillars. The eyes of the faithful moved naturally toward the apse (a semicircular area at the end of the nave), where the assembled clergy sat on either side of the bishop's throne (*cathedra*), behind the altar table, where the Eucharist would be consecrated. The space, adapted from Roman lawcourts, easily led the imagination to a gathering of God's heavenly court. Homilists often referred their audience to the significance of seeing the bread and wine arrive, rest on the altar, and become Christ's body and blood. After the fifth century the altar space and eucharistic blessings became increasingly separated from the people by curtains or screens, to intensify the awareness of and respect for God's presence.

Art for walls, ceilings, floors, and eventually altar screens was borrowed and heavily adapted from imperial styles of representation. Christ appeared as emperor (Pantocrator [Greek *pantokratōr*, "universal ruler"]) and saints as his royal court, echoing images from Revelation. From the fourth century, Christian communities chose to adorn their worship spaces in ways that reminded gathered worshipers of the communion they have with Christ and the saints. Portrait images gazed directly at worshipers to emphasize their actual presence among fellow believers still on earth.[32] Depictions of Bible stories and of martyrs continued the older didactic style of Christian art. Martyrs' shrines sometimes had a sequence of episodes in fresco or mosaic recounting the hero's (or heroine's) story. However, observers sought more from these pictures than a mere story: Christians participated in a "visceral seeing," which drew viewers into the story, made static representations take on an animated life, and then entered into the viewer.[33] All those hours during the liturgy could be spent wandering the church, meditating and communing with the holy figures in perpetual attendance in the church.

The Eucharist was the centerpiece for tasting and touching. With great awe, Cyril of Jerusalem invited new initiates to "taste and see that the Lord is good" (Ps. 34:8) in the Eucharist. Here in their hands and on their tongue and lips was the savor of Christ himself. Drawing attention to the corporeal experience of the sacrament, Cyril declared, "When we taste, we are bidden to taste, not bread and wine, but the sign of the Body and Blood of Christ."[34] The tongue is trained and guided by faith; the hands enthrone the bread-body so no crumb falls carelessly to the floor. Carefully the believers touched the body to their eyes before eating it. After receiving the blood, the faithful are to treasure the remaining moisture on the lips by dabbing it on other sense centers to sanctify them.

CONCLUSIONS

The mystical unity of heaven and earth celebrated in the regular liturgy of the church did not guarantee church attendance or Christlike lives. Curiously, the more Christians explored the wonder of God's presence in worship, the more awe and dread apparently drove many Christians away from frequenting the altar for the Eucharist. Their participation revolved around the words, actions, and images associated with the liturgy, which all their senses, except taste, enjoyed. When it came to thinking and living in accord with the mighty, transformative gifts of God, mere humans were cautious. Put less charitably, some were not interested in God interfering with their comfortable lives. All sorts of people with all sorts of reasons sought entry into the family without fear from earthly powers. Once again the orthodox insistence upon openness rather than strict purity of the "family" demanded enormous practical and intellectual effort to give a meaningful account of Christian life. What difference did being a Christian make outside of the liturgy, once one dried off from baptism or digested Christ's body and blood? If the church is composed of believers at different levels of commitment and understanding, how can the church best minister to all? The next chapter looks at the challenges to transformation of self, which contact with God was supposed to engender.

QUESTIONS FOR DISCUSSION

1. What difference does it make to think of church as a people or as a place?
2. How do various images of the church explore its purpose and relations among its membership?
3. How did early Christians develop newcomers and integrate them into the people of God?
4. How did early Christians experience and explore the way church connects the local and earthly to the universal and eternal?

SUGGESTED FURTHER READING

Hellerman, Joseph H. *The Ancient Church as Family: Early Christian Communities and Surrogate Kinship*. Minneapolis: Fortress Press, 2001.

Mazza, Enrico. *Mystagogy: A Theology of Liturgy in the Patristic Age*. Translated by Matthew J. O'Connell. New York: Pueblo Publishing Co., 1989.

Wainwright, Geoffrey, and Karen Beth Westerfield Tucker, eds. *Oxford History of Christian Worship*. New York: Oxford University Press, 2006.

8

Cultivating Life in Christ

INTRODUCTION

The complex interaction with the sights, fragrances, textures, sounds, and tastes of worship offered a sensuous banquet of paradise insofar as believers were prepared to receive it. Preparation to live in the Lord daily was an equally complex operation, which sought to coordinate heavenly and earthly dimensions within the human person. Shifting perspective from the *ekklēsia* to individual believers, this chapter will examine Christian formation. There were stumbles; there were breathtaking performances of love. Each believer struggled to make sense of failures and successes, of desires and actions, and to bring these into closer step with Christ. What blocks or distorts members' heartfelt longing for God? What remedies, if any, are at hand when a member sins and damages relationships with fellow believers and God? How do members discover and take advantage of the ways God offers to sculpt them into greater likeness to him? How do they learn to discern good from evil, the path toward God from the path away from him?

These questions led to reflections on pastoral care and training (*ascesis*). Individual believers bore the responsibility (with help from spiritually mature brothers and sisters) to dedicate themselves to turning, or conversion, of the whole person ever more toward God. Early Christians built upon the ascesis already proved to sustain believers through day-to-day challenges as well as the extraordinary tests during persecution. With the rise of professional ascesis in monasticism, systematic approaches to prayer identified spiritual roadblocks and offered methods for dismantling them in order to proceed on one's journey in God. This chapter comes full circle to the *ekklēsia* once more by considering how such formation could take place only in the company of fellow believers. When zealous individuals congregated with like-minded believers, new patterns for thinking and living in Christian community developed.

ASCESIS: TRAINING AND RETRAINING IN THE CHRISTIAN LIFE

Definitions and Goals

Ascesis may call up images of gaunt figures, bizarre self-torture, and wild settings. It may prompt disgust at artificial or even inhuman renunciation of relationships and pleasures. The term *ascesis* may evoke disdain at the seemingly self-centered obsession with one's own salvation, which apparently prefers a holier-than-thou love of God to a humble love of neighbor. Or ascesis may be so unfamiliar as to conjure none of these responses. On the fringes, some of those stereotypes held true, from the truly crazed (who became object lessons about the need for moderation and the moderating company of others) to those deemed exceptional vehicles for God's teaching, healing, and intercession. There were the stylites, who spent years living on pillars, preaching and praying. There were desert monks said to live only on the weekly Eucharist. But these extremes were not the mainstream experience of ascesis among early Christians.

Simply put, ascesis meant training or practice applied toward some goal, be it the Olympics or philosophy or the Christian life. A review of the New Testament easily demonstrates that early Christians were ascetics from the start. Existing philosophies certainly informed the way ascetic thought and practice developed among early Christians. The Platonic return of the soul to God escaping from material shadows (or fleshly prison) to spiritual reality, beloved by the gnostics, remained a powerful, if carefully tailored, image for orthodox Christian life. Stoic analysis of the internal impulses, which deceive and distract individuals from their appointed places in nature (or reason, logos), proved to be a useful resource as well. Among the basic ascetic practices, Christians took into account parallels in non-Christian medical and religious recommendations. Eating too much clouds the mind and makes the body sluggish. Too much sex robs the body of vital energy. Serving the gods often requires refraining from sexual activity. Simplicity in life and the avoidance of luxury contribute to one's ability to handle crises calmly and to perceive one's duty to God and fellow human beings.

Early Christians assumed that life in Christ required effort. After baptism, Christian life involved both God and man, both grace and works. From Origen to Gregory of Nyssa and even Augustine, pastors connected the Israelites' Red Sea crossing and journey across the wilderness to the promised land with Christian baptism. Baptism (crossing the Red Sea) is a saving gift; however, God did not snap his fingers and materialize the people immediately in the promised land. The faithful faced challenges and recovered from mistakes throughout their journey. Christian life is a cooperative effort to know and choose God in daily life with God's help. Whenever reading pre-Reformation writings that connect human activity with salvation (e.g., almsgiving), it is well to recall that such texts assume a baptized audience, where Christ was already in some way regenerating fallen human beings. Without God's initial gifts and transforming grace, humans could do nothing to return to God. Christians, then, bore a sacred responsibility to guard, cultivate, and share the gifts through love of God and love of neighbor.

When Christians professed full-time commitment to the faith as "philosophy" (love of wisdom), they did so while being certain that their ascetic orientation was directed toward Wisdom, who was Christ himself, not a faceless and distant God. Christ alone, who was born, died, and rose again, imparted the "happy life," an object all Greco-Roman philosophies pursued, but imperfectly, according to the Christians. In Christ, philosophy no longer belonged to the elite with the education and leisure to pursue it, but even to the "unlettered" (i.e., those without an elite education). Christians took the culturally mediated assumptions of the philosophical life and read them through the lens of Scripture and Christ in order to fine-tune both the practices and their meanings. Christ's passion and death highlighted the countercultural ideals of humility, obedience, patience, and openness to self-emptying suffering. Christ's own incarnation and bodily resurrection further distinguished Christian ascesis. Instead of escaping the body, the body played a positive role for progress into the likeness of Christ. Worship, sacraments, reading and reciting and praying with Scripture—all became intertwined with loving service toward others in a truly human life. Humans are psychosomatic creatures, whose whole being is involved in knowing God.[1]

Ascetics hoped for a life where distractions of body and soul would dissipate to the point that they might participate, even if fleetingly, in the glory of God (2 Cor. 3:18) and see God (as the pure of heart; Matt. 5:8). Maturity manifested itself in a profound sensitivity to both good and evil and the call to teach what one had learned. Ascetics assumed that God's plan for humanity in Christ aimed for a restored, transformed, even divinized human nature. Beginning with God's gifts in the incarnation and baptism, humanity could finally cooperate with God to achieve trusting fellowship among humans and communion with God. Thus ascetic life practiced and prepared for the resurrection.

Sex, Chastity, and Love

For many early Christians, preparing for the resurrection involved a self-conscious withdrawal from the customs of the preresurrection world as taught in Scripture. Among the oddities that some early Christians practiced, not for a little while but for life, was the "life of angels," as suggested by Jesus' description: "For in the resurrection they neither marry nor are given in marriage, but are like angels in heaven" (Matt. 22:30). The renunciation of marriage (and sexual activity) likewise drew on the apostle Paul's recommendation that Christians focus on readiness for Christ's return by not seeking marriage (1 Cor. 7:25–35). Celibates, in Paul's assessment, avoid worry and anxieties that detract from "devotion to the Lord" (7:35). Although some voices repeated a kind of body-hatred spiel, orthodox proponents of virginity and celibacy in the fourth and fifth centuries interpreted the biblical standards and honored tradition with more finesse. Virginity (condition of never having married nor had sexual intercourse) and celibacy (vowed renunciation of marriage and sexual intercourse) attracted Christians of both genders and were honored categories of laity within the church. From the early Christian perspective, however, focusing on sex misses the point. Stepping away from established social roles and their accompanying distractions, Christians cultivated unselfish love in part through publicly vowed ("professed") asceticism.

One argument for virginity was waged through negative depictions of the horrors of marriage replete with graphic lists of worries to which Paul had merely alluded. In his treatise *On Virginity*, a young Gregory of Nyssa outlined the pressures that bedevil even the best of married couples as they maintain and increase family honor and wealth (3). The gnawing fear of death reveals how the beloved's face and voice will one day be gone. Trying to cheat death and keep the family line going, the couple bears children, which in turn often results in death for the baby and mother. If children should survive, parents can never truly be at ease. Each stage in their child's life will have its own tribulations. There is also the abuse and heartbreak of truly troubled marriages.

On the positive side, virginity for Gregory and others meant escaping a treadmill of trouble and embracing, at the cost of customary ambitions, the vision of God: "The real Virginity, the real zeal for chastity, ends in no other goal than this, namely the power thereby of seeing God."[2] Fallen humans wrestle endlessly with desires, which wander from our innate but damaged desire for God. Gregory observed that the distractions arising from marriage are many, but they are not primarily due to physical pleasure.[3] Marriage tends to direct one's energies to transitory things that are destined to fall short of their promises for stability, companionship, and happiness. Marriage also represents bondage to the demands of fallen society as well as the chaotic impulses of the fallen self, both of which mask real human flourishing. Through Christ's incarnation and resurrection, body-soul humans are freed from self-created delusions and distractions, freed to discover their true selves again as beings created in the image of God. Virginity as a central component of ascetic life aims at participating in a stage-by-stage reversal of the consequences suffered by the first humans in the fall, starting with marriage, and returning to tranquil contemplation, fellowship, and service of God.[4]

Extreme proponents of virginity eloquently wove a tapestry of the joys and privileges of virgins. Jerome of Stridon (ca. 347–419) presented virgins as eligible for the highest prize or crown of heaven, echoing athletic and martyr imagery (*Letter 22 to Eustochium*). Woe to those who passed up the opportunity to be a virgin by marrying or who failed in their vows! To Christians who, like earlier pagans, complained that if all adopted virginity, then humanity would disappear, Jerome retorted that the whiners would also blame virginity for the disappearance of prostitutes, adulterers, and curiously, "wailing infants in town or country." Taken out of context, as Jerome often is, this is callous: who could lump sex abusers with babies? Jerome did, yet he was looking toward a future promised to all Christians, but practiced by a few now:

> What others will hereafter be in heaven, that virgins begin to be on earth. If likeness to the angels is promised us (and there is no difference of sex among the angels), we shall either be of no sex as are the angels, or at all events which is clearly proved, though we rise from the dead in our own sex, we shall not perform the functions of sex.[5]

As nasty as his sarcasm can be, Jerome was not a baby hater, but rather was preoccupied by a longing to allow Christ's transformation of the body in the resurrection to begin even in this life. Early Christian commentators assumed that the time for populating the earth (and of scripturally sanctioned polygamy) was past. Instead, Christians needed to busy themselves making children of God out of the existing population. Jerome's impatience (and contempt) arose from his difficulty in fathoming why any Christian would turn down an opportunity to start the resurrected life in the here and now. His eagerness to defend his cause provoked others to moderate Jerome's claim that marriage was only good for producing future virgins (see Augustine, *On the Good of Marriage*, pp. 188–89).[6]

John Cassian explored the significance of chastity in developing the capacity to love others. For early Christians, chastity was the virtue of purity in relationships, based on the discipline of self-control. It could be practiced by the married as well as the celibate. Cassian was talking about ascetic chastity and assumed that monks had given up marriage and sexual activity.[7] Though people today might think of chastity as an artificial and dangerous repression, many monastic teachers saw it as God's work to transform the ascetic discipline of self-control into a graced condition of freedom from self. Unfettered from the idolatry of self and selfish desires, chastity allows humans to resume the "natural" (prefall nature) human sociability that focuses upon God, other humans, and their well-being. Rather than promoting antisocial behavior, chastity in concert with other ascetic disciplines promotes self-giving love.[8] Cassian's *Conferences* (12), for all its blunt discussion of sexual fantasies and genital sensations, operates on the premise that chastity is intertwined with divine and selfless love. Divinely granted chastity opens the possibility for the monk to "receive others as Christ and to meet them on the ground of their needs rather than the monk's own."[9]

Ordinary Ascesis

Ordinary Christians engaged in ascesis under three conditions: preparation for baptism (see chap. 7 above), observation of penitential seasons, and the retraining of penitents. In preparing his catechumens for life as a Christian, John Chrysostom compared prebaptismal instruction to wrestling practice. Soon-to-be Christians would learn to recognize the "moves" of future demonic opponents and practice both offensive and defensive maneuvers of body and soul "in order that, when the contest comes on, we may not feel strange, nor become confused, as seeing new forms of wrestling; but having already practiced them amongst ourselves, and having learnt all his methods, may engage in these forms of wrestling against him [Satan] with courage."[10] Baptism was a beginning not merely in life as a child of God, but also as an athlete in daily competition against manifold opponents, within and without, who threatened to lure the believer away from God.

Despite bishops' best efforts at rousing homilies, insightful catechetics, and leaders' own attempts at modeling Christian life, many believers managed to limp along more or less complacently in their Christian walk. The dual trends of encouraging baptism widely and of stressing the Eucharist as a highly charged encounter with God resulted in declining eucharistic participation even as the population became more "Christian." Many of the baptized were reluctant to prepare themselves for approaching Christ at the altar. Also, there were many more enjoyable things to do than spend several hours at the liturgy every Sunday. Preachers across the empire lamented and lambasted those who liked to sleep in on Sunday morning or go to public entertainments. Some minimalists would sneak out of the liturgy when the penitents and catechumens were dismissed.

One tool that seemed amenable to both frustrated pastors and commitment-challenged laity was the rhythm of the church year, with its focus upon Easter/the Pasch. The nightlong Easter vigil was the primary festival for baptisms. Full-fledged Christians had long shared in the disciplines of fasting and prayer, accompanying baptismal candidates in the period preceding their initiation. But the disciplines that had been a sign of solidarity with the candidates in the *Didache* of the early second century increasingly served as a concentrated, penitential conditioning for baptized laity to prepare for receiving the Eucharist at the Pasch. Customs for the Forty Days, or Fast season (Lent), varied but included food restrictions, such as limiting what one could eat (only vegetables, grains, water). For the rank-and-file *humiliores*, this was hardly a big shift, given that their diet rarely exceeded the fasting menu in the first place. Aristocratic Christians, on the other hand, were offended by these limitations.

Pastors repeatedly taught that the care of souls—or better, for the whole person—took advantage of physical disciplines as tools. Ascesis was not supposed to be an end in itself, nor was it cover for gnostic scorn of material bodies. God created the psychosomatic human being to work best when the soul is willingly aligned with God and so directs the body in ways that accord with divine goodness. Preachers readily echoed and drew inspiration from classic prophetic themes in the Old Testament to emphasize that worship and ritual life are worthless when believers try to use rituals to distract God from noticing obstinate sinful behavior. John Chrysostom taught that keeping the fast only in terms of food worsened the believer's spiritual health "when we abstain from food but do not abstain from sins; when we do not eat meat but devour the homes of the poor; when we do not get drunk from wine but become intoxicated by wicked desire; when we continue without food for the entire day but pass all of it [the day] at wanton spectacles."[11] Physical disciplines began the task of realigning the soul's guidance of the body so that the two would no longer fight with each other, but join in close ranks to combat evil and do good.

Seasonal ascetic disciplines involved an important communal element in restoring relationships and serving one another. Leo I of Rome (mid-5th c.) pointed out that any progress believers made in Lenten disciplines disintegrated completely if they tried to partake of the paschal Lord's Supper while refusing forgiveness to another believer. Reaching out to needy brothers and sisters and making peace with enemies were crucial counterparts to personal disciplines (*Sermon 49* [*On Lent*] 11.5–6). Fasting in physical and moral terms offered ample opportunities to redirect the food, money, and time usually consumed away from the self and toward others. Thus Lenten homilies reaching back to the second and third centuries repeatedly urged the natural pairing of almsgiving with fasting in contributing to the church's health and believers' purification from sins. For sin disrupts and damages not merely the individual sinner, but also relationships among believers.

LIGHT (*LEVIS*) AND HEAVY (*GRAVIS*) SIN

Early Christians agreed that any sin of itself makes a human unworthy of God. However, sin in the baptized not only offends God; it also harms the believer. Thus early Christians distinguished between sins as one might assess wounds or illnesses: is it life-threatening or not? Heavy sins threatened irreparable damage, a mortal wound, to baptismal grace and represented a rupture with fellow believers if left untended. Lighter sins revealed feebleness in the faith analogous to a sprained ankle or a cold: not life-threatening, but worthy of attention in order to speed recovery and prevent complications. Within the Roman Catholic Church, these categories are known as venial and mortal sins.

Sacrament of Repentance

Baptism, though more widespread than in prior centuries, remained a difficult commitment well into the fifth century. At baptism Christians rejected the "devil," which meant all idolatry and immoral influences, including attending the theater, horse races, and other games. The ideal baptized Christian was supposed to turn instead to pastimes that sought God and loved neighbors. Ascetic renunciation envisioned a positive embrace of the alternatives to evil. However, when baptized believers committed serious (*gravis*, or heavy) sins, the church defended, against some who claimed otherwise, sinners' access to reformative grace through confession and repentance.[12] Serious sins involved variations on idolatry, murder, and adultery. By the fourth and fifth centuries, penitents usually approached voluntarily and not nearly so often as bishops desired. On the one hand, forced confession rarely resulted in true repentance; on the other, there were too many serious sinners for a bishop or priest to track them all down.

As early as the *Shepherd of Hermas* (early 2nd c.), Christians worried about whether the Lord would forgive serious sins committed after baptism. By the end of the second century, the hope for a second "washing" resided in a formal process of public repentance, since there could be only one baptism. Over the course of debates about whether the church should be a community of the perfect and devoid of the lapsed, most of the Great Church sided cautiously with God's mercy and preferred a view of church as a mixed society, dedicated to the healing and education of its varied members. Yet even at the beginning of the fifth century, John Chrysostom felt the need to assure the baptized that they still had access to forgiveness even if they fell into heavy sins.[13]

Chrysostom had in mind not only those who felt overwhelmed by their sins, but also believers who outright refused to recognize as sins what the Christian tradition considered sinful. To many, multiple marriages meant opportunities to improve one's status, dignity, and wealth, not polygamy and adultery. Some believers chafed at equating astrology or protective charms (often with Christ's name inscribed) or love potions with idolatry. Seriously injuring or killing a slave had its economic costs for non-Christians; for a Christian, such violence incurred a hefty spiritual cost too. Family planning in Greco-Roman society generally countenanced abortions; Christian tradition unequivocally named these as murder or attempted murder, with specific penitential consequences.

Confession and repentance were viewed in terms of healing, purification, and restoration to full participation in the church. For ordinary (light) sins, Augustine assumed that face-to-face reconciliation with victims, almsgiving, fasting, and prayer would allow the Spirit to repair the sinner (*Enchiridion* 70–76). Heavy sins required drastic measures of quarantine (forbidding communion at the Eucharist and with the worshiping congregation) and therapy (penance) in order to restore the sinner to fellowship with the church and with God. As noted above with Leo I and John Chrysostom, early Christians saw firsthand the extensive brokenness that issued from heavy and light sins among fellow believers. The demonic wrestling opponents that Chrysostom highlighted to his catechumens generally attacked the mouth: hurtful speech that killed or maimed people and their relationships.

PENITENTIAL PROCESS

One influential format for dealing with heavy sins comes from Basil of Caesarea in Cappadocia. Those who confessed to heavy sins would undergo a four-stage program lasting generally from five to twenty years, or one's deathbed, whichever came first. Penitents began as "weepers" outside the church each Sunday and at major festivals, seeking intercession from the faithful who were entering the church. Then they would serve a period as "hearers" at the back of the church before reaching the status of "kneelers," who focused on prayer during the liturgy. From there they would "stand" and worship with the faithful, barred only from communion in the Eucharist until fully restored. Offenders from the presbyterate (deacons, priests, and bishops) were generally deposed permanently to the laity.

Penitents underwent a public and progressive reentry to the church and its worship until the period was completed and the penitent could be readmitted into full communion with the church in the Eucharist.[14] The process lay almost entirely in the hands of the bishop, who was repeatedly counseled in church documents to handle cases mercifully and tenderly. Bishops had wide latitude in assessing acts and intentionality, and applying an appropriate mode of reorientation for individuals who confessed their sin. Despite the growing body of official instructions on penitential procedures in this period, Augustine voiced a common sentiment: that "[bishops] are not to take account so much of the measure of time as the measure of sorrow" when assigning and monitoring the penitential regimen for a contrite sinner.[15] Similarly, bishops were counseled to restore penitents whenever they discerned that a reorientation had occurred rather than to insist slavishly upon completion of a fixed period.

PRAYER AND PERFECTION

Even if a believer had not committed some form of murder, adultery, or idolatry, early Christians recognized that, in a sense, all humanity is in recovery mode. Believers experience and succumb to the lure of sin until the resurrection. Professional ascetics developed sophisticated systems for assessing Christian health and for prescribing regimens that addressed specific conditions. Yet because God had created humanity in his own image and subsequently became human in Christ, Christians aimed for more than avoidance of temptation and sin. They respected humanity's innate desire to seek God and believed that God also desired to draw men and women to himself. As Gregory of Nyssa observed: "The perfection of human nature consists perhaps in its very growth in goodness" so as "to be known by God and to become his friend."[16]

Diagnosis of Distractions

Given the intensive experience of professional ascetics, or even a new believer's toddling first steps in contemplating God during a long worship service, early Christians noticed that paying attention is hard. The Eastern liturgies of St. John Chrysostom and St. Basil (originating in the fourth and fifth centuries) are equipped with eight cues for the priest or deacon to cry out "Attend!" or "Let us pay attention!" Wandering attention also leads to seemingly accidental sins. From little children to mature adults, humans often find themselves wondering why in the world they just did some stupid or hurtful thing. Instead of mumbling "I don't know" and throwing up their hands, ascetics dug deep to figure out the inner roots of sinful acts and the graceful resources for combating them.

Although differing in intensity, pastoral care and monastic ascesis shared a model for spiritual health care: evaluating symptoms and diagnosing causes, rooting out illness and cultivating health. Paying attention grows from restructuring one's environment. It is a sort of spring cleaning and decluttering of physical, emotional, and spiritual distractions. Addressing both those who sought to live their baptismal vows in intentional communities and those in ordinary life, Basil of Caesarea recommended an extended retreat. There among like-minded believers, participants might benefit from the temporary removal of business pressures, non-Christian associates, and the hubbub of the marketplace in order to focus upon rooting out old habits and instilling new ones.[17] With the help of spiritual advisers, believers could be trained to "see" what ailed them, what patterns of distractions interfered with their orientation toward God.

Evagrius of Pontus (ca. 345–399) gave shape to a system of diagnosis and therapy for distractions that underlies both Eastern and Western Christian traditions. The primary diagnostic tool consisted of eight evil thoughts or passions that twist and distort humanity's created capacity to desire and love God. Adapted by Western Christians, the thoughts show up as the seven deadly sins. The evil thoughts are not sins at all, but rather attitudes that create a friendly environment for breeding sins. They are interchangeably attributed to the inattentive self and to demons. Left undiagnosed, and therefore unchecked, the demons or thoughts could break a believer's commitment to God and a godly way of life.

Evagrius listed thoughts whose distractions arise first from natural functions or needs of the body that spin out of control: *gluttony, avarice, fornication.* These produce anxieties over having enough food, clothing, or shelter to preserve life, fussiness over the little that one has, and regret or fantasies about what one has given up. Other thoughts can descend in a dangerous cascade out of those anxieties or regrets. Thus, *sadness, anger,* and *restlessness/acedia* can result in desperate or self-righteous excuses to quit the battle. Finally, the dangerous thoughts of *pride* and *vainglory* sneak up on the careless who begin to take satisfaction in their progress, compared to others, and then imagine what they, rather than God, have accomplished.[18]

Scripture and Prayer

Creating an awareness of one's struggles and symptoms was the foundation for tailoring a recovery plan. Regular praying with Scripture supplied both diagnoses and a whole pharmacy of remedies that aimed at awareness of and communion with God. Contemplation of Christ through Scripture imparted dynamically the "mind of Christ," as exhorted by Paul and generations of early Christians. The third-century *Apostolic Tradition* (42.18) recommended seven prayer breaks over the course of each day as well as a daily gathering of believers. These time-outs would keep Christ present to believers and help them resist temptations. Christians monks used these regular hours in tandem with repetitive labor conducive to prayer in order to fulfill another of Paul's counsels: "Pray without ceasing" (1 Thess. 5:17).

> *Scriptural Interpretation* remained embedded within a life of scripturally rooted prayer. The fruits of contemplation would be tested against the accepted tradition of the church with a spiritual adviser and with fellow believers through conversations. Thus, multiple interpretations of passages were honored since the Spirit might reveal something particular to the experience and needs of a believer or group. This method, used by Christians influenced by Alexandrian traditions derived from Origen, adapted philosophical methods for contemplating authoritative texts to the practice of Christian prayer (see chap. 5 above). In the fifth century, methods borrowed from grammatical and rhetorical studies, often associated with Antioch, became a source of conflict in the christological debates (see chap. 10 below).

First- to third-century documents recommended regular meditation on the passion and resurrection of Christ and the Lord's Prayer. By the fourth and fifth centuries, the book of Psalms became the primary vehicle. In his *Letter to Marcellinus* (mid-4th c.), Athanasius of Alexandria offered a detailed guide to praying psalms, derived from Egyptian monastic thought and practices. Athanasius explained that the Spirit composed the psalms through the original authors, but graciously inspires an additional "writing" within believers as they pray the psalms. The psalms allow the pray-ers to step into the questions, accusations, anxieties, joys, self-revelations, praises, and encounters with God that the psalmist has experienced and make them their own. Through the Spirit (and usually with a spiritual adviser) the psalms become a mirror so that "he who wants to do so can learn the emotions and dispositions of the souls, finding in them [the psalms] also the therapy and correction suited for each emotion."[19] The one immersed in this prayer becomes like a harp tuned and plucked by the Spirit through the psalms. Athanasius listed psalms according to particular days of the week, temptations, and physical/emotional/spiritual conditions as a resource to individual believers and their spiritual advisers. The musical component of chanting psalms further enriched prayer because it united and directed the whole person—body and soul—toward God. Communal psalmody, which most Christians practiced, united individual believers into a concrete expression of church that is a foretaste of eternal worship.

The Vision of God

What was needed to keep the Christian not necessarily free of temptation, but less liable to surrendering, was to acquire virtues that opposed specific evil thoughts. Although contemplative prayer belonged theoretically to all Christians, it was analyzed and practiced most assiduously among monks and nuns. However, these ascetic methods and ideals were quickly integrated into pastoral care because pastors were increasingly drawn from ascetic ranks from the fourth century onward.

Contemplative prayer consisted of listening to God after stilling, or at least ignoring, the chattering of evil thoughts and the tumult of sensations as far as possible. Disciplines geared toward developing stillness were called *praxis* and created openness for *theoria*, or contemplation, of God. The two were inextricable components of Christian life because, as John Cassian (early 5th c.) recounted, the soul keeps spinning like a mill wheel (*Conferences* 1.18). In prayer and in life the believer must exercise discipline to choose what thoughts to grind or foster as well as the actions that proceed from the thoughts. Will believers fall prey to obsessions fed by evil thoughts? Will they instead be directed toward virtues that allow God to transform believers into greater likeness to himself? Praxis trains humans to function (in body and soul) more and more according to their original purpose: to know and relate to God. Praxis must not cease; it continues in order to keep the believer receptive to God.

At prayer, the ascetic's movement from rooting out distractions to a state of attentive focus could, by divine gift, escape the limits of verbal, visual, or conceptual images. Ascetics called such explicit communion with God "pure prayer" or "prayer of the heart." Christian mystical traditions explored and tested what it might mean to "see" God when human senses surely fail to register divine data. Two scriptural images predominated to make similar points about how finite humanity might experience something of the infinite God: God's presence with Moses in the darkness atop Mount Sinai, and the brilliance of Christ's transfiguration into his divine glory. Anchoring these mountaintop encounters is the fact, emphasized by most authors, that graced visionaries must come down from the mountain to teach and serve others, even as Moses and Christ did.

Gregory of Nyssa, in his allegorical treatment of *The Life of Moses*, chose the image of darkness to describe intense and experiential knowledge of God that exceeds our sensory capacities. On Mount Sinai, Moses "drew near to the thick darkness where God was" (Exod. 20:21). The believer engaged in praxis may receive a divinely graced boost to the soul so that it might "see" God in this supersensory darkness. Beyond the limits of our physical and mental sensors is the more real reality of God. Gregory's approach to divine revelation is known as negative, or apophatic, theology. It is negative because one first asserts positive statements about God, then strips these away in recognition of the concepts' innate limitations when applied to God. For instance, God is love, but the reality of divine love exceeds and bursts what humans mean by *love*. Therefore one can conclude "God is not love" (as humans conceive love) because experience of God makes clear how inadequate is the human term *love*. Similarly this is apophatic (unspeakable) because no words or images suffice to convey the experience, nor may it be appropriate to divulge the experience to those at earlier stages in their journey.

Although Gregory traced Moses' ascent to God from visible light (the burning bush) to supersensible darkness on Mount Sinai, others focused on encountering Christ in the light of the transfiguration, which is his resurrected glory. In his *Conferences*, John Cassian built on Evagrius's love of fiery light for describing the communion of believer and God in pure prayer. Leaving behind distractions, the believer climbs the mountain of the transfiguration with Jesus and beholds "the glory of his face and the image of his brightness." Because it permeates the whole person, body and soul, Christ's glory becomes the conduit for communion and conversation beyond words between God and the believer. "The mind is aware of [pure wordless prayer] when it is illuminated by an infusion of heavenly light." While the light uncovers and communicates the believer's hidden longings, it also enables the believer to enjoy an intimacy with God that afterward is too concentrated to express in words. Christ's purifying and divinizing light suffuses the believer and transforms the person's whole life (speech, interactions, thoughts) into prayer. The light does not disappear after the gifted moment, but accompanies, strengthens, and shapes the believer in the daily task of turning from distractions "to spiritual things, until one's whole way of life and all the yearnings of one's heart become a single and continuous prayer."[20]

Although monks treasured visions of God that came to them individually, their preparations for and their living out of the impact of pure prayer owed much to their relationships with others. Progress in praxis and *theoria* could not happen without the aid of teachers and companions dedicated toward the same end. We need to dispel images of monks and nuns as absolutely cut off from other humans or the world beyond their communities. Early Christians organized themselves in many ways to foster the inner life, but the structures and rationales they adopted recognized the human need for others.

COMMUNAL ASCESIS

Apart but Not Alone

Monastic vocabulary as it was developing in the fourth and fifth centuries suggests a variety of lifestyles marked by intentional separation from ordinary life. At the same time these terms (in both masculine and feminine forms) assumed a corresponding attachment to God aided by the fellowship and instruction of like-minded ascetics.

MONASTIC VOCABULARY IN THE FOURTH AND FIFTH CENTURIES

anchorite (*anachōrētēs*): one committed to *anachrōrēsis* ("withdrawal") and thus moving outside ordinary civilized space both physical and social (term first applied to draft dodgers and tax evaders in hiding). An anchorite lived in a detached dwelling called a cell.

cenobite: monk living in a *coenobium* rather than a separate dwelling.

elder (*presbyteros/a*) or old man/woman (*geron/geronta*): a recognized wise leader and spiritual guide for less experienced ascetics in the communities.

Father/Mother (*abba* [or *apa*]/*amma*): formal address for elders.

hermit: wilderness or desert (*eremos*) dweller; often equivalent to anchorite.

monastery (*coenobium* or *koinonia*): both the building complex and the community of monks.

monk (*monachos/a*): one who lives alone.

renouncer/renunciant (*apotaktikos/a*): one who renounced living an ordinary life or specific aspects (e.g. social relations, property, foods).

virgin (*parthenos*): sometimes used exclusively for nuns, but applicable to virgin monks as well.

The classic anchoritic settlements in lower Egypt attracted hundreds of monks, where they were certainly not "alone." Most monks were involved spiritually and economically with local villages or cities and churches. In Egypt before the Aswan Dam, the boundary between civilization and wilderness was marked by the Nile's floodplain, which could be a matter of yards, not miles.[21] At times monks played significant roles as spiritual advisers, hospital staff, missionaries, and bodyguards for bishops. Being "alone" or "withdrawing" referred less to an antisocial outlook or geographic distance, than to a distance of the heart from cultural norms, which often distorted the pursuit of human flourishing. Submitting to a monastic lifestyle continually reminded monks of the disjunction between God's desires for humanity and society's complacency.

Bishops and monastic elders were particularly concerned about the temptation for vowed ascetics to try this endeavor without companions or guides. The ideal of the lone hero in the wilderness battling with demons made for rampant best sellers among early Christians, such as Athanasius's *Life of Antony* (of Egypt) in both Greek and Latin, and Jerome's Latin accounts of Paul the Hermit and Hilarion. On the ground, the isolation proved risky and flew in the face of the social aspect of being church. Only in extraordinary circumstances would elders allow a monk to take on a solitary lifestyle, and usually only after candidates had thoroughly proved themselves stable in praxis and *theoria* over the years or decades. Cautionary tales abounded about hermits whose premature solitude ended in self-deception and madness. John Cassian recounted the view of an anchorite, John, who left a twenty-year stint of solitary life in favor of communal asceticism because the monastery provided fewer distractions and greater peace (*Conference* 19).

The greatest hermits garnered their reputation of holiness precisely from the witnesses who benefited from the saints' wisdom and prayers. Antony of Egypt (ca. 251–356) is supposedly an exemplar for solitary desert ascesis, but at the same time his story (*Life of Antony* ca. 356–358) and letters reveal his influence and interaction with believers and unbelievers, ordinary believers and apprentice monks. Time and again Antony withdrew from civilization to confront demons in their wilderness home. Each stage of conflict brought God's greater presence and wisdom to Antony as well as people hopeful for his intercession, healing, and teaching. Not even a twenty-year seclusion in an abandoned fort deep in the Egyptian desert prevented the arrival of visitors and disciples, with whom he would at times converse. When Antony finally emerged, he embarked upon a public career as a teacher of divine mysteries, a peacemaker, an encourager of persecuted Christians, and a defender of orthodoxy.

In the big picture, not even anchorites or hermits were entirely isolated, but they had renounced, withdrawn from, and revised customary social and economic relationships and values.[22] Furthermore, all monks assumed the necessity of some sort of community where they could learn, teach, and serve one another.

Benefits and Challenges of Community

The majority of ascetics gravitated toward group settings to pursue their longing for God. There were several reasons related to both faith and practicalities. Over his lifetime, Basil of Caesarea (in Cappadocia) produced some of the earliest rationales for ascetic life in community in his *Askētikon*. In the face of sensationalized heroics of desert hermits, Basil cautiously defined "renunciation" and "withdrawal" in terms that emphasized the interior battle for tranquility. From his own experience, the actual framework for accomplishing the ultimate Christian goal to love God and neighbor (*Longer Rules* 1–2) required companions, not solitude (*Longer Rules* 5–8). Humans are social by nature and their life should be characterized by fellowship (*Longer Rules* 3). Obviously, with others not around, loving neighbors becomes a vacuous mental occupation rather than the fulfillment of God's command. Brothers and sisters need teachers by word and example. They need help to identify and correct weaknesses that the individual might happily ignore. Vital biblical virtues such as humility, patience, generosity, and so on have no room to grow without the presence of others, who inevitably tempt a believer to react in pride, impatience, anger, and greed. The different gifts (charisms) are granted by the Spirit to individuals edify the community, but isolated from others and their gifts, the gift is useless, like a buried treasure. Alternatively, brothers and sisters bring various gifts and insights for the benefit of all through the Holy Spirit in their midst.

> For if something is obscure, it is more easily uncovered by the labour of several looking into the matter together, since, according to the promise of our Lord Jesus Christ, God bestows on us the finding of what we seek (Matt. 7:7) through the teaching and reminding of the Holy Spirit (John 14:26).[23]

Basil's vision is that of the church: only through communal sharing and interdependence among variously gifted (and variously needy) believers may the fullness of the body of Christ be realized.

CONCLUSIONS: FROM INDIVIDUAL BACK TO COMMUNITY

Ascesis within monasticism was a natural intensification of Christian life in the company of zealous and wise brothers and sisters. Nameless generations of holy men and women had come and gone over the earlier centuries: some wanderers, some functioning through their families or in official capacities in the church, some resident advisers and protectors. They formed the ranks from whom martyrs were drawn. In the fourth and fifth centuries, both Christian and non-Christian sources attest to monasticism's greater visibility, range of activities, and compelling attraction to even the highest ranks of the Roman aristocracy.

An important counterweight to the stereotype of monks longing for spectacular encounters with God lay in the insistence in ascetic literature upon the basic orientation of all Christians toward both God and neighbor. All Christians needed vigilance to notice the more humble and easily missed opportunities that offered themselves whenever believers encountered fellow humans. Contemplative ascetics understood that Christian life expresses love of God through love of neighbor, as troublesome as neighbors often can be. Basil of Caesarea declared, "Whoever loves his neighbour makes good his love for God, who receives the favour as done to himself."[24] For all the attention dedicated to pure prayer, at least as much was dedicated to the imperative for hospitality. From the most reclusive hermit to an ascetic dwelling on a busy city street to an ordinary Christian, no discipline ever took precedence over serving those in need, materially or spiritually. So while light and darkness continued to be rich images for pondering how humanity and God might interact, everyday life brought concrete opportunities to "see" Christ in those who hungered, thirsted, were naked, sick, or imprisoned (Matt. 25:34–40). This leads to considering how early Christians thought about and created social patterns through which they might be conformed to Christ and by which they might serve Christ through others. Let us see how the inner life of early Christians made a mark on the world around them.

QUESTIONS FOR DISCUSSION

1. How were Christian formation and training both individual and communal activities?
2. Why did early Christians involve the body so heavily in the "spiritual" life?
3. What ambiguities accompanied ascetic assessments of marriage and virginity?
4. How did Christians conceive of the connections among prayer, the moral life, and knowledge/experience of God?

SUGGESTED FURTHER READING

Brown, Peter R. L. *The Body and Society: Men, Women, and Sexual Renunciation in Early Christianity*. New York: Columbia University Press, 1988.

Elm, Susanna. *Virgins of God: The Making of Asceticism in Late Antiquity*. Oxford: Clarendon Press, 1994.

Harmless, William. *Desert Christians: An Introduction to the Literature of Early Monasticism*. New York: Oxford University Press, 2004.

Wimbush, Vincent L., and Richard Valantasis, eds. *Asceticism*. New York: Oxford University Press, 1995.

9

Cultivating Humanity

INTRODUCTION

The world of early Christians was urban and multicultural. They were facing issues familiar to people today: the instability of families, the cutthroat drive for fame and fortune, the homeless and refugees, disease, and poverty. When early Christians walked the streets of their cities and towns, what did they see, and how did they see it? From a Christian perspective, what did they consider to be wrong with their society? How did they see Christ-shaped alternatives to human disparities? How did they filter "normal" Greco-Roman ways of assessing humans and human good through Christ?

At no time did pastors or monks fall under the delusion that their ideals about the inner life and human potential in Christ would create God's kingdom on earth, but they were impelled to try. Worship, ascesis, and contemplation offered tools for believers to open themselves to graced awareness of God's transformative presence. Day-to-day living, for monks and ordinary Christians, consisted of baby steps forward, stagnant drudgery, and some spectacular slipups. Nevertheless, imperfect Christians, inspired by the glimpses of God and a transformed humanity, explored how to express their inner identity in the world around them. Christians after the persecution found themselves with more opportunities for shaping ways of thinking and being human in accord with their faith. Starting with relationships in the home and proceeding to social and economic relations, this chapter will consider how early Christians connected their views of humanity to their world.

THE HOME FRONT

The home was the locus of creating and forming citizens as much for Christians as for non-Christians. The relation of husband to wife and parents to children said a lot about the priorities and worldview that members carried from the home to society. Here preachers hoped that believers would practice embodying Christian ideas about being human in relation to existing social structures. At the same time that ascetic lifestyles were taking the Christian world by storm, celibate bishops defended the good of marriage and drew a moving image of the family as church.

Christian Marriage

Christian ideals for marriage mirrored Jewish and pagan ideals, such as having children for the good of the community and lifelong companionship. However, remarriage, especially after divorce, bothered Christians more than non-Christians because Jesus taught that it constituted adultery (Mark 10:2–12; Matt. 19:3–9, Luke 16:18). Additionally, having multiple marriages, even if the spouse had died, was deemed serial polygamy. The church had its own disciplinary penalties for all kinds of adultery, and although stiff, they maintained the church's dogged hope for forgiveness and conversion of sinners. Disregard of marriage on two fronts generated homilies and treatises defending marriage: worldly realists for whom marriage was a tool for personal advancement, and zealous proponents of virginity.

Most fourth- and fifth-century pastors underscored Christ's own defense of marriage (Matt. 19:3–9) as based on God's plan for humanity to exist in a single, lifelong, male-female companionship, geared toward raising families. This idealistic picture of marriage did not necessarily reflect reality. Pastors regularly decried when Christian marriages bowed to cultural pressures for worldly success. John Chrysostom begged families, "You must consider that marriage is not a business venture but a fellowship for life," in the model of Christ's mystical union with the church (Eph. 5:32–33).[1] Similarly Asterius, bishop of the provincial capital of Amaseia in northern Asia Minor, looked upon his congregation's marital patterns with alarm. He angrily upbraided parishioners "who outfit yourself in wives as blithely as a change of clothes, . . . marrying abundant resources and trafficking in women."[2] Even in smaller administrative centers like Amaseia, upward mobility in status and wealth depended upon strategic marriages. Asterius advised Christians to think of divorce as a breach of contract, not with a spouse or spouse's family, but with God. Pastors passionately, but rather fruitlessly, counseled Christian men to resist relying upon Roman law as a cover for their lack of self-control and fidelity.[3] Asterius argued that what should bind a man and wife together in God is a treasure worth more than the next promotion.

ROMAN LAW AND DIVORCE

Roman law allowed divorce by mutual consent without any penalties. But if only one spouse took the initiative, there were penalties for divorcing without a legal cause (e.g., criminal activity, adultery). To limit divorce, Christian emperors introduced penalties, which could be exile, limits on remarriage, or the loss of the betrothal gifts and dowry (for the wealthy, this was usually valuable real estate). Until Theodosius II (ruled 408–50), Roman law treated adultery (sex with another man's wife) and other sex outside of marriage as a fact of life for husbands, but a heinous crime for wives, in order to preserve legitimate progeny. The Theodosian Code (438) made the grounds for divorce virtually the same. But the civil law never quite coincided with the stricter interpretations of marriage under which the church operated.

Marriage for Asterius contained the potential for recovering a sense of God's ideal for communion in the face of a sin-shattered world. Marriage is "a single union of body and soul so that disposition mingles with disposition, and flesh is in some way bound together with flesh."[4] An affectionate marital relationship is so important to Asterius that he used the term *diathesis* to indicate an unusual intensity of love and attachment shared by soul mates.[5] John Cassian used *diathesis* to describe a rare friendship that rises above even the generous love (*agapē*) owed to all: "*Diathesis*, or affection, is shown to very few, to those who are linked by a similarity of behavior and by the fellowship of virtue."[6] *Diathesis* characterized Jesus' attachment to the beloved disciple in the Gospel of John. On occasion ardent seekers of God share in a mutually self-giving love oriented toward each other's progress in divine perfection, and this, for Asterius, was the precious potential of Christian marriage.

FRIENDSHIP AND THE AGE OF MARRIAGE

Age discrepancy was a practical hurdle to friendship for many first marriages. Friendship required a match of equals in interest, maturity, education, capability, and so forth. Among the *honestiores* (nobility) and those *humiliores* (lower-class folks) who often imitated them, the law allowed girls to be married as early as age twelve, but more often they waited till the midteens to late teens. Men tended to contract marriages once they were established in a career, around twenty-five to thirty. Though groomed for the job better than today's teenagers, a young wife usually had a lot of maturing to do before a husband would begin considering her to be a meaningful conversation partner and friend. Indeed, non-Christian moralists like Plutarch believed that a good husband bore the responsibility of teaching his wife so that she could grow into a fulfilling marital companion.

For Augustine, humans naturally recognized the social goods of marriage: children and companionship. Christians alone enjoyed marriage as a holy thing (*sacramentum*) or divine mystery, which God established between the man and woman in marriage (*On the Good of Marriage* 32). Augustine carefully moderated between the assertions of the popular monk Jovinian (380s) who saw no difference in status between celibacy and marriage and Jerome's venomous tirade against marriage (393).

Augustine argued that marriage was certainly a good and created aspect of original humanity. It could raise husband and wife above bodily desires and childbearing. Marriage supplied a lifelong context for growth in love regardless of the conditions of parenthood, old age, or childlessness. Sexual activity in marriage is possible but not necessary (*The Good of Marriage* 3). Augustine admitted that sexual intercourse between a husband and wife for pleasure rather than to produce children is a venial or light sin—better than adultery, but not as good as procreative sex or continence (6). Still, beyond procreation, Christian marriage for Augustine was a symbol of the unity and harmony toward which God leads the church (18–21).

That being said, controversies (from 411 and onward) over the human capacity to do good drew Augustine's attention almost exclusively to the negative role of sexual desire and activity in marriage. In trying to figure out just what the sin of Adam and Eve was, and how it damaged and spread to all humanity, Augustine concluded that sexual desire and its consummation was the point of contact for humanity's inheritance of the first humans' sin. Adam and Eve's abuse of their powerful will to choose and do what is good degenerated into an existence buffeted by desires (concupiscence) that spun out of control. The devastated will in fallen humanity especially demonstrated its frailty in the craziness of sexual desire and intercourse. Because marriage allowed sexual activity, it put married couples at risk every time they submitted to the explosive effects of the postfall sexual drive. Thus, according to Augustine, married believers fell short of the ideal of celibate and virgin ascetics, who could strive for similar goods as in marriage, fellowship, and a sacramental status, but without the distractions of sexual activity—theoretically.

Nonetheless, Augustine created a middle ground between the absolute exaltation of sexual continence (Jerome), and those vowing continence being valued equally alongside sexually active married believers (Jovinian).[7] In a dig at those who thought only continent ascetics were real Christians, Augustine reminded believers that sexual continence was not the only or even the highest virtue in the Christian life. Surely obedience to God and readiness for martyrdom resided within married Christians as well as ascetics. Ultimately, Augustine's insight into the universal power of sin made the superiority of celibate ascetics merely a theory, thus dismantling any practical differences between the potential for holiness in the two statuses. For Augustine, the social nature of humanity meant that whether married or celibate, a truly godlike human being flourishes only in fellowship with others on the same journey.[8]

The fourth and fifth centuries witnessed a serious effort to situate sexual activity in marriage in relation to original human existence before the fall. Some argued that if humanity is supposed to enjoy the life of angels in the resurrection (with no marriage; Mark 12:25), then God must have created Adam and Eve to enjoy communion and live as virgins (Jerome's ardent position). Genesis does not speak of Adam and Eve having sex until after the fall; Eve's "desire" for her husband is part of the curses (Gen. 3:16), and intercourse occurs as soon as they leave Eden (4:1). Therefore, having sex and creating children were symptoms of the fall or a sort of consolation prize.[9]

The other position, that of Augustine and others, tried to explain how sex, which even within marriage is so closely identified with sin, was part of God's good initial creation. God planned on human couples having sex, as was clear by his command: "Be fruitful and multiply, and fill the earth" (Gen. 1:28). However, something about the fall—there were lots of theories about this—severely damaged the potential to experience the emotions and sensations associated with all sexual activity, even in marriage. Consequently, fallen humans, baptized Christians too, were playing with fire whenever sex was involved, but marriage could direct desire into venues for truly human sanctity within the fellowship of husband, wife, and when possible, children. Thus even with the theoretical elevation of ascetic continence, practically speaking, virtue and godlike lives could occur in either type of life.

Formation in Christian Families

Flipping the earliest model of church as family, Christian leaders examined how the family itself was a little church, with the same potential for formation in holiness as austere monks. Monks told cautionary tales of venerable elders whose holiness was put to shame by families plying asceticism in normal village settings, where distractions were greater than in monasteries or the wilderness.[10] For example, the Egyptian Abba Paphnutius taught some visiting priests to observe how "in every station of human life there are souls pleasing to God, doing deeds in secret with which God is delighted," for God, as it were, sees the "inner monk" even among the married or simple farmers.[11]

When encouraging ascetically minded believers to take their faith-life to the next level by adopting virginity, John Chrysostom suggested that marriage and family were in a sense obsolete. However, as a pastor caring for his diverse flock, Chrysostom emphatically advocated the "little church" of the family in *Homily 20 on Ephesians* (Eph. 5:22–33).[12] Because of the additional

social pressures associated with life among less committed Christians, Chrysostom remarked that, done well, the Christian family "will surpass all others
in virtue."[13] He specifically challenged the assumed superiority of ascetics by
stating that married couples and parents whose goal is to "be perfectly one
both with Christ and each other" will "rival the holiest of monks."[14] He saw
rich opportunities within the family to do away with the concept of "mine,"
echoing the moralist Plutarch (ca. 45–120), but grounding his image in Paul's
counsel that the body of each spouse is under the other's authority (1 Cor.
7:4).[15] Family members can learn how to detach themselves from striving for
money and honor by attaching themselves in everyday life to God by the practice of virtue, especially hospitality, even as Abraham and Sarah had done.

Preaching on Colossians 4:18, Chrysostom maintained that families derive
their holiness from the mystery of marital love divinely created to be "an image
. . . of God himself."[16] The man and woman united in marriage make a complete human existence. By their physical intercourse, the resulting "child is a
bridge connecting mother to father, so the three become one flesh."[17] Even
barren but sexually active husbands and wives enjoy this completeness because
of the act of intercourse, which is an important expression of their overall
communion with each other. All this frank sex talk made his audience squirm,
but Chrysostom chided them for being ashamed of the good of marriage while
treating the financial and bawdy approaches to sex without embarrassment.

Within the little church of the home, Chrysostom advised father and
mother to preside over the faith and character formation of their flock. Like the
church, families should pray, read Scripture, fast, and serve the needy together.
Individuals who have had little choice in belonging to a particular family unit
must learn through practice to love and serve one another in Christ, just as
the church at large must do. Child-rearing was a divine art for Chrysostom as
well as a political one. In his tract on Christian parenting, *Address on Vainglory*,
child-rearing becomes an opportunity and sacred duty to "fashion . . . these
wondrous statues for God."[18] Likewise as good governors, parents must guard
and strengthen their children's sensory "gates" (ears, eyes, etc.) from input that
could warp and harm their development. In this way sons and daughters will
learn the art of good self-governance that contributes to both heavenly and
earthly citizenship.

Christian parenting included retelling Bible stories in age-appropriate
ways and pausing occasionally to ask the children questions about characters'
actions and motivations or to let children tell the stories in their own words.
Chrysostom counseled parents to teach by their own example in helping
young children sing psalms and Christian hymns. This formation was common to girls and boys. As the children matured, parents were responsible for
cultivating behavior and appearance in line with the situations specific to their

gender. For instance, adolescent boys, who more often encountered lewd culture, required better supervision and role models in order to avoid popular entertainment, parties, and the peer pressure to sow wild oats. Girls' formation continued directly under their mothers at home. It focused upon wise use of household resources and renouncing economically and morally destructive self-decoration (makeup, clothing, perfume, hairdos, and jewelry).

Chrysostom pleaded with parents to choose spouses on the basis of Christian virtues, not bank accounts or blue-blooded pedigrees (*How to Choose a Wife*). Young men needed to understand the importance of a future wife's internal beauty, which would last far longer than the external. Pastors across the empire hoped that parents would start inviting clergy to be present at the wedding ceremony and that wedding festivities would avoid drunken excesses and raunchy entertainment. Traditional weddings were so pagan, in all the moral and religious senses, that church law prohibited clergy from watching wedding entertainment and the laity from dancing (Synod of Laodicea, ca. 390, canons 53–54). Except for the occasional wedding for pastors' children, Christian marriages were not routinely held in churches until the medieval and Byzantine periods. When children entered the family, Chrysostom argued that Christians should start naming their children after biblical heroes and saints rather than pagan deities, heroes, and relatives.[19]

In practice, Christian leaders had an uphill battle in giving marriage, family, and child-rearing practical Christian significance. Christian parents of the upper class faced particularly difficult questions in how to handle their sons' formal education, which was geared toward public careers. For the most part, pastors did not ask parents to bypass ordinary education, but they made recommendations about how the education should be supplemented through the church and at home. Reorienting the purpose of education was a top priority, as was redefining success with a view toward the kingdom of God rather than Rome's kingdom, Christian though it might claim to be. Above all, education must serve character development and growth in virtue, not the pursuit of human glory in one's career. In his *Confessions*, Augustine blamed the link between education and ambition for his own years of self-deception about the value of stylish language. Succumbing to the system, he valued elegance despite his discomfort with the way it so often twisted the truth and perpetuated falsehood. The brilliant young Augustine scorned the simplicity and downright barbarity of Scripture, though it contained divine truth. Yet for the purpose of future family honor and wealth, his parents dedicated all their resources, plus some, to gain Augustine the best education money could buy.

Much later in life, Augustine taught that a Christian should focus upon how formal education provides resources for knowing God through reading, understanding, and teaching Scripture (*On Christian Teaching* 2). Basil of

Caesarea (in Cappadocia), boasting an even better education than Augustine, urged Christian students to soak up the lessons about virtue and truth found in the classics of pagan literature—as long as such study is done in conversation with a Christian adviser, such as himself (*Address to Young Men on the Right Use of Greek Literature*). Education should be a tool in preparing the Christian to live, and not merely know, Truth. Basil thought that in conversation with other educated Christians, discerning students should pursue truth in non-Christian learning like bees gathering the finest nectar from the best flowers (*Address* 4).

How successful were these bids to shift family priorities? We do not know much about the family life of most of the population, who did not write about themselves as did the elite. The evidence points to the lower classes imitating the upper classes in making advantageous matches in trades and marriages wherever possible and according to their means. Yet the recommended bookish devotional activities need not have required literacy since memorizing Scripture, especially the psalms, was within the capability of all who attended worship regularly. Nevertheless, Chrysostom faced objections that too much Bible reading with the children would make them monks and useless to the family's future.[20] Being a Christian family still required more reshaping than most Christians were willing to undertake. Those that did often ended up raising sons and daughters who opted for service in the church as clergy and ascetics.

CLASS AND GENDER

Early Christians adapted existing family structures in two ways, creating continent "families" of ascetics and redirecting ordinary marriage and parenting toward the service of society through the Christian worldview. What else in the broader society was capable of being transformed into the likeness of true human existence? Today, modern Westerners may shudder at the limitations to freedom, the denigration of human dignity, and the evident hypocrisy of the church, which accommodated rather than revolted against ancient norms, particularly regarding slaves and women. However, looking through the eyes of the late ancient world, the situation was more complex.

Christian leaders of the fourth and fifth centuries were concerned to promote a Christian view of all humans as human. In contrast to prevailing theories in science and philosophy (as well as the day-to-day experience of most people), Christians resisted seeing gradations of subhumanity that allowed only free, elite males to be fully human. Aristotle's position derived from harsh realities: the only people with the leisure and resources to exercise the highest human faculties (intellect and authority) were elite males. Christians took a long view of humanity anchored in divine creation, the troubled realities of the fall, and final perfection in the resurrection. Between the fall and the incarnation, between baptismal rebirth and resurrection, Christians struggled with how to embody Paul's troubling exclamation regarding membership in God's family: "There is no longer Jew or Greek, there is no longer slave or free, there is no longer male and female; for all of you are one in Christ Jesus" (Gal. 3:28).

Ordinary Constraints

In the late ancient Mediterranean world, everyone in society was constrained to particular roles over which individuals had little choice. It was almost always tougher to be in a lower class than a higher one. Elite women had more power and freedom in many areas than did women and men in the lower classes. Those with the greatest apparent power and freedom, elite males, found themselves bound, for the good of family and city, to responsibilities many wished they could shed. Imperial legislation in the third century made the local elite class, the decurions who served on the city council, hereditary in order to combat alarming desertions. Without a sizable decurion class, towns were prey to deterioration, and the imperial governors were less able to collect taxes. After Constantine's generous tax breaks for clergy, many elite protected their resources by becoming Christian clergy or monks. Frustrated family members also saw their clan's fortune disappear into the churches, charitable foundations, and monasteries when devout widows of the elite refused to remarry and became vowed nuns. Nevertheless, legal restrictions, peer pressure, and the weight of prior generations' expectations contributed to a feeling among many *honestiores* (the "more honorable" class) that they too were trapped.

Slavery, mostly domestic, could provide stability, education, professional skills, food, clothing, and shelter that many peasants, day and seasonal laborers, and refugees envied. Industrial slavery like mining was handled by convicts. On large estates slaves often worked beside free peasants. Certainly slavery had its brutal side, and slaves were pieces of property; even ecclesiastical legislation had to address the penitential procedures for Christians who harmed or killed their slaves. Yet being a slave had a temporary quality. Emancipation in the Roman world was a regular opportunity for slaves. A slave could buy his freedom. A master could free a slave woman in order to marry her. Owners could emancipate slaves in their will or release those whom they could no longer afford to support. Some owners anticipated profitable relations with well-trained and entrepreneurial former slaves. From the perspective of the *honestiores*, little distinguished the status of slaves from the mass of free men and women. Together they were the *humiliores*, the lowly, humble ones.

Slaves could and did change status in visible ways, but gender differences remained. Sexual differentiation was viewed according to roles in continuing the species. Aristotle's carefully observed and reasoned analysis of nature in *On the Generation of Animals* led him to conclude that males provided the architect and blueprint for offspring while females supplied the raw material. Using a culinary metaphor, Aristotle believed that the male provided the recipe and heat energy to cook the female ingredients for a little "bun in the oven." From this, he reasoned that women and men complemented each other in society as well as in the family, offering sets of male-female polarities that are recognizable today: active/passive, ruler/ruled, man about town/ woman of the house, self-controlled/emotional, and so forth. Taken to an extreme, conventional ancient thought excluded women (and nonelite men) from wielding authority or having an intellectual life—that is, being human to the fullest extent. But conventional thought, as well as Christian thought, had to take into account real women who often did not fit into convenient categories. Furthermore, Christians had to interpret and adapt conventional thought on the basis of their own biblical worldview. What they saw drove depictions of women in two directions.

Demonizing Women

Christians acknowledged that Christ had initiated a new era, dispersing his Spirit and making full children of God regardless of gender or other social divisions. For Christians, being human was all about being created in God's image (Gen. 1:26–27). Male and female seemed subsequent to basic human nature (1:27; 2:21–25). Questions directed toward the cultural status quo started here. Commentators did not agree about how or whether female humans bore God's image. Gregory of Nyssa thought that humanity was created fully in the image of God and then secondarily given gendered and embodied distinctions. Augustine and Chrysostom reasoned that the male-female creation subsequent to the creation of humanity according to God's image meant that women inherited the rational image with the capability for virtue and goodness, but only men received the full image, which entitled them to rule in society and in the home.

The figure of Eve, and her daughters, represented all that was dangerous in leading men away from God, in the pattern of Eve. Eve's fate after the fall clearly supported and illustrated the social reality of women in the ancient world, officially limited in scope of action and focused upon the family. Male ascetics, in writing about their own experiences, despaired at the persistence of sexual thoughts and sensations that arose in conjunction with tempting women. Nothing, it seemed, was more powerful than the desires associated with sexual pleasure, marriage, family, and making a living, as represented by women. Evagrius of Pontus warned, "The sight of a woman is a poisoned arrow; it wounds the soul and injects the poison, and for as long a time as it stays there, it causes an ever greater festering."[21] Yet lust (or fornication) was never deemed the most powerful of the evil thoughts; it was simply a very easy one to identify. Women were "demonized" in ascetic settings because the male authors had to admit their own deep-seated weaknesses. Many ascetics arrogantly assumed victory over fornication when in fact they merely hid from it until real, remembered, or imagined women uncovered that the battle was not over.

On the other hand, early Christians had to take into account the kind of humanity to which men and women, slave and free, were equally destined in the final resurrection. On the ground was already plenty of startling evidence of the resurrection in progress. Amazed observers celebrated that holiness of life, the most important aspect of being human, knew no constraints by class or gender.

Transformations and Transpositions

The real threat for Christians was not one's accidental birth into a class or gender but ignoring the opportunities to grow in true humanity and god-likeness. Although they usually occupied different physical spaces within the church building, rich and poor, noble and lowly, male and female—all received the very same baptism and approached the same altar for receiving the same Eucharist. Grappling with cultural givens about who and what marks real human flourishing, Christians talked about real slavery or real femininity being a state of mind. Many who might be considered free, rich, powerful, and virtuous (by worldly standards) often turned out to be the opposite when considered from God's perspective.

Real slavery marked those who mistakenly saw themselves as free and under their own authority. The rich and powerful hid from their true status as the biblical Prophets and Psalms so often warned. Yet not a few eyebrows were raised when Asterius of Amaseia went so far as to state, "O man, nothing is your own. You are a slave, and what is yours belongs to your Lord."[22] Trapped by sins and possessions, the elite refused to see their own neediness and their responsibilities to God and fellow human beings. John Chrysostom warned that at the end of life's play, the external masks come off to reveal the internal beauty, freedom, and riches or decay, slavery, and poverty which is one's true self (*Homily 6: On Lazarus and the Rich Man*).

In his *Life of Antony*, Athanasius highlighted the power of divine wisdom, which breaks down class barriers. The monk Antony could read and write, but he had not the opportunity for the extensive education that marked the lettered elite. When curious philosophers came to test Antony, they left astounded at how "cultured" his demeanor, speech, and insight were. Augustine found this particularly damning in his own case before converting to Christianity. After hearing Antony's story, an anguished Augustine exclaimed to a friend: "What is wrong with us? . . . Uneducated people are rising up and capturing heaven and we with our high culture without any heart—see where we roll in the mud of flesh and blood."[23] The life of the church witnessed the continuing legacy of Paul's contention that "God's foolishness is wiser than human wisdom" (1 Cor. 1:25). Mainstream piety practiced across classes could derail trends within Christianity led by elite intellectuals and emperors, such as occurred during the gnostic (see chap. 6) and christological (see chap. 10) debates.

Moving from class to gender, early Christians believed that both male and female could participate in a transformed humanity where relationships were characterized by self-giving love that outstripped the desire for personal satisfaction through sexual activity or worldly prominence. True humanity knew no gender, but until the resurrection, male and female bodies would continue to have some social distinctions. More important, behavioral marks of gender were no longer fixed by one's birth status. Constrained by the gendered vocabulary of Greek and Latin, Christians tried to redefine humanness by making it accessible to all in a way that non-Christian philosophy never tried to do on such a large and practical scale. The pinnacle of human excellence in both Greek and Latin derived from a concept of maleness instead of using roots for humanity (Latin *homo*; Greek *anthrōpos*). Virtue (Latin *virtus*; Greek *andreia*) refers specifically to the masculine human: *vir* in Latin and *andros* in Greek. Christians argued that in the revised version of virtue, "womanly" humans failed to take advantage of the power Christ offered to grow in his image while "manly" humans did.[24] Gregory of Nyssa's apparently offensive call for all Christians to birth themselves "male" (as rational and virtuous) is rooted in a then-countercultural claim for women's equal access to full human excellence in Christ (*Life of Moses* 2.3–4).

God's ideal for true, divinized humanity could be seen from the Virgin Mary to martyrs to female ascetics. Besides functioning as the guarantee of Christ's humanity, Mary marked the shift toward new potential for Eve's daughters: Mary's obedience overthrew Eve's disobedience; Mary's virginity reflects Eve's original condition, untroubled by sexual concupiscence. Because of Mary, God came in the flesh to reverse the damage of the fall. The growing devotional attachment to Mary elaborated her role as a female pioneer of divinization and a model for men as well. Mary successfully combated the serpent, which defeated Eve. For this reason, Cyril of Alexandria (mid-5th c.) proclaimed, "Through you [Mary], every faithful soul achieves salvation."[25] Another Cyril, of Jerusalem, earlier commented that whereas

Eve (and all women) had their first "birth" from a man, Adam, Mary turned the tables, for men and women now owe their true "birth" to a woman, the Mother of God (*Catechetical Lectures* 12.29; 10.19).

In Christ, females could become male and transcend what the fallen world considered weak and worthless in order to become exemplary human beings. The valor and sheer physical endurance of women martyrs such as Blandina (also a slave), Perpetua, and her slave Felicitas (see chap. 4) bore witness to something new at work in humanity as a whole. Gregory of Nyssa recorded his sister Macrina's life precisely because it would prove a model of "the greatest height of human virtue," breaking free of the limiting categories of gender.[26] Here was a woman who embodied what God desired for humans and made possible: Christian "philosophy." She used her prodigious learning, including classical philosophy and Scripture, to guide the education of her younger brothers. She applied her zeal in Christianity to give up material markers of her class, living on par with her newly freed slaves and convincing her mother to do the same. She was a patron and benefactor for the region, directing the distribution of family grain stores during a famine, opening her home to orphaned or abandoned children, organizing and leading a full-blown ascetic community, and healing suppliants. But where her "manliness" showed forth most impressively for Gregory was in facing death: her own and that of her family members. Her solid hope of the resurrection allowed her to practice all the virtues of a real philosopher, including cheerfulness at her impending death. Macrina was the constant "man," bringing stability to those suffering from "womanly" instability around her, including the international churchman Gregory, who fell apart emotionally as his sister lay dying. Women could, and often did, shame men by demonstrating the heights of *vir*-tue.

SEEING AND BEING HUMAN

Early Christians saw a set of pressing needs in their own society that does not entirely accord with what twenty-first-century Westerners think crucial, such as slavery and the status of women. For the most part, premodern Christians did not think that class and gender interfered with being human to the extent that abuse of resources and blindness to suffering did. Christian social thought grew out of noticing things that did not accord with key biblical ideas about how humans transformed in Christ should see and relate to one another.

Much of what we know about the social issues with which Christians were struggling meets us in homilies. Preachers taxed their rhetorical skills to teach and urge Christian attitudes and actions among the faithful. Pastors, sensitive to the gamut of interest and understanding among listeners, crafted their exhortations accordingly. What can look like wild inconsistencies in the motivational schemes within homilies are actually strategies designed to persuade the faithful on the basis of things about which they cared, from the petty to the sublime. Preachers threatened damnation for the stubborn and proffered divine honor for the status-conscious. But they fervently hoped that the faithful would eventually be moved to act out of love and humble conformity to Christ.

Ascesis had already captivated believers from all classes. This grassroots workforce independently or in cooperation with the local bishop provided much face-to-face service to a variety of needy. Most preaching then was directed toward nonascetics of all classes, but with a special focus upon the elite. When leaders in the church looked around, they saw what the traditional elite generally had not: people who slipped through the traditional safety nets of family, patron, and civic membership. The preachers' job: (1) make the needy and their needs visible, (2) situate sin and suffering in a Christian context, and (3) create motivation to meet those needs. The elite were both the problem and the solution: a problem because pastors viewed traditional ways of using power and money as sinful, a solution because they had both the financial and social resources to make further "Christian" changes to society.[27]

Looking but Not Seeing

For most people in the history of the world, the scenario Jesus depicted in the parable of Lazarus and the Rich Man (Luke 16:19–31) was not quaint. Lazarus was a faceless beggar, reduced to a passivity from which he could not be roused, even by dogs licking his sores. It was blunt reality and so was a popular platform from which to preach about poverty and wealth. Without pain relievers, antibiotics, vaccinations, and the whole system of modern medicine, life was (and is) painful and subject to sudden brushes with death, poverty, and neediness. Broken bones and simple infections could reduce strong workers to beggars. The periodic revolts or incursions of non-Roman people into the empire created desperate captives and sudden refugee populations belonging to no family or patron or city. Even the elite contributed to the have-nots by cannibalizing each other: the very powerful overcoming the less powerful of their ranks by force, contrived lawsuits, and usurious loans. The uncomfortable relevance of Lazarus and the Rich Man lay in the fact that the streets of most large towns and cities were lined with all sorts of Lazaruses, whom few were eager to notice. Like that rich man, most people would pass by the destitute and deformed and diseased, anxiously avoiding physical and visual contact while perhaps dropping them some coins.

Pastors wrestled with why the needy and their needs were not seen. Gregory of Nazianzus (d. 391) discerned that many did not want to admit that such a situation could easily be their own. If there were any recognition of others' unsought suffering, then people would have to face their own fragile control over health, wealth, and friendship. That recognition is painful and terribly inconvenient; it might mean a fundamental change of ingrained attitudes and behaviors. Altruistic support of the needy was neither a traditional nor profitable investment of the elite's resources. Humans would much prefer to think of their prosperity as their birthright, a kind of reward for personal excellence or the fruits of their own efforts. From that perspective, suffering of any type becomes the fruit of sinfulness and laziness—basically a divine judgment. Gregory shuddered at how self-satisfied penny-pinchers passed by the needy and concluded that "the suffering of these people is God's work. . . . Let them be sick, let them suffer, let them be unfortunate. Such is God's will!"[28] "No!" shouted Gregory and other preachers. The root of the blindness resided in the fall of Adam and Eve; its cure depended upon letting Christ dispel the blindness in order to recover the relationships that support true human existence through an interdependent community.

Perceiving Diamonds in the Rough

Early Christians argued that humans are "diamonds in the rough" if one knows how to look at them discerningly. Preachers tried two central tactics to dispel moral blindness. First, they tried to make their audience feel others' pain by "seeing with their ears" the people intentionally unseen by the eyes. Second, they sought to reveal the innate kinship of all humanity. One moving example is Gregory of Nazianzus's *Oration 14: On the Love of the Poor*, preached in the 360s to help his friend Basil address the desperate situation of lepers in the region of Caesarea in Cappadocia. Gregory directed his full rhetorical and theological arsenal to reveal both the shared weakness of humanity and the human dignity of those from whom society generally flinches. Both conditions converge in Christ, who is the source of human dignity in creation and who dignified human weakness by sharing it for human salvation.

THE BASILIAD

Basil developed an episcopal complex at Caesarea, which his friend Gregory of Nazianzus called a "new city." Its ambitious range of services hints at what was happening throughout the church, giving beliefs about human well-being concrete expressions. The Basiliad's importance as a center for worship and social services contributed to the gradual relocation of downtown Caesarea, from its ancient location to its new environs surrounding the church and associated residence, hospital (staffed by trained professionals, often ascetics), guest house, poorhouse, barns, and workshops.

Gregory, like other socially conscious bishops, pushed his audience to "walk in the shoes" of the poor. Lepers encapsulated the whole spectrum of the human potential for suffering through poverty (9). At one level, scarce resources cause anxiety as well as physical suffering, but usually one has friends or family who can cover a short-term need. A worse level of poverty entails long-term illness or disability, which prevents one from work and increases the sense of being a helpless burden to others and useless to dependents. The nadir of human suffering combines the first two levels and introduces the condition of utter dehumanization. Leprosy (and other conditions) make one a horror, treated as dead, and cast out of homes and cities.

Gregory believed that opening one's eyes to suffering could teach hard-hearted humans "reverence and humanity from our common weakness" by recalling our own susceptibility.[29] Vulnerability should remind those who dare to be called by Christ's name of their Lord's own loving embrace of weakness, suffering, and poverty for our sake (15). Imagine what it is like to beg, to see one's body fall apart, to see former friends turn away, to have one's family treat you as if you are not there, to pull your decaying carcass to the church to beg. Imagine, preachers called to the elite, what it is like to be hungry, what it is like to be enslaved to "patrons" whose usurious loans have become chains. Basil of Caesarea, angered and alarmed at the effects of famine and ensuing disease among his weakened population, graphically described what no one really wanted to see: the gradual marks of starvation upon human bodies. After initial stages of pallor and weakness, "the eyes are sunken as if in a casket, like dried-up nuts in their shells; the empty belly collapses, conforming itself to the shape of the backbone."[30] Small wonder no one wanted to look at this condition and see the human form so desecrated. The human being is reduced to an identity of disease and want.[31]

Early Christians looked to Christ's incarnation, death, and resurrection to undo the impact of Adam's sin upon subsequent humanity. Christians baptized into Christ's death and resurrection were to practice their Christlikeness rather than their fallen Adam-likeness. No longer blinded by social divisions and suffering, Gregory of Nazianzus urged his hearers to view humanity, especially those whom Christians were tempted to ignore, with sight restored by what both the healthy and ill share: creation in the image of God, morality, Scripture, worship, sacraments, hopes in Christ, and inheritance of divine glory (14). Gregory tightly connected a sanctified use of possessions (18) with fulfilling God's plan for humans to "become a god to the unfortunate, by imitating the mercy of God" (26). Only with clear vision would it be possible for believers to live and progress in likeness to the image of God "to become a child of God, a fellow-heir with Christ, even (I make bold to say) to become yourself divine" (23).[32]

Managing God's Wealth

One would think that the challenge to become divine would be an attractive motivation to shift from giving extravagant banquets and plying money for influence, to becoming a godlike patron of Christ in the needy. Not so for most. Society, especially the elite, resisted blurring the lines between themselves, the *honestiores*, and the *humiliores*. When preachers railed about the need to alleviate the dreadful suffering of fellow humans through neglect or profiteering, their prime adversaries in the fight were cultural attitudes that defined whom the elite were bound to help and what counted as a good investment.

Few elite of the late Roman Empire looked upon their possessions except as tools to enhance family power and honor. Generations of "Carnegies," "Rockefellers," and "Gateses" were expected to continue and exceed earlier generations' reputation for philanthropy. Spending was not a problem; indeed, it was common for the elite to fall into financial ruin while in pursuit of a reputation for splendor and lavishness. Spending in particular ways was an investment in relationships. *Do ut des* (I give so that you may give) shaped the rationale for all sorts of transactions (loans, gifts, jobs, pulling strings, etc.). The wealthy worked hard to put each other into debts of honor and of finances. They were equally competitive in pooling resources through strategic marriages. Public reputation rested upon well-maintained temples and roads, water supply, baths, public buildings, festival entertainment, and feasts. These services depended not upon tax revenues, but upon the wealth of each city's council of decurions, who carefully labeled their accomplishments in fancy inscriptions on walls and pavements. Think about the ire raised against a mayor today when potholes mar the roads or snow removal is not up to citizens' standards. Shame rather than losing an election motivated the elite. Wealth, class, and honor entailed a high-stakes pledge to the community, fellow elite, and one's family name.

The first job for preachers was to fix upon the souls of all hearers that all things come from God and as such are good, yet never truly one's own. The second was an adjustment of the proper use of wealth: to support and enhance life as part of an existence oriented toward God. After the fall, the value of goods became ambivalent because abundant possessions, even inherited ones, were tainted with sin. Gregory of Nazianzus noted that wealth was often accumulated through dishonest and even violent means, with people operating according to "the conqueror's law" rather than the "creator's."[33] After the fall, humans must learn to assess how much is enough for one's own needs and responsibilities so that the rest can be disbursed for the good of others. Arguments about the necessary and the superfluous resulted in vicious attacks and detailed depictions of what the elite considered "necessary" for their status.

Asterius of Amaseia lambasted rich Christians for investing in exquisite silk garments embellished with Bible stories instead of clothing and honoring their poor brothers and sisters, who are even more precious because they are images of God (*Homily 1: On the Rich Man and Lazarus* 1). Given relative prices at the time, one fancy silk garment equaled the cost of fifty ordinary garments for *humiliores*. Basil of Caesarea and John Chrysostom made enemies when they baldly accused the elite of theft and murder for preferring to share the wealth with fellow elites rather than with those in desperate need.

Although appearing to push a communal socialism, most bishops were more interested in shifting the recipients of the elite's competitive spending. Instead of munificence for the purpose of negotiating relationships with peers and superiors, pastors offered the poor as recipients, through whom one could establish a favorable relationship with God. An important passage for John Chrysostom was Jesus' countercultural advice to invite guests who could never return the favor: "the poor, the crippled, the lame, and the blind" (Luke 14:12–14).[34] However, when considering that these outcasts are Christ himself, the rewards are immense, even if delayed, because it is God who becomes, in a manner of speaking, the human benefactor's debtor.

Because the expenditures of the elite had little trickle-down effect for the masses, preachers questioned the very actions that were the basis of much traditional honor. Playing on the elite's horror of shame, Gregory of Nazianzus pointed out how ignoble it was to develop such refined tastes in food, clothing, and shelter while the poor lack even the poorest quality of all three:

> Why do we feast in the face of our brothers' and sisters' misfortunes? . . . Surely we must either give all things away for Christ's sake, so that we may follow him truly, taking up our cross, so that we might take our flight unburdened towards the world above, well equipped and held back by nothing, so that we might gain Christ at the expense of all else, exalted through humility and made rich by poverty; or else we must share our goods with Christ, so that our possession of them may at least be sanctified by our possessing them well, by our sharing them with those who have nothing.[35]

A Christian redefinition of honor and wealth derived from investing in an eternal and heavenly future rather than a worldly one. Preachers pointed out that if one yearned to be praised in the emperor's presence, who then would refuse the greater opportunity to be lauded in God's own court by a crowd of thankful poor bearing witness to one's generosity and kindness? Or who would dare to face the Judge of all with carefully hoarded gold rather than witnesses to one's generosity and love? Only a few might be convinced to sell all and live an ascetic life, but by using traditional motivations, preachers hoped to convert existing leaders into more Christlike attitudes and actions.

CONCLUSIONS

A pagan Roman of the third century arriving by time travel to his home-town a century later would see some remarkable and shocking changes to city life wrought by Christianity. Bishops, elite laity, and professional ascetics founded and served in new social services to clients that an old Roman would scarcely recognize as worthy of aid. These Christians saw their reshaping or invention of social institutions to be a natural outgrowth of their beliefs.[36] To do nothing betrayed the incarnate Christ, who took on human weakness, even if these efforts and institutions could never eliminate the effects of fallen human nature.

Bishops hoped to alter perceptions of the existing social and economic dif-ferences so that interaction among people would better reflect the community of the church as brothers and sisters in Christ. Across the Christians world, new or more widespread institutions sought to cooperate with God's original and ultimate plan for humanity on the local, face-to-face level. The elite and political leaders faced the greatest demands to adjust their sights, rationale, and actions to their Christian faith. While distinctions would continue to exist, Christians tried to redirect class, wealth, and gender differences in order to humanize and so divinize themselves and others, not dehumanize. Early Christians within an empire, heirs and neighbors to other empires, could be flexible about the variety of ways human beings organized themselves. The task for Christians, regardless of their social structures, was to find ways to form and exercise virtue as humans created in the image of God. Even the barbarians who converted to Christianity shamed civilized, Roman, so-called Christians by their adherence to the faith and their self-control despite a very different civilization.

Christian social action was heavily dependent upon its portrayal of humanity created and re-created in God's image. Knowing God revealed true humanity. It should come as no surprise, then, that figuring out what it meant for Jesus Christ to be divine and human was a highly charged endeavor.[37] Glimpsing God's intended reality for humanity in the person of Christ incarnate and resurrected strongly suggested how humans should treat one another in the interim. Concentrating on the unity of the divine-human Christ motivated preachers like Gregory of Nazianzus to sacralize the decayed and suffering poor, through whom Christ's own suffering and victory bore witness.[38] In Christ, God himself had condescended to be and be seen in the poor, whose treatment would determine entry into the Father's kingdom (*Oration 14* 39, cf. Matt. 25:31–46).

Such homilies in the context of the sacraments and of the ever-present, suffering poor encouraged images of a shared experience between God and humanity in Christ. They also raised serious and long-standing questions. To what extent did the Son of God truly experience and dignify human existence, even suffering and scorn? If encountering, touching, and serving the needy are indeed points of real contact with Christ, what does that mean for him to be God? The old quandary about how spirit and matter, God and creation intersect bubbled up anew. The debates focused squarely on the inner life of God and the person of Jesus Christ. They threatened the very stability of an already-stressed empire both in the arguments and in the attempts to enforce conciliar decisions.

QUESTIONS FOR DISCUSSION

1. Why was marriage controversial for early Christians? What Christian significance did pastors locate within marriage and family life?
2. Where do early Christians' concerns about human good differ from what many today would identify? Why?
3. What arguments and motivational tactics did pastors employ to transform the economic habits of the elite to include the poor?

SUGGESTED FURTHER READING

Brown, Peter R. L. *Poverty and Leadership in the Later Roman Empire*. Hanover, NH: University Press of New England, 2002.
González, Justo L. *Faith and Wealth: A History of Early Christian Ideas on the Origin, Significance, and Use of Money*. Eugene, OR: Wipf & Stock, 2002.
Hunter, David. *Marriage, Celibacy, and Heresy in Ancient Christianity: The Jovinianist Controversy*. New York: Oxford University Press, 2007.
Nathan, Geoffrey S. *The Family in Late Antiquity: The Rise of Christianity and the Endurance of Tradition*. New York: Routledge, 2000.

10

Jesus Christ

Divine and Human

INTRODUCTION

Mention Christology over coffee today, and the conversation is likely to lapse into embarrassed silence, glazed looks, and a hurried observation about the weather. In the fourth and fifth centuries, the topic could come up while buying groceries and would result in heated debates, exchanges of competing hymns and slogans, and even brawls. Why, people wondered, did Jesus not know what the Father knows? How can Jesus and the Father be one? Is Christ really like us? But don't we want a Christ who is *not* like us? How can God enter personally into humanity? How can God be born or bleed or die? But if God was not born, if he did not bleed and die, then how are we saved?

Imperial stability teetered on understandings of Christ. Emperors, try as they might, could not control the outcome of the councils they called. Why? With its inherent limitations, language could not fully express experience and knowledge of God. Building a portrait of God that was accurate, or at least not incorrect, was key to avoiding idolatrous understandings of God. If competing understandings of God were to be adapted by different peoples within the empire, then they might become rallying points for dissension, disobedience, and even open revolt.

Ecclesial stability also teetered on understanding the identity and saving work of Christ. A good portrait of God needed to maintain communion with earlier brothers and sisters of the church, who handed down multiple overlapping images of Christ in teachings and worship. It needed to honor the rule of faith that had long been crucial to Christian belief and practice. Deeply influenced by their worship, sacraments, Scripture, and fellowship in the church, Christians found themselves searching for ways to make language serve their insights. Although believers had always adapted philosophical and religious language from their culture, there came a point when those very tools began to cause more disputes than they resolved. Both ancient philosophy and Scripture spoke of an unchanging, transcendent God. Much of Scripture, however, also told the story of a God very much involved in his creation. Moreover, if God is transcendent, then how can Jesus be regarded as divine? If Jesus was not divine, then how could he save us from our sins? If Jesus was divine, and he was begotten by God the Father, then were Christians really honoring Jewish Scripture's insistence on the absolute unity and oneness of God?

Thus, early Christians had to reflect carefully upon the received tradition that Christ could be worshiped as God without compromising either monotheism or divine transcendence. Attempts to find language that achieved that delicate balance heightened the tension about how divine transcendence in Christ could relate to mere humanity.[1] This in turn required addressing salvation; for whatever Christ is and does determines who we are, how we are saved, and the end to which God desires to bring us.

DIVINE-HUMAN DATA

Meeting God Materially

At every eucharistic assembly, believers saw and heard the priest or bishop raise the bread and wine and say some form of the words of institution handed down by Paul:

> On the night when he was betrayed [the Lord Jesus] took a loaf of bread, and when he had given thanks, he broke it and said, "This is my body that is [broken] for you. Do this in remembrance of me." In the same way he took the cup also, after supper, saying, "This cup is the new covenant in my blood. Do this, as often as you drink it, in remembrance of me." (1 Cor. 11:23–25)

The newly baptized received emphatic teaching that this truly is Christ's body and blood, which provides direct communion with Christ. In turn, the Eucharist created communion with Christ's body, the church.

In worship, the lyrical nature of hymns, prayer, and art created an environment that held the paradoxical insights of Christian belief in tension. This ritually mediated knowledge of God had been the mainstay of the rule of faith, which perpetually tested how far human intellectual categories could be applied to the mysteries of the faith. Ephrem the Syrian (ca. 306–373), beloved poet and hymnographer, reflected upon the mysterious but comforting reality that Christ's presence in the Eucharist mirrors his incarnation. He envisioned Mary crooning to baby Jesus: "Dwell in bread and in those who eat it. In hidden and revealed [form] let your church see You as [does] the one who bore You."[2] Ephrem elsewhere exclaimed, "Blessed is the Vineshoot that became the cup of our salvation. / Blessed also is the Cluster, the source of the medicine of life. / Blessed also is the Ploughman Who Himself became the grain of wheat that was sown and the sheaf that was reaped."[3] What is consumed is Christ himself and his salvation: healing, spiritual nourishment, and divine communion. The invisible God was visible in Jesus Christ, popularly represented on the one hand as the fierce, yet human, universal Ruler (Pantocrator), and on the other as a child sitting on the Virgin Mary's lap—a child who nonetheless bore the label *ho ōn* (the Living One) to translate the Hebrew YHWH. The invisible God was also reflected in his children, baptized and anointed as "Christs," as well as in the scriptural Word of God and the recitation of the creed.

The regularity with which believers heard and experienced God's crossing of the divine-human divide offers a hint at the familiarity most active believers had with encountering God in material things. Knowing and reflecting upon God as frightfully transcendent yet lovingly present was an even more important element in the debates when one considers the actual voting members of councils: bishops high and low from urban and rural areas, whose theological training and acumen varied greatly.[4] Nonetheless their ordinary liturgical duties kept issues of Christ and salvation rooted in preaching Scripture and presiding over sacraments. The daring language and experience of Christian worship risked bending both scriptural and philosophical sensibilities to the breaking point when addressing the incarnation.

The Root of Controversies: "For I Am God, and Not Man" (Hos. 11:9, Septuagint)

While it frequently describes God as possessing human (anthropomorphic) characteristics, Jewish Scripture is adamant that those characteristics must be understood only as metaphors.[5] They are symbolic language being used to convey something true about God's character, intent, and actions. They do not describe God's physiology or suggest that God is in any way limited by space or time. Christians, however, believed that symbols of God's anthropomorphic rescue of humanity throughout Israel's past became astonishingly concrete in the person of Jesus Christ. Jesus, the incarnate Son of God, was God's salvation: he was the very thing that the Israelites could discern only partially. The author of Hebrews noted this well when he wrote, "Long ago God spoke to our ancestors in many and various ways by the prophets, but in these last days he has spoken to us by a Son" (1:1–2).

Models for describing how and why God entered humanity in Jesus Christ affected how believers understood their communion with God in worship. For if one approached the bread and wine expecting, as most Christians did, to receive Christ himself, then how different could that corporeal expression of God be from the incarnation? However, if God cannot travel together with matter in a human body, then worship largely becomes a moral, intellectual, and spiritual exercise. It ceases to be a transformative communion with God, leading toward the bodily resurrection of the dead.[6] Salvation becomes spiritualized human improvement rather than intimate union with God. Disputes with gnostics in the second and third centuries led many to resist this spiritualizing tendency, yet the question persisted: To what extent can God really experience humanity and its limitations?

When the early Christians employed philosophical concepts to describe divinity, they did so in order to extend biblical understandings about holiness. Scripture placed anthropomorphic descriptions of God changing his mind, acting emotionally, or doing something new within a broader understanding of his divine steadfastness and love. Philosophy provided a vocabulary for expressing that broader understanding. Scholarship of the last century frequently drew too sharp a contrast between the God of Scripture and the god of philosophy. Fresher views reveal many competing understandings of transcendence and the terms used to describe it.[7] Moreover, just as ancient philosophy did not possess a unified vision of absolute transcendence, it is wrong to suggest that writers of the Old Testament had little sense of God's transcendence. Be it Greek philosophers or Isaiah or Job, all attested that God does not need creation in order for him to exist; nor does he require anything but himself to have a complete identity. By embracing Greek concepts of divine immutability (God does not change) and impassibility or *apatheia* (God does not suffer), early Christians were able to describe the relationship between creation and a perfect (complete) God.

IMPASSIBILITY (*APATHEIA*)

This is not "apathy," a listless indifference. It is a Stoic term describing an ideal state in which the divine cosmos and virtuous humans avoided irrational and self-serving passions (the *pathē*) while cultivating rational and selfless motivations (good passions: *eupatheiai*). *Pathē* included fear, desire, distress, gratification. *Eupatheiai* such as joy, caution, and hope should supplant *pathē*.

For Christians, God's *apatheia* was revealed in the incarnation when the Logos "emptied" himself (*kenōsis* of Phil. 2:7) in "radical attachment" to others.[8] This was an "apathetic" plan in utter consistency with God's Old Testament commitment to saving others. The *kenōsis* was motivated by the Logos's selfless, good passion (*eupatheia*) of love, and was untroubled by any self-serving passion (*pathos*). The incarnation never suggested to Christians that God was unreliable, incomplete, or changeable, but instead highlighted God's firm commitment to humanity and creation. God's difference from humanity, such as holiness and impassibility, bespoke his ultimate power to be entirely in charge. Nothing external to God could move or affect or manipulate or "create" him, and so impassibility denoted God's utter freedom of acting and being.

While God in his holiness and impassibility might draw near to humanity out of love, however, a question remained: How near might God come? It is one thing to say that God is love (1 John 4:8, 16), but quite another to consider whether God suffered and died. Debates almost always derived from attempts to honor God's alien majesty and to protect God from the degradation inherent in any contact with creation's variety, limits, and changeability. Jesus Christ was the unavoidable stumbling block; he was also the point around which divine-human boundaries were defined.

JESUS CHRIST, SON OF GOD

Developments to the Fourth Century

Most of the early descriptions of Christ lurch from divine to human emphases according to the context in which questions arose. When some teachings appeared to threaten Christ's solidarity with humanity, opposition treatises stressed the absolute necessity of the Son's full and real humanity. Likewise, when the extent or kind of divinity Christ enjoyed was called into question, the response consisted of arguments in support of Christ's complete divinity.

Reacting to doubts about Jesus' role in the covenant, the first generations of Christians claimed that Jesus enjoyed divine status not simply as a human being or prophet, but instead as the descended and reascended Christ, the creating Word of God. The earliest Christians emphasized the Son's existence before his incarnation. At the same time that they accepted Christ's divine status, most Christian writers took for granted the basic barrier between divinity and creation. Some Christians, operating under Platonic models, agreed that divine transcendence could not be retained in the material world, especially not in a body. They often represented the divine Christ's job as one of messenger, teacher, model, or a subordinate type of divinity capable of interfacing with creation without, so to speak, infecting the transcendent Father. Yet most also insisted, to the confusion of non-Christians, that this divine Christ suffered and died.

Oddly enough, doing the math to make 3 = 1 was not the trickiest nor the only hurdle to overcome when speaking of one God in trinity (Father, Son, and Holy Spirit). Conflict arose over how to recognize all the limitations of human existence within the Son without somehow causing the very definition of the one God to fall apart. Third-century Patripassionists (proponents of a Father-suffering theology) were accused of imagining the Son so intimately united with the Father that Christ's suffering was experienced by the Father. Not so, others contended; the Father cannot suffer and remain God. On the other end, subordinationists preserved the Father's transcendence and a threefold contour to God, but were accused of doing so at the expense of demoting the Son and Holy Spirit from real divinity.

Radical attempts at strict monotheism utterly failed at the popular and intellectual levels for the same reasons that Christians in the first generations had differentiated themselves from Jewish monotheism. Sabellius of Rome (early 3rd c.) took the threefold language of worship and Scripture to be indicative of God's actions, not his inner being. The Sabellians, or Modalists, protected God's oneness by seeing Father, Son, and Holy Spirit as "modes" of God's plan of salvation (the economy). In this model, the one God swaps masks to play the roles of Creator, Redeemer, and Sustainer as needed, and so led back to Patripassionism. Like Patripassionism, modalism failed to accommodate general belief in the distinctiveness of Father, Son, and Spirit.

Origen suggested that while these "jobs" in the economy (plan) of salvation helped explain the way humans experienced the threefold God, the biblical and ritual names (Father, Son, Spirit) more truly described each person's distinct identity by their relationships to one another. However, because Origen assumed humanity to be originally and ultimately spiritual, he avoided the potential outrage to divine transcendence that a divine-human Son otherwise provoked.

So it was that fourth-century Christians already had a partial language and set of models (and lots of questions) for discussing one God, who nevertheless consisted of distinct members. Tertullian's Latin formula—one divine substance (*substantia*, essential stuff that makes something what it is) and three persons (*personae*, individual participants in the divine category)—became the foundational wording among Latin speakers for the Trinity. Fourth-century Eastern Christians adopted a similar Greek formula, one divine essence (*ousia*, base reality or what something *is* from the verb "to be") and three individuals (*hypostases*, freestanding members of a species; or *prosōpa*, persons). But in the long term, it was much more difficult to enunciate the relationship of the divine and human qualities in Christ than to figure out how three can equal one. The more thorny issue always lay in how the essence of God-ness could be preserved when one also believed that the Son of God was born, suffered, and died.

What Kind of God-ness Does the Son Have?

In the interest of protecting God's oneness and transcendence, Arius (ca. 260–336), a well-liked priest in Alexandria, Egypt, embarked upon a mission that led to his condemnation in 325 at the Council of Nicaea. He wanted to make sure that believers understood Christ's job as a created but divine mediator between the uncreated and created dimensions. Everyone agreed that Christ is the "enfleshment" (incarnation) of the only begotten Son of God. Arius contended that since the Son derived his existence from the Father, who is unbegotten and has no origin, there was an essential difference between the two. Begotten-ness and unbegotten-ness are two planes of being, two "substances," two *ousiai*. *Begotten* meant that the Son had some sort of beginning like all creatures, making him unlike the Father, who is eternal.

Arius and his successors made thorough lists of scriptural passages that supported Christ's difference from the Father. For example, Psalm 45:7–8 was understood to show that God anointed Christ "with the oil of gladness beyond your companions," thus establishing that Christ had a creaturely nature (like his "companions"), not a divine one. Oddly enough, Jesus' claim that "the Father is greater than I" (John 14:28) was used by Arius's opponents to argue that the difference between Father and Son was only one of degree, not the "stuff" of his basic nature.[9] Although he agreed that the Son was the Father's divine partner in creation and conveyed the invisible God to that creation, Arius considered it impossible for the Son to know the Father fully. So for Arius, the Son was God, but of a subordinate kind, who could interact with lower creation and still be a buffer to protect the transcendent Father from change and decay.

The conclusion reached against the Arians at the Council of Nicaea (325), and affirmed more adamantly in the Council of Constantinople (381), was that the Son shares the *same* divine *stuff* (*homoousios*) with God the Father, as does the Holy Spirit. The wrangling revealed that alternative hypotheses for recognizing the Christ of faith "according to Scripture" were at stake. The battle was not won by stacking up biblical evidence until one side tipped. Nor did it consist of a mere clash of exegetical methods.[10] When theologians latched onto nonbiblical terms like *homoousios*, it was not to preempt Scripture. The goal was to highlight what Scripture really meant when viewed through the apostolic witness to Jesus. Against a hypothesis that read Christ as a creature sent to save by offering knowledge of God and his moral example, *homoousios* seemed to preserve what the bishops attending Nicaea and later Constantinople instinctively felt to be so important to human salvation: God's complete presence and involvement in the Son's saving work.

THE NICENE-CONSTANTINOPOLITAN CREED

We believe in one God, the Father all-powerful, Maker [of heaven and of earth, and] of all things both seen and unseen; And in one Lord Jesus Christ, the [only begotten] Son of God, (the Only) begotten from the Father [before all the ages], (that is from substance of the Father, God of God,) light from light, true God of true God, begotten not made, consubstantial with the Father, through whom all things came to be, (both those in heaven and those on earth); for us humans and for our salvation he came down [from the heavens] and became incarnate [from the Holy Spirit and the Virgin Mary], became human, [and was crucified on our behalf under Pontius Pilate; he] suffered [and was buried] and rose up on the third day, [in accordance with the Scriptures; and he] went up into the heavens [and is seated at the Father's right hand; he], is coming [again with glory] to judge the living and the dead[; his kingdom will have no end]. And in the (Holy) Spirit[, the holy, the lordly, and life-giving one, proceeding forth from the Father, coworshiped and coglorified with Father and Son, the one who spoke through the prophets; in one, holy, catholic, and apostolic church. We confess one baptism for the forgiving of sins. We look forward to a resurrection of the dead and life in the age to come. Amen].

(Parenthetical words are only in the 325 creed.) [Words in brackets are additional or replacement material from 381.][11]

The Nicene Creed built upon existing baptismal confessions (also called symbols) that expressed the rule of faith. As the story of the faith into which one entered into communion with both God and God's people, little had changed for most believers. The symbol of Nicaea depicted how God acts on humanity's behalf in a spare format. The version from 381 makes it clear that leaders wanted to ground the creed even more solidly within the story portrayed in Scripture. Gleaning from several symbols known to them, the delegates added several details about the mission of the Son, the role of the Spirit, and the nature of the Spirit-formed people.

Settling that the Son of God is *homoousios* with the Father turned attention toward understanding how the Son's intrinsic, raw, transcendence could exist in the same "container" with its disintegrating opposite, or any container whatsoever. The more some thought about the claim, the more reckless the term seemed to be. If the Son is *homooousios* with the Father, who suffers and dies in Christ? The ensuing debates demonstrated the lingering pressure to maintain respectful separation between God and humanity and to subject this relationship to reason. At the same time, believers recognized humanity's limited capacity to describe the transcendent God, who revealed himself mystically and dynamically in the life of the church—a God who might exist and act outside humanly conceived parameters "for us humans and for our salvation." Tradition pushed biblical and philosophical envelopes, suggesting that the holy and transcendent God, through the consubstantial (*homoousios*) Son, could handle contact with change and suffering, and that, for the purpose of salvation, God chose to suffer.

JESUS CHRIST, THE INCARNATE LOGOS

It is crucial at the outset to recognize that all participants in the christological debates shared a commitment to Christ somehow being both God and Man (Greek *anthrōpos*; Latin *homo*: "human person," or "humanity" categorically including males and females). Both sides in the controversy started from the experience of worship, where the enigma of Christ continually presented itself. Furthermore, they were anxious to avoid creating a "monster," a being neither completely divine nor completely human. The heart of the issue had to do less with objective curiosity about the phenomenon of God than with a passion to know God.

At the end of the fourth century, Gregory of Nazianzus wrote with an urgency that foreshadowed the gravity of future discussions as well as established the vocabulary that was to raise serious questions: "For what [Christ] has not assumed He has not healed; but that which is united to His Godhead is also saved; . . . but if the whole of Adam's nature fell, then it must be united to the whole nature of the Begotten One, and so be saved as a whole."[12] Much rested upon what "assumed" and "united" and "saved" could mean: Does the divine Son slip on the nasty cloak of human nature? Does the Son simply project himself through it (like "assuming" an identity)? What kind of unity between divine and human natures will save humanity "as a whole"? At stake was a comprehensive picture of how humanity is saved and what saved humanity will be.

The two primary perspectives in this controversy have been labeled according to the cities where participants received their intellectual and faith formation: Antioch in Syria and Alexandria in Egypt. As a corrective to long-held assumptions about the positions of Antiochenes and Alexandrians, we will lay out the old understandings and why the new ones better represent what separated the two sides. There follows a survey of issues as they unfolded in the fifth century between the two protagonists: Nestorius of Constantinople for the Antiochenes, and Cyril of Alexandria for the Alexandrians. This involves considering what models each perspective proffered for putting together divine and human natures in Christ before proceeding to the models of salvation that ensue from particular understandings of Christ.

Antioch and Alexandria

Scholars of the post-Enlightenment era cultivated a liking for the Antiochenes because they seemed precursors to the modern, rationalist focus on the human Jesus and on so-called objective, "historical" interpretation of Scripture. And some Antiochene interpretations even severely limited the extent to which Jewish Scripture could have any Christian or Christ-centered meaning.[13] However, these "literal," "historical," and "allegorical" categories were derived from the methods and teaching of rhetoric and literature (see chap. 5), which were clearly used by Alexandrian exegetes as well. The biblical foundations for discerning Christ were built with the same tools of interpretation yet governed by differing hypotheses of the faith.[14] In line with modernist tastes, Antiochenes were assumed to care more about history and human realities in their exegesis, and consequently about Christ's concrete humanity, than did Alexandrians. It is now apparent that an overarching desire to protect divine transcendence led Antiochenes to keep the divine element in Christ aloof from his human carrier, whom they called the "assumed man" or "the man Jesus."[15]

THE ANTIOCHENE AND ALEXANDRIAN SCHOOLS

"Schools" in antiquity did not have a specific address but rather a pedigree of central teachers and disciples through whom the "school" would continue. The scholar-monk Diodore of Tarsus (died ca. 390) is considered to be the founder of a distinctive literary-rhetorical approach to understanding Scripture. After Diodore, the chief Antiochenes were Theodore of Mopsuestia (392–428), Nestorius (d. ca. 451), and Theodoret of Cyrrhus (ca. 393–ca. 466). The Alexandrian school had its roots in a philosophical-mystical methodology originating with Origen. Heirs to Origen and this method were the Cappadocian fathers (Basil of Caesarea, Gregory of Nazianzus, Gregory of Nyssa) as well as those local to Alexandria: Athanasius (ca. 295–373), Didymus the Blind (ca. 313–398), and above all, Cyril (ca. 378–444).

The Antiochenes accused the Alexandrians of promoting an undisciplined confusion of divine and human boundaries. Alexandrians seemed to glory in an overbearing divine Logos, who obliterated the composite Christ's lowly and fragile human nature. Such a Christ, it was thought, would not share the same humanity that we do. Yet in reality, the Alexandrian traditions radically envisioned an intimate communion of God and humanity in Christ despite the difficulty in conceptually preserving divine transcendence in the presence of intact human nature. Salvation for the Alexandrians depended upon a Christianized version of divine *apatheia* that could give rise to Cyril's cherished phrase: God the Logos "suffered impassibly" (*Scholia on the Incarnation* 35).

The real Antiochenes and Alexandrians can now emerge as two schools of thought that differed not over rational, historical interpretation versus irrational, fantastic interpretation. Nor were they pitting the historical human Jesus against a Christ who lost his humanity to the engulfing Logos. Antiochenes so keenly felt the gulf between God and creation that they actively discouraged any sacramental understanding, scriptural interpretation, model of Christ, or eschatological hope that suggested possible overlap of created and uncreated realities. The Antiochenes' distinction between the divine and human natures in Christ was related to their resistance to Alexandrian scriptural interpretation. Theodore of Mopsuestia, an Antiochene, believed that the two covenants (Old and New), and their Scriptures, had to be kept distinct so that the teachings and reality of the first covenant would highlight the novelty of the new covenant.[16] Antiochenes ridiculed Alexandrians for reducing the whole of Jewish Scripture to a fused symbol for Christ, even as they mocked the Alexandrian Christ for being a sacrilegious fusion of the divine and human.

Antiochenes applied themselves to discovering the intent of smaller, coherent units of Scripture, such as a psalm or book of the Bible, especially in order to develop moral teachings. Alexandrians tended to speculate on the relationship of the pieces to the universal story of Scripture and its Author, who remained dynamically and flexibly present in the text. The conflicting approaches to God's proximity raised questions about Scripture and Christ. Was Christ only in some places in Scripture, or united with the whole of Scripture? Was Christ's divinity only in parts of the man Jesus? Or was God fully present through the Son in Jesus?

How Can *Homoousios* Go Both Ways?

Once the church established that the Son is *homoousios* (of the same divine stuff) with the Father, believers in the fifth century witnessed the pendulum swing between the Antiochene separation of divine and human natures in Christ and the Alexandrian union of natures.

The Antiochenes burst into public notoriety when the priest Nestorius of Antioch became bishop (patriarch) of Constantinople in 428. Nestorius followed the beloved Antiochene traditions of Diodore of Tarsus and Theodore of Mopsuestia, though he lacked their charisma. The new bishop's pastoral instincts and scholarly concern for meticulous language led him to correct his parishioners' devotional language for the Virgin Mary. Growing out of third-century practices, many Christians, especially in the East, cherished calling upon Mary the *Theotokos*—literally, God-bearer—and understood her to be Mother of God. The trouble with Theotokos was what such devotion implied about Jesus Christ. For Nestorius, imagining a second birth for the Logos as a human was tantamount to bringing back the old tales about gods having sex with humans and bearing children. Surely it was time for a responsible pastor to set things straight. While forbidding use of the title Theotokos, Nestorius counseled his flock to use the terms "Christ-bearer" or "Man-bearer" to avoid confusing the border between God and humanity.

Proclus, a priest in Constantinople and later patriarch there (434–446), publicly contradicted his superior with a resounding homily on Mary the Theotokos. He defended a union of human and divine natures in Christ for the purpose of human salvation. With Nestorius present and fuming, Proclus regaled the assembly with artful, exuberant praise of Mary the Theotokos, who is the locus for God becoming a human being. The Logos, through Mary, wove his humanness within her womb, which he called "the workshop of the union of the natures."[17]

Not to be outdone, Nestorius patiently (so he thought; others felt it to be condescending) chided the mistaken practice in his *First Sermon against the Theotokos*. Surely when God stoops down to raise fallen humanity, he explained, it is no different from one healthy human being picking up a hurt brother or sister. No one would say that the two become one except that the whole person touches and becomes "one" by lifting the fallen one. The unity of Christ is apparent from the experience of the church at worship, where he receives all love, honor, worship, blessing, praise, adoration—even if further reflection on how salvation takes place requires a careful recognition of the team effort (Logos and human being). So Nestorius concluded:

> I revere the one who is borne [the assumed man] because of the one who carries him [the Logos], and I worship the one I see [the assumed man] because of the one who is hidden [the Logos]. God is undivided from the one who appears, and therefore I do not divide the honor of that which is not divided. I divide the natures, but I unite the worship. Attend to what is said here. That which was formed in the womb is not in itself God. That which was created by the Spirit was not in itself God. That which was buried in the tomb was not in itself God. If that were the case, we should manifestly be worshipers of a human being and worshipers of the dead. But since God is within the one who was assumed, the one who was assumed is styled God because of the one who assumed him.[18]

Following standard philosophical categories, Nestorius could not imagine that human nature (*physis*) could exist apart from a concrete human being. A nature that exists only in the mind would be like centaurs and mermaids: entertaining notions, but not real. Consequently, Nestorius insisted that the incarnation had to be a conjunction forged by goodwill between an existing human being and the transcendent Son, the Logos. The man Jesus in Christ was *homoousios* with humans, but not with the Logos, in order to make clear that "the Godhead is not susceptible to passion."[19]

Cyril of Alexandria found this sort of representation to be dangerous. He wanted to move past the obvious (God is impassible) to tackle the less obvious: how to contemplate the truly human experiences of the incarnate Logos. Throughout the controversies, Cyril was inspired by the Christ hymn in Philippians, naming Christ's preexistent equality with God the Father. The divine Christ nevertheless emptied himself into his own humanity and thus into death. Within ancient thought, impassibility as a divine characteristic was consistent with immutability because many assumed that change within perfect divinity had to mean a change for the worse, as suffering and death surely were. If one is already perfect, there is no place to go but down. What if, thought Cyril, the experience of self-limitation within a complete human existence was really a self-consistent act (entailing no essential change) of omnipotent divinity? What if the feelings and experiences proper to being fully human, even pain and death, did not involve a change *for the worse* in the Logos?[20]

According to Cyril, the Logos in his humanity was aware of and experienced what human beings term negative sensations (*pathē*; e.g., hunger, fear, grief, and pain), but these did not take control of him as they usually do in fallen humanity. Because this was the divine Logos's own humanity, he was able to direct and transform weakness into glorified humanity. Since the concept impassibility tried to describe how free and powerful God is, then God seeking out human experience for the purpose of saving humanity is consistent with his depiction in Scripture. God is not changed when the consubstantial Logos embraces humanity into himself. God freely chooses and powerfully accomplishes acts of salvation that proceed from his unchanging character.

COMMUNICATIO IDIOMATUM

The "communication of idioms" is the technical term for describing Jesus Christ, the Son of God and Logos, as both divine and human. In Christ, one can equally apply the "idioms" or characteristics of both divinity and humanity. For example, in Christ, God was born; a human being forgave sins.

Along these lines, Cyril could venture to say that the incarnate Logos "suffered impassibly" because there was no threat that God himself changed as a result of his human experiences. Therefore the Logos did really experience two "births": eternally begotten of the Father, and then born a human being through the Virgin Mary. The Logos was not hovering separately in the vicinity, but truly underwent the confinement and development of a fetus, even while being the unconfined ruler of the universe. As God the Logos incarnate, he was born and went through a normal progression of self-understanding and maturation, as Cyril surmised, so as not to frighten fellow human beings whom he came to save.[21]

Cyril envisioned the Logos meeting and engaging his creation as a real human being whose "personality" (as we might anachronistically call it) drew seamlessly and inextricably from both components of his being. People regularly say "I" when referring to what different parts of their bodies are doing (e.g., I'm thinking or eating or hurting). Christ, too, in divinity and humanity can say "I" as a single being. Christ's actions, thoughts, and fears were that of the Logos experiencing his creation from the inside. The resulting "one incarnate nature of God the Logos" did not obliterate human nature but instead enriched and transformed it into what God wanted all along for these beings created in his own image.

In sum, Antiochenes and Alexandrians had legitimate concerns about the implications of distancing God and humanity in Christ or of placing them in direct contact with each other. The Antiochenes asserted that transcendent divinity would overwhelm and change human nature if the two were too close. Christ then would be all divine Logos, having absorbed paltry humanity. Their worst fears were confirmed when Eutyches, a proponent of extreme Alexandrian Christology, affirmed that the incarnate Christ is not *homoousios* with our humanity because the Logos swallows it up. Most Christians, including Alexandrians, believed that Eutyches went too far. His position was rejected at the Council of Chalcedon (451). On the other hand, the objections raised by Cyril revolved around Nestorius's logically and grammatically precise statements about what the divine Logos does and what the human Jesus does in Christ. Keeping the divine Logos distinct from the man Jesus (if only theoretically) created a troubling image. The Antiochene model asserts that Christ is *homoousios* with humanity through the man Jesus, but the Logos is *homoousios* only with the Father. This reduced Christ to either a corporate title under which the man Jesus represents, so to speak, the divine CEO, or a being suffering from a very literal split personality.[22] The Antiochene model of collegial unity rather than a natural, personal union prompted uneasiness about the extent to which the Logos was simply a mentor for his human companion. The two models forged new meanings through contrasting terms, which like *homoousios* drew their technical meaning from outside of Scripture in order to bring greater clarity to the Christ of Scripture.

Vocabulary of the Debates

Fluency in ancient Greek would be of only some help in untangling the way early Christians tried to describe the identity and role of Christ. The theological meanings of the words were forged in debate and with constant reference to how these words expressed the truths of Scripture. The fact of the matter was that, until the debates, many of the words used in various contexts could sometimes mean opposite things.

Alexandrians and Antiochenes alike were dedicated to finding language to convey adequately that when believers encounter Christ, they encounter a single center of will and action. The two sides differed over the identity of the primary agent in Christ: the assumed man for Nestorius and the Logos for Cyril.[23] Antiochenes preferred to denote the stability and unity of Christ by using *prosōpon* (person), which literally meant a theatrical mask or a person's face, but was developing into a juridical concept of a legal person (Latin *persona*). In contrast, Cyril of Alexandria used *physis* (nature) to imply the unity of the acting and encountered incarnate Logos. When Cyril of Alexandria employed his trademark phrase "*one* incarnate *nature* (*mia physis*) of God the Logos," he could still distinguish two kinds of stuff, intact divine and human natures (*physeis*, plural) that come together in Christ.

Cyril apparently overworked the term *physis* to mean the individual who is Christ as well as to distinguish the divine and human natures in Christ; Nestorius overworked *prosōpon*. This was more problematic because using *prosōpon* in theological discourse by this time usually meant a distinct individual or person, such as the three *prosōpa* of the Trinity. The incarnation brought the *prosōpon* of the eternal Logos into a relationship with the *prosōpon* of the man Jesus, who had a specific beginning in time. However, according to Nestorius, believers meet Christ, interact with him, and are saved by him as a single *prosōpon*. Upon reflection, believers can (and should) acknowledge the plural reality of the divine and human *prosōpa* who exist compositely within the visible Christ. Which *prosōpon* was in charge? The assumed man.

In its condemnations of Nestorius and his teachings, the Council of Ephesus (431) swept away using *prosōpon* to talk about the relationship of God and Man in Christ. *Prosōpon* was relegated to the job of distinguishing the three persons who comprise the one God. The Council of Chalcedon (451) adopted *hypostasis* (freestanding individual) in favor of *physis* to identify the single center of acting and being that is Christ the Logos after the incarnation. *Physis* remained to assert the reality affirmed earlier in the Nicene-Constantinopolitan Creed that the Son is "true God from true God" (divine nature) who nevertheless "became incarnate" and "became human" (human nature).[24]

IMPLICATIONS FOR SALVATION

Two patterns emerged and solidified in early Christian thought about Christ:
the incarnation as a joint association of the Logos and a human being (Antiochene model), or as God himself present in his own humanity (Alexandrian).
From these sprang distinctive models for thinking about who does the saving
in Christ and of what that salvation consists. Is salvation the result of God
giving humanity gifts (grace) or of God giving himself?[25] If humanity receives
gifts for overcoming the limitations of human nature, then direct contact with
God is not necessary. On the other hand, if humanity receives God himself in
order to become a new type of divinized humanity, then union is unavoidable.
Both Antiochenes and Alexandrians agreed that the end condition of humanity would exceed even the goodness of humanity before the fall.

Salvation through the Assumed Man

Antiochenes represented human origins and destiny in two stages: The age
of Adam (now) and the age of the new Adam (future hope made possible in
Christ).[26] The fall was not a separate stage but is yoked with the creation
to describe humanity's situation since the beginning: prone to change and
gradually burdened by accretions of sin over time. To accomplish salvation, a
human being just like us needs to be involved in the process, not a generic or
theoretical human nature. Humanity can proceed to the next age as evolved
humans, thanks to the assumed man's perfect use of the divine gifts from the
Logos. Humans must imitate Christ's efforts and make a similar good use of
divine gifts.

Nestorius made clear that the assumed man is the acting self in Christ,
elevated and graced by the indwelling of the Logos. The incarnation was
analogous to the making of prophets, but in its fullness was unique in human
history to this point. With the Logos's grace, the assumed man in Christ is
the second Adam, who pioneers human salvation, as Nestorius described:

> Our nature, having been put on by Christ like a garment, intervenes
> on [humanity's] behalf, being entirely free from all sin and contend-
> ing by appeal to its blameless origin, just as the Adam who was formed
> earlier brought punishment upon his race by reason of his sin. *This
> was the opportunity which belonged to the assumed man*, as a human being,
> to dissolve, by means of the flesh, that corruption which arose by
> means of the flesh.[27]

Jesus' exemplary manifestation of obedience, even to death, led the way for
the rest of humanity to advance to a similar path of moral excellence for which

humanity was destined. Theodore of Mopsuestia (to whose teachings Nestorius clung) favored scriptural images of salvation in Christ, such as the firstborn of creation (Col. 1:15), the firstfruits of the resurrection (1 Cor. 15:20,
23), the pioneer of salvation (Heb. 2:10).

In this scenario there was no need to adjust what impassibility meant
because the preexistent Logos did not suffer. Only the assumed man suffered
and was rewarded for it by receiving divine honor. In hindsight there was
something alarming about this Antiochene position when it began to sound
like gnostic Christian texts. For instance, Diodore's exegesis on Christ's cry of
dereliction ("My God, my God, why have you forsaken me?" Ps. 22:1) iden-
tifies the cry coming from the body, which suddenly discovered itself abandoned by the Logos on the cross.[28] Both the *Apocalypse of Peter* and the *Second
Treatise of the Great Seth* made sport of orthodox Christians for ignorantly
attributing that cry to the divine operator of Christ when in fact it emanated
from the earthly shell as a discarded tool.[29] Theodore of Mopsuestia at least
believed that although he could not die, the Logos went so far as to stay near
the assumed man as he died.

The Antiochene view of salvation noted that while humanity had previously participated (to its detriment) in the body of Adam, the resurrection will
complete the baptismal and eucharistic foretaste of union in the second Adam,
the body of Christ. God intends humans to enjoy communion in Christ, but
not in the Logos. The exalted Christ will pass on the Logos's grace to the rest
of humanity, who may then achieve the new norm for being human. Christian
hope for Antiochenes consisted of freedom from the mortal and unstable condition of the first humans, which allowed them to err. Until then, sin still dom-
inates human life. Believers must strive within the church, which is the body of
Christ, to make their best use of grace to reach that condition of the new Adam
for which they long: full participation and union in the body of Christ.

Sharing God's Life

Drawing from third-century resources like Irenaeus of Lyons, most Christians employed the audacious claim that salvation consisted in God promoting
human nature into himself (*Against Heresies* 3.19.1). This approach, favored
by the Alexandrians, risked an edginess that hearkened back to the old days
of the faith. Through inspired prophecy, hymns, and polemics, early generations of Christians had playfully and reverently imagined God not playing
by the rules of holiness and transcendence that were understood only in part
before the incarnation.

Alexandrians held out for the Logos to be the sole, acting self who "self-
emptied" (see Phil. 2:7–8) as a supreme act of power in order to transform

the human race by his living a human life. The Logos lived and died within a human existence, which he created for himself.[30] Salvation is a top-down operation resulting from the Logos's union with all humanity by means of his own humanity. Cyril's favorite scriptural depictions of human salvation highlight human beings becoming gods (Ps. 82:6) and children of God (John 1:12). The incarnation restored and elevated humans into even greater likeness to their original creation in the image of God (Gen. 1:26–27), making them "participants in divine nature" (2 Pet. 1:4, my trans.). For Cyril, the future for humanity is, in some sense, to be in God, not merely with him. Antiochenes feared that humanity would be changed by a union with the Logos, but that was the point for the Alexandrians. The human race needs change.

The emphasis on communion and divinization did not materialize out of arrogant wishful thinking. Instead, its roots sank deeply into the way the church had thought about what is wrong with humanity. Athanasius of Alexandria's landmark treatise *On the Incarnation of the Word* (mid-4th c.), set the tone for recognizing the significance of the Logos taking on his very own humanity. The incarnation marked the point at which humanity entered into a new relationship with God. For Athanasius, the fall of Adam and Eve was a turning from God to self. Humanity detached from its "power" source slipped into a spiral toward death: the ultimate death of annihilation. Readers today might think of it as pulling our own plug. No longer aware of who God is or who we are as beings created in the image of God, humans hide from impending non-existence by occupying themselves in sin. Certainly there was a legal transgression which put humanity under a death sentence (eventually the primary focus for western Christians) due to Adam and Eve eating the forbidden fruit (Gen. 3). Equally serious for Athanasius was the essential damage to all humanity: the slow decomposition and death (un-creation) of the entire human race, compounded by the viciousness with which disintegrating humans treated each other.

Salvation then requires a full re-creation, putting humanity through the original mold which is the Logos, for he is the Image of God (Col. 1:15). Like the Antiochenes, Athanasius and subsequent Alexandrians saw that salvation involved renewed knowledge of God in Christ who revealed properly human ways of flourishing. Yet that example and teaching accomplished little without first (to use a computer image) God reprogramming the hopelessly compromised human hard drive. Only then could humans access and use the information of their own God-reflecting identity. Second, God must die to destroy death as both a corrupted condition and a legal sentence. God the Logos, who first created humanity, must personally live out human life as intended by God, recreate human nature, and die for humanity's disobedience (see Recapitulation in chap. 6). Therefore, for Athanasius and subsequent Alexandrians, the pre-existent Logos emptied himself into his very own "flesh" or human nature. This is not foreign to the divine Logos, seeing that humanity, though damaged, originated from the Logos and is by nature marked by the Logos's image.

While his Antiochene opponents objected that humanity is destroyed in the union and participation model, Cyril argued that humanity is rescued and then transformed into what it is supposed to be:

> For if [the Logos] had not suffered for us as man he would not have achieved our salvation as God. . . . For he who did not know death descended into death alongside us through his own flesh so that we too might rise up with him to life. And coming back to life he despoiled Hell, not as a man like us, but as God alongside us and for us in the flesh. Our nature is enriched with incorruptibility in him as the first, and death has been crushed since it launched a hostile attack against the body of Life itself.[31]

Salvation begins in the restoration of the first Adam ("enriched with incorruptibility in him as the first"). The incarnate Logos as the second Adam has drawn humanity into God's own life so that there is henceforth a godlike humanity. What humanity needs for salvation, in Cyril's view, is God living out a real human existence.

The Alexandrians believed that God the Logos somehow suffers and dies. Salvation would be impotent without God's personal involvement. Until he created his own human existence, the Logos could not suffer and die. But in his self-created humanity, suffering, dying, and all other naturally human experiences became his own. Divine transcendence took on limitation in order to transcend, so to speak, the limitations of divinity for the purpose of transforming human weakness into divine life.[32]

The end product of salvation for Cyril is a humanity that can enjoy real sonship with the incarnate Son. Through the incarnation, the Logos became a natural brother to all humanity. Through his death and resurrection, the Logos brings his human siblings into the intimacy of his unique sonship to the Father by grace. It is not a gift conferred through a mediator, the assumed man, who himself received the gift of sonship. Instead, it is a relationship extended by and within the Son directly.[33]

Cyril never claimed that divinization (*theōsis*) involved humans shifting from human stuff to divine stuff (*ousia*). Yet the Logos participates in our humanity to the same extent that he participates in the Trinity. Through the concept of participation or communion, Cyril anchored the Logos in a dual *homoousios*: with the Father, as in the Nicene Creed, and with us humans. Following Cyril's line of thought, the definition of Chalcedon (451) declared that "one and the same Son, our Lord Jesus Christ . . . [is] *consubstantial* with the Father as regards his divinity, and the same *consubstantial* with us as regards his human-ity."[34] Salvation is entry into a fellowship with the triune God that restores and enhances the intimacy enjoyed by the first humans before the fall.

CONCLUSIONS

With varying vocabulary and analogies, most Christians understood that a God-initiated and a God-completed salvation stood at the base of what it meant to be Christian.[35] The Nestorian version of Antiochene theology was not the mainstream, but represented a scholarly approach taken too far. Between the condemnation of Nestorius at Ephesus (431) and Cyril's death (444), Cyril showed flexibility in the terms he employed in order to preserve the notion of unity in the incarnate Logos that made salvation possible.[36] What motivated Cyril's Formula of Reunion (433) in the aftermath of Ephe-sus was his desire for levelheaded leaders to get past esoteric jargon in order to agree with the Nicene tradition. Somehow the divine Logos, the Son of God, the Only Begotten, became a real human being through a second birth by Mary the Theotokos, in order to save humanity. Earlier Cyril had pushed for "one incarnate nature of God the Logos," but he was willing to equate his favored "one nature" (*mia physis*) phrase with hypostasis.[37]

Most of the so-called Nestorians (the Orientals of Syria and Persia) agreed to this depiction of a single-person Christ. A few speculators eventually received posthumous condemnations against themselves or some of their writings: Nestorius at Ephesus in 431; Theodore of Mopsuestia, Theodoret of Cyrrhus, and Ibas of Edessa at Constantinople II in 553. Extreme Anti-ochenes' writings persisted in calling Christ "one thing and another" (Logos and assumed man) rather than the church's consensus at Chalcedon that Christ is "one and the same" in his divinity and humanity.

Nestorius was distracted in his grand plans for reforming the church through his position at Constantinople. His desire to keep his flock techni-cally precise in their devotional actions, language, and thought clashed decid-edly with most of the church. His demand for exacting language could not succeed when the object, God, by nature exceeded the verbal and conceptual capacities of human beings. Proclus of Constantinople had said as much in his homily on the Theotokos: "The Son became man (he himself knows how— to explain this miracle is beyond the power of speech)." That this happened, rather than how, was central to salvation for "had the Word [Logos] not dwelt in a womb, the flesh would never have sat on the throne."[38]

Early Christian thought about God, Christ, and salvation followed a gen-eral rule: while it is necessary to say that *X* is the case (God became a human being) and why X is the case (to save humanity), the faith does not require a static and exact understanding of how X actually happens. The limits of human understanding are at the same time rich opportunities for continuing speculation based upon believers' life in God.

God's presence in the lowly material of bread and wine in the Eucharist offered a regular drama and experience of God's paradoxical entry into the world of matter and change. However for Nestorius, believers had to exercise great care to avoid overstating what happens in communion. When Jesus claimed that eating his flesh and drinking his blood allows communion with him (John 6:22–59), for Nestorius, this meant no more and no less: communion in the flesh and the humanity of Jesus Christ, but not God.[39] In contrast Cyril pointed out that Christ promises

> the Eucharistic reception of the holy flesh and blood, which restores man wholly to incorruption. . . . Accordingly, the holy body of Christ endows those who receive it with life and keeps us incorrupt when it is mingled with our bodies. For it is not the body of anyone else, but [it] is thought of as the body of him who is Life by nature, since it has within itself the entire power of the Word that is united with it.[40]

In this text, Cyril warned believers not to absent themselves from the life-sustaining participation in the Logos himself through his body and blood. Shored by the paradoxical strains of Scripture, homilies, and hymns, most Christians felt their experience of the faith supported the Cyrillian models of Christ and salvation. The incarnation allows for no tidy solution, but rather, a mystery to savor and explore.

QUESTIONS FOR DISCUSSION

1. Why was impassibility such a central issue for Christians as they delved into their long-standing claim that Jesus is God?
2. How were the Antiochene emphases in thinking about the faith different from Alexandrian ones? How did this show up in their approaches to Scripture and Jesus Christ?
3. How did the Antiochene and Alexandrian models of Christ result in distinctive models of salvation?

SUGGESTED FURTHER READING

Behr, John. *The Nicene Faith*. 2 parts. Vol. 2 of *Formation of Christian Theology*. Crestwood, NY: St. Vladimir's Seminary Press, 2004.

———. *The Way to Nicaea*. Vol. 1 of *Formation of Christian Theology*. Crestwood, NY: St. Vladimir's Seminary Press, 2001.

Fairbairn, Donald. *Grace and Christology in the Early Church*. Oxford Early Christian Studies. New York: Oxford University Press, 2003.

Gavrilyuk, Paul L. *The Suffering of the Impassible God: The Dialectics of Patristic Thought*. New York: Oxford University Press, 2004.

Epilogue

Partings

In 431, as episcopal caravans headed toward the Council of Ephesus, Vandals were pillaging North African estates and forging a simulacrum of the empire they had just torn asunder. In 451, even as he prepared for the Council of Chalcedon, Theodoret of Cyrrhus worked tirelessly to offer hospitality to those fleeing the Vandals and other tribes pouring across the Western empire's undefended borders. The western half of the empire was slowly descending into chaos. Nestorius, embittered by his deposition and continued exile, described the chaos as God's punishment of the empire for enforcing his deposition and exile. While less prone to see himself as the center of God's activity in the world, Salvian of Marseilles also described the barbarian invasions as the wrath of God. Writing from what is now southern France, and as an eyewitness to the events he described, Salvian placed the blame squarely upon the moral failure of so-called Christians who, hiding from the reality of injustice on the one hand and invasions on the other, flocked to bloodfests, horse races, and bawdy shows at the circuses. Augustine, too, was distressed by the indifference of Christians to a Christlike lifestyle. However, he was less concerned with locating the wrath of God in particular events than he was with the natural, if painful, ebb and flow of governments in this fallen world.

Regardless of the reasons why, the collapse of the western portion of the empire made it increasingly difficult for diverse Christians to remain in contact with each other. Distinctive characteristics of Christians in the East and the West ceased to enrich the church and instead contributed to further mistrust and splintering. Distance made hearts grow more suspicious and, looking back, the fifth century marked a parting of ways. No one at the time would have believed that the separation would become permanent, just as no one could have believed that the Roman Empire would cease to be. Nevertheless, over the centuries the splintering of the church, and of Mediterranean civilization more generally, would become ossified into the medieval west and Byzantine east.

The seeds of this parting were planted well before Christianity entered the scene. Empires can hold separate cultures together for only so long. Ancient civilizations in Egypt, Syria, and Mesopotamia historically and culturally dwarfed their Roman conquerors. When conditions became unsettled, political allegiance to Rome frayed. Christianity contributed to the rending of the imperial fabric when Roman emperors outlawed views of Christ that had become part of the "national" identity of these ancient and still-distinct peoples. As contact between them became less frequent, mutual prejudices held by Greeks and Latins increasingly colored the way they looked upon each other. These attitudes petrified within the two cultures as former imperial territory fell under the tumultuous "rule" of barbarians. Each side came to regard itself as the true heir to the apostolic church.

The christological controversies of the fifth century brought this animus to the fore. In short, the questions that began this survey (Who is Christ? What does it mean to follow him?) can now be seen as contributing to the ever-widening chasm between East and West. Latin Christians grew increasingly frustrated with their Greek brothers and sisters, believing that they had philosophized to death the simple statement of faith that Jesus Christ is fully divine and fully human. Moreover, as the debates continued and underwent new and more convoluted permutations, Latins and Greeks developed different understandings of how the debates were to be resolved.

Both parties subscribed to the same decision at Chalcedon. However, it soon became apparent that their agreement resulted from equivocation more than from a true sense of harmony. Greek theologians increasingly focused on exploring the divine nature of Christ: what God does and how God is present in Christ. From Chalcedon through today, Greek Orthodox theology has dwelt on what it means to be in union with God. On one level, this is a christological issue. On another level, it is a soteriological issue, for Greek Orthodoxy has frequently described salvation as union with God, or divinization. The Latin West, on the other hand, would become increasingly concerned with the nature and limits of our humanity. Again, this is both a christological and soteriological question. Augustine and Pelagius argued bitterly over whether humans have any active role in a saving relationship with God. Augustine said no. The fall of Adam and Eve has corrupted all human will to the point that we cannot do anything to merit our own salvation. We are utterly dependent upon the saving work of Christ. In contrast, Pelagius said yes. God would not demand from us something that we cannot accomplish. If God tells us to act in a way that is pleasing to God, then it must be possible to act in that way. To say that we cannot please God would be to say that God is unjust, demanding from us what we have no hope of fulfilling. These questions of original sin, grace, and free will emphasize the human nature of Christ and the limits of our humanity.

Despite fundamental differences in their concerns and approaches, Pelagius and Nestorius shared a kindred spirit. The Antiochene and Alexandrian models of Christ revealed equally contrasting models of salvation. Pelagian views of human life relate well to Nestorius's two-person Christ. For both, the responsibility of salvation weighed heavily upon humanity to follow Christ's pioneering path of virtue. Giving God full credit for salvation, Augustine anticipated a Cyrillian destiny for humanity: unity with the Trinity in the resurrection. However, Augustine's attention as a pastor and thinker came to rest on powerless humanity, forever dependent upon divine grace. Consequently, his real impact upon Western Christianity would be to disown union with Christ (divinization) and to leave the door open for extreme pessimism about human potential even when assisted by divine grace.

The fifth-century councils (Ephesus and Chalcedon) showed how difficult it was for the church to operate as a transcultural family. Syrian and Mesopotamian Christians took up the "Nestorian" cause in honor of the former bishop's personal holiness and that of earlier Antiochene theologians. Some leaders moved beyond the limits of imperial authority and entered the well-established Persian Christian communities. The Persian Christians (so-called Nestorians) would have a distinguished future in tireless missions as far as China and India. They regularly held honored posts among the Persians, early Islamic Arabs in Persia (before the 9th c.) and the Mongols (13th c.), some of whom had been converted to Christianity.

Allegiance to the blessed memory of Cyril led to resistance to Chalcedon and the empire that enforced it. To Cyril's followers, the formula appeared to allow Nestorian vocabulary. Feeling that Cyril had been betrayed, whole regions (especially Egypt) threatened ecclesiastical and political secession. So began the non-Chalcedonian church. The Chalcedonians would call this church Monophysite (the Eutychian fused, single nature), even though "Miaphysite" (one subject or hypostasis) would be a more accurate rendering of the Cyrillian position. Desperate and frustrated emperors alternatively coerced unity among Christians or simply pretended that unity existed. Some negotiated new statements of faith (often rejected as heretical). Others sought unity by designating and persecuting a common enemy. These attempts continued until the seventh century, when Islamic Arab invaders tipped the scales in non-Chalcedonian lands like Egypt and Syria, and the lands fell forever from the control of Constantinople.

Contrary to the views of Cyril's followers, Chalcedon actually did adopt and remain relatively faithful to his views. In great part, their suspicions were due to the adoption of Leo I's *Tome* (a doctrinal letter to Patriarch Flavian of Constantinople) among Chalcedon's documents. And here another difficulty in being one church arose. The West took Leo I's *Tome* to be definitive of the council's intent. This would allow later Western Christians to think that the bishop of Rome had single-handedly resolved the Chalcedonian debate. Western self-congratulations should have been more muted. At the council, Leo's *Tome* was accepted only because it agreed with Cyril's theology. In subsequent negotiations with "Monophysites," Chalcedonians regularly offered to exclude the *Tome* from the council's supporting documents.

Ecumenical councils became sore points for the bishop of Rome. Rome had bristled at (and rejected) a canon of Chalcedon that recognized the church of Constantinople (and its bishop) as holding privileges equal to Rome, because Constantinople was the new imperial capital. Although not the first to promote papal primacy, Leo believed that Rome had a unique honor among all other churches. Papal tradition asserted that the church at Rome was heir to the apostle Peter's designation as the "rock" on which Jesus would "build [his] church" (Matt. 16:18). Honor rested on succession to Peter, Rome's first bishop, not the ebb and flow of imperial capitals. In a move rejected by the East, Rome would eventually move beyond honor to claim final jurisdiction over the entire Christian church. The Roman patriarchs adopted a fatherly attitude toward other patriarchs and expected to oversee their disputes, just as Leo thought he had overseen the disputes concerning Nestorius and Eutyches.

With the fall of the Western empire, Rome's monarchical ideas about the role of the bishop of Rome had room to become realities. After enough snubs from the East to its authority, Rome, the lone patriarchal outpost in the West, became accustomed to looking West and functioning as the remaining presence of the defunct western empire. Without regular contact, Latins and Greeks lost interest in each other except when they trod on each others' toes. Different practices led to different theologies, and Eastern and Western Christians eventually entered into a state of schism that lingers to this day between the Roman Catholic Church and the Chalcedonian Orthodox churches.

Notes

Chapter 1: "The One to Redeem Israel" (Luke 24:21)

1. Ekkehard W. Stegemann and Wolfgang Stegemann, *The Jesus Movement: A Social History of Its First Century*, trans. O. C. Dean (Minneapolis: Fortress Press, 1999), 141–42; Lester L. Grabbe, *Judaic Religion in the Second Temple Period: Belief and Practice from the Exile to Yavneh* (London: Routledge, 2000), 170–75.
2. Grabbe, *Judaic Religion*, 150–70.
3. E. P. Sanders, *Judaism: Practice and Belief, 63 B.C.E.–55 C.E.* (London: SCM Press, 1992), 119–45.
4. N. T. Wright, *The New Testament and the People of God*, vol. 1 of *Christian Origins and the Questions of God* (Minneapolis: Fortress Press, 1992), 291–97.

Chapter 2: "Are You the One Who Is to Come?" (Matt. 11:3)

1. See N. T. Wright, *Jesus and the Victory of God*, vol. 2 of *Christian Origins and the Questions of God* (Minneapolis: Fortress Press, 1996), 523–26.
2. Ibid., 125–31.
3. Johannes C. De Moor, "The Targumic Background of Mark 12:1–12: The Parable of the Wicked Tenants," *Journal for the Study of Judaism in the Persian, Hellenistic, and Roman Period* 29 (Fall 1998): 63–80.
4. Larry W. Hurtado, *Lord Jesus Christ: Devotion to Jesus in Earliest Christianity* (Grand Rapids: Wm. B. Eerdmans Publishing Co., 2003), 114.

Chapter 3: "Go Therefore and Make Disciples" (Matt. 28:19)

1. Luke Timothy Johnson, *The Writings of the New Testament: An Interpretation*, rev. ed. (Minneapolis: Fortress Press, 1999), 265–66.
2. *The Martyrdom of Justin, Chariton, Charites, Pæon, and Liberianus, Who Suffered at Rome* 3; in *ANF* 1:306.
3. Justin, *1 Apology* 23; in *ANF* 1:171.
4. Tertullian, *Apology* 32; in *ANF* 3:49.
5. *The Acts of Thecla*, in Bart D. Ehrman, *Lost Scriptures: Books That Did Not Make It into the New Testament* (New York: Oxford University Press, 2003), 113–21.
6. *The Acts of Thecla* 12; in Ehrman, *Lost Scriptures*, 116.
7. *The Acts of Thecla* 41; in Ehrman, *Lost Scriptures*, 121.
8. Howard Clark Kee, *Miracle in the Early Christian World: A Study in Sociohistorical Method* (New Haven: Yale University Press, 1983), 252–89.
9. *Acts of John*, trans. Knut Schäferdiek; in *New Testament Apocrypha*, vol. 2, *Writings Relating to the Apostles; Apocalypses and Related Subjects*, ed. Wilhelm

Schneemelcher, trans. Robert McLachlan Wilson (Louisville, KY: Westminster John Knox, 1992), 176.

10. Justin, *Dialogue with Trypho* 2–8; in *ANF* 1:195–99.

11. Melito of Sardis, *On Pascha: With the Fragments of Melito and Other Material Related to the Quartodecimans*, translated, introduced, and annotated by Alistair Stewart-Sykes (Crestwood, NY: St. Vladimir's Seminary Press, 2001).

12. Deborah Bleicher Carmichael, "David Daube on the Eucharist and the Passover Seder," *Journal for the Study of the New Testament* 42 (1991): 45–67; John Hainsworth, "The Force of the Mystery: Anamnesis and Exegesis in Melito's *Peri pascha*," *St. Vladimir's Theological Quarterly* 46, no. 2–3 (2002): 107–46.

13. See N. T. Wright, *The New Testament and the People of God*, vol. 1 of *Christian Origins and the Question of God* (Minneapolis: Fortress Press, 1992), 280–99.

14. Richard Bauckham, "The Worship of Jesus," in *The Climax of Prophecy: Studies on the Book of Revelation* (Edinburgh: T&T Clark, 1993), 118–49, esp. 133–40.

15. "Epistle of Ignatius to Polycarp" (longer version), 3; in *ANF* 1:94.

16. "Epistle of Ignatius to the Ephesians" (longer version); in *ANF* 1:49–58.

Chapter 4: *Christianus/a Sum*: I Am a Christian

1. Tertullian, *Apology* 40; in *ANF* 3:47.

2. *The Annals of Tacitus* 15.44.3, 7, ed. H. Furneaux, 2nd ed., ed. H. F. Pelham and C. D. Fisher (Oxford: Oxford University Press, 1907; reprint 1979), 374–75.

3. Suetonius, *Life of Nero* 16.2, Loeb Classical Library (New York: Macmillan, 1914), 110, my trans.

4. Tacitus, *The Histories* 5.5, trans. W. H. Fyfe, rev. D. S. Levene, Oxford World Classics (New York: Oxford University Press, 1997), 235.

5. *The Martyrdom of Pionius* 5; in *The Acts of the Christian Martyrs*, ed. and trans. Herbert Musurillo (New York: Oxford University Press, 1972), 142–43.

6. Tertullian, *Apology* 39; in *ANF* 3:47.

7. Clement, *Exhortation to the Greeks*, 1; in *Clement of Alexandria*, trans. George William Butterworth, Loeb Classical Library (New York: Macmillan, 1919), 27.

8. Clement, *The Instructor* 1; in *ANF* 2:209.

9. Tertullian, *To Scapula* 2; in *ANF* 3:106. On tax-paying, see idem, *Apology* 42.

10. Tertullian, *To Scapula* 2; in *ANF* 3:106.

11. Origen, *Contra Celsum [Against Celsus]* 8.73, trans. Henry Chadwick (New York: Cambridge University Press, 1953), 509.

12. *Epistle to Diognetus* 5; in *ANF* 1:27.

13. Origen, *Against Celsus* 8.66, trans. Chadwick, 502.

14. Justin, *1 Apology* 13; in *ANF* 1:166–67.

15. Justin, *2 Apology* 13; in *ANF* 1:193.

16. Tertullian, *On Idolatry* 14; in *ANF* 3:70.

17. Cyprian, *On the Lapsed* 7; in *ANF* 5:439.

18. Cyprian, "Letter 51 To Antonianus about Cornelius and Novatian" 16; in *ANF* 5:331.

19. G. W. Bowersock, *Martyrdom and Rome* (Cambridge: Cambridge University Press, 1995), 1–21.

20. Ignatius, *Letter to Smyrnaeans* 4; in *ANF* 1:87–88.

21. The letter from the Christians of Lyons and Vienne is found in Eusebius, *Church History* 5.1–2; in *NPNF*² 1:211–18.

22. Tacitus, *The Histories* 5.5, trans. Fyfe, 235.

23. Eusebius, *Church History* 5.1.35; in *NPNF*² 1:215.

24. Eusebius, *Church History* 5.1.11; in *NPNF*² 1:212.

25. Eusebius, *The Martyrs of Palestine*; in *Eusebius, Bishop of Caesarea: The Ecclesiastical History and the Martyrs of Palestine*, trans. H. J. Lawlor and J. E. L. Oulton, vol. 1 (London: SPCK, 1954), 331–33.

26. Maureen A. Tilley, "The Ascetic Body and the (Un)making of the World of the Martyr," *Journal of the American Academy of Religion* 59, no. 3 (Fall 1991): 467–79.

27. Eusebius, *Church History* 5.41; in *NPNF*² 1:215.

28. Ignatius, *Epistle to the Trallians* 10; in *ANF* 1:70.

29. *Martyrdom of Pionius* 1; in Musurillo, *Acts*, 134–35.

30. Origen, *Exhortation to Martyrdom* 4.37, trans. Rowan A. Greer, Classics of Western Spirituality (New York: Paulist Press, 1979), 41–79.

31. Origen, *Exhortation to Martyrdom* 37–38, trans. Greer, 69–70.

32. *Letter of the Smyrnaeans on the Martyrdom of Polycarp* 17; in *The Apostolic Fathers*, pt. 2, vol. 3, ed. and trans. J. B. Lightfoot, 2nd ed. (London: Macmillan: 1889, repr., Peabody, MA: Hendrickson Publishers, 1989), 394, my trans.

33. M. Therese Lysaught, "Witnessing Christ in Their Bodies: Martyrs and Ascetics as Doxological Disciples," *Annual of the Society of Christian Ethics* 20 (2000): 239–62.

34. *Martyrdom of Pionius* 22; in Musurillo, *Acts*, 164–65.

35. See Elizabeth Castelli, *Martyrdom and Memory: Early Christian Culture Making* (New York: Columbia University Press, 2004), 50–67.

36. Lysaught, "Witnessing Christ," 246–47.

37. Origen, *Exhortation to Martyrdom* 30; trans. Greer, 62.

Chapter 5: Scripture: From Jewish to Christian

1. See the insightful discussion by Theodore G. Stylianopoulos, "The Nature of Holy Scripture," in *The New Testament—An Orthodox Perspective: Scripture, Tradition, Hermeneutics*, vol. 1 (Brookline, MA: Holy Cross Orthodox Press, 1997).

2. Tertullian, *The Chaplet* 3; in *ANF* 3.95.

3. See the discussion by James R. Davila, *The Provenance of the Pseudepigrapha: Jewish, Christian, or Other?* Supplements to the Journal for the Study of Judaism in the Persian, Hellenistic, and Roman Periods 105 (Leiden: E. J. Brill, 2005); and Marinus de Jonge, *The Pseudepigrapha of the Old Testament as Christian Literature* (Leiden: E. J. Brill, 2003).

4. Annette Yoshiko Reed, "'Jewish Christianity' after the 'Parting of the Ways': Approaches to Historiography and Self-Definition in the Pseudo-Clementines," in *The Ways That Never Parted: Jews and Christians in Late Antiquity and the Early Middle Ages*, ed. Adam H. Becker and Annette Yoshiko Reed, Texts and Studies in Ancient Judaism 95 (Tübingen: Mohr Siebeck, 2003), 189–231.

5. Rodney Stark argues from a sociological standpoint that Diaspora Jews in the empire likely comprised the largest pool of converts well into the 3rd century; see his "Paul and the Mission to Hellenized Jews," in *Cities of God: The Real Story of How Christianity Became an Urban Movement and Conquered Rome* (San Francisco: HarperOne, 2006), 119–39. On Christian polemic against Judaizing

Christians, see Robert L. Wilken, *John Chrysostom and the Jews: Rhetoric and Reality in the Late Fourth Century* (Los Angeles: University of California Press, 1983).

6. Antti Marjanen, "Montanism: Egalitarian Ecstatic 'New Prophecy,'" in *A Companion to Second-Century "Heretics,"* ed. Antti Marjanen and Petri Luomanen, Supplements to Vigiliae christianae 76 (Leiden: E. J. Brill, 2005), 196–99, 207–8, 210.

7. *Epistle to Diognetus* 11; in *ANF* 1:29; emphasis added.

8. Harry Y. Gamble, *Books and Readers in the Early Church: A History of Early Christian Texts* (New Haven: Yale University Press, 1995), 126–27.

9. Harry Y. Gamble, "The New Testament Canon: Recent Research and the *Status Quaestionis*," in *The Canon Debate*, ed. Lee Martin McDonald and James A. Sanders (Peabody, MA: Hendrickson Publishers, 2002), 290.

10. Eusebius, *Church History* 6.12; in *NPNF*[2] 1:258.

11. John Behr, *The Way to Nicaea*, vol. 1, *Formation of Christian Theology* (Crestwood, NY: St. Vladimir's Seminary Press, 2001), 13, 35–48.

12. Martin C. Albl, *And Scripture Cannot Be Broken: The Form and Function of the Early Christian "Testimonia" Collections* (Leiden: E. J. Brill, 1999), 97–158.

13. Behr, *Way to Nicaea*, 25.

14. Justin, *Dialogue with Trypho* 56; in *ANF* 1:223.

15. Heikki Räisänen, "Marcion," in *Companion to Second-Century "Heretics,"* 113–16.

16. Irenaeus, *Against Heresies* 4.26.3; in *ANF* 1:498.

17. Origen, *On First Principles* 4.2.7 (Latin); in *Origen: On First Principles*, trans. G. W. Butterworth (New York: Harper Torchbooks, 1966), 283. "Watchings" are all-night prayer services more commonly translated as "vigils."

18. Origen, *Against Celsus* 6.4, trans. Henry Chadwick (New York: Cambridge University Press, 1953), 319.

19. *Homily XII on Exodus* 2; in *Origen: Homilies on Genesis and Exodus*, trans. Ronald E. Heine, Fathers of the Church 71 (Washington, DC: Catholic University of America, 1982), 368–69.

20. Origen, *Against Celsus* 7.20.

21. Frances M. Young, *Biblical Exegesis and the Formation of Christian Culture* (Peabody, MA: Hendrickson Publishers, 2002), esp. "Part II: The Bible as Classic" and "Part III: Language and Reference."

22. Origen, *Against Celsus* 6.5, trans. Chadwick, 319–20. *Against Celsus* 6.1 shows the elites' narrow sense of public good.

23. Young, *Biblical Exegesis*, 17–27.

24. *Homily V on Exodus* 5; in *Origen: Homilies on Genesis and Exodus*, 283–84.

25. Young, *Biblical Exegesis* 1–5, 186–213.

Chapter 6: Heresy: Congregational Dynamics and Theological Method

1. For positive and negative definitions of "proto-orthodox" respectively, see Larry W. Hurtado, *Lord Jesus Christ: Devotion to Jesus in Earliest Christianity* (Grand Rapids: Wm. B. Eerdmans Publishing Co., 2003), 494–95; and Bart D. Ehrman, *Lost Christianities: The Battles for Scripture and the Faiths We Never Knew* (Oxford: Oxford University Press, 2003), 13.

2. *St. Irenaeus of Lyons: Against Heresies, Book 1*, translated and annotated by Dominic J. Unger, rev. John J. Dillon, Ancient Christian Writers 55 (Mahwah, NJ: Paulist Press, 1992), 21–22.

3. Tertullian, *Against the Valentinians* 1; in *ANF* 3:504.
4. Tertullian, *Prescription against Heretics* 3.2, ed. R. F. Refoulé, Sources Chré-tiennes 46 (Paris: Les Éditions du Cerf, 1957), my trans.
5. Karen L. King, *What Is Gnosticism?* (Cambridge, MA: Belknap Press of Harvard University Press, 2003), 24–25.
6. Ptolemy, *Letter to Flora*, in Epiphanius, *Panarion* 33.3.1–33.7.10; in *The Panarion of Epiphanius of Salamis*, vol. 2, *Books II and III*, trans. Frank Williams (Leiden: E. J. Brill, 1993), 198–204.
7. See Karen L. King, "Why Is Gnosticism So Hard to Define?" in *What Is Gnosticism?* 5–19. Also, Michael Allen Williams, *Rethinking "Gnosticism": An Argument for Dismantling a Dubious Category* (Princeton, NJ: Princeton University Press, 1996).
8. See the cautionary discussion about the relationship between the fourth-century texts and their potential second-century versions, in Hurtado, *Lord Jesus Christ*, 533–37.
9. Johann Ferreira, *The Hymn of the Pearl: The Syriac and Greek Texts with Introduction, Translations, and Notes* (Sydney: St. Paul's Publications, 2002).
10. *Apocryphon of John*, trans. Frederick Wisse, in *Nag Hammadi Library in English*, ed. James M. Robinson, rev. ed. (San Francisco: HarperOne, 1990), 104–23.
11. The name derives from the title "Lord God of Hosts" (YHWH Sabbaoth).
12. *Nag Hammadi Library in English*, 222–23.
13. *Apocalypse of Peter*, in *Nag Hammadi Library in English*, 372–78.
14. *The Second Treatise of the Great Seth*, in *Nag Hammadi Library in English*, 363–71.
15. Williams, *Rethinking "Gnosticism,"* 199–201.
16. Philip Rousseau, *The Early Christian Centuries* (New York: Longman, 2002), 103–21.
17. Tertullian, *Prescription against Heretics* 3.5, my trans.
18. Irenaeus, *Proof of the Apostolic Preaching* 6, translated and annotated by Joseph P. Smith, Ancient Christian Writers 16 (Westminster, MD: Newman Press, 1952), 51. Other summaries can be found in Irenaeus, *Against Heresies*, e.g., 1.10.1 and 3.4.2.
19. Irenaeus, *Against Heresies* 3.3.1; in *ANF* 1:416.
20. Williams, *Rethinking "Gnosticism,"* 201.
21. Tertullian, *Prescription against Heretics* 11.3, my trans.
22. Tertullian, *Prescription against Heretics* 14; in *ANF* 3:249–50.
23. Origen, *On First Principles*, Preface 2–3; in *Origen: On First Principles*, trans. G. W. Butterworth (New York: Harper Torchbooks, 1966), 1–2.
24. For a valuable overview of the various approaches regarding divine transcendence that rubbed shoulders among the major Greco-Roman philosophies, see Paul L. Gavrilyuk, *The Suffering of the Impassible God: The Dialectics of Patristic Thought* (New York: Oxford University Press, 2004), 21–63.
25. Tertullian, *Against Marcion* 1.2; in *ANF* 3:272.
26. Tertullian, *Against Marcion* 1.9; in *ANF* 3:277.
27. Tertullian, *Against Marcion* 1.17; in *ANF* 3:283.
28. Plotinus, *Enneads* 2.9, "Against the Gnostics; or Against Those That Affirm the Creator of the Cosmos and the Cosmos Itself to Be Evil," in *The Enneads*, trans. Stephen MacKenna, abridged edition and notes by John Dillon (New York: Penguin, 1991), 108–32.
29. Irenaeus, *Against Heresies* 1.10.3, trans. Unger, 50.

30. Tertullian, *Against Marcion* 3.8; in *ANF* 3:328.
31. John Behr, *The Way to Nicaea*, vol. 1, *Formation of Christian Theology* (Crestwood, NY: St. Vladimir's Seminary Press, 2001), 123–24.
32. Parallels drawn from Irenaeus, *Proof of the Apostolic Preaching* 32–34, trans. Smith, 68–69. See also 1 Cor. 15 for resurrection, esp. vv. 21–22, 42–49; and Irenaeus, *Against Heresies* 3.21.10 recapitulation: analogy of the two Adams.
33. Irenaeus, *Proof of the Apostolic Preaching* 12, trans. Smith, 55.
34. Irenaeus, *Against Heresies* 3.18.1; in *ANF* 1:446.
35. Irenaeus, *Against Heresies* 3.18.7; in *ANF* 1:448.
36. Irenaeus, *Against Heresies* 5.16.2; in *ANF* 1:543.
37. Irenaeus, *Against Heresies*, Preface to book 5; in *ANF* 1:526.

Chapter 7: *Ekklēsia*: The People of God

1. Augustine, *Confessions* 8.4, trans. Henry Chadwick (New York: Oxford University Press, 1991), 136.
2. L. Kreitzer, "The Messianic Man of Peace as Temple Builder: Solomonic Imagery in Ephesians 2:13–22," in *Temple and Worship in Biblical Israel*, ed. John Day (New York: T&T Clark, 2005), 484–512. See also Bernard F. Batto, "The Covenant of Peace: A Neglected Ancient Near Eastern Motif," *Catholic Biblical Quarterly* 49, no. 2 (April 1987): 187–211.
3. Augustine of Hippo, *On the Words of the Gospel*, Matt. 8:8, "*I am not worthy that thou shouldest come under my roof,*" etc., *and of the words of the apostle*, 1 Cor. 8:10, "*For if a man see thee who hast knowledge sitting at meat in an idol's temple*"; in *NPNF*[1] 6:298–304.
4. Riemer Roukema, "The Good Samaritan in Ancient Christianity," *Vigiliae christianae* 58 (2004): 56–74.
5. Augustine, *Answer to Faustus, a Manichean* 12.14–21, intro. and trans. Roland Teske, *The Works of Augustine: A Translation for the Twenty-First Century*, ed. Boniface Ramsey, part 1, vol. 20 (Hyde Park, NY: New City Press, 2007), 135–39.
6. Leo I, *Sermon 26: On the Feast of the Nativity* 6.2; in *NPNF*[2] 12:137. On father and sons, see 6.4; in *NPNF*[2] 12:138.
7. *Didascalia apostolorum* 8; in *The Didascalia Apostolorum in Syriac*, vol. 1, *Chapters I–X*, trans. Arthur Vööbus, Corpus scriptorum Christianorum Orientalium 401, Scriptores Syri 176 (Leuven: Secrétariat du Corpus scriptorum Christianorum Orientalium, 1979), 90–98.
8. *Didascalia apostolorum* 9; in Vööbus, 100.
9. John Chrysostom, *Homily 3: On the Statues* 1.
10. John Chrysostom, *Homily 21: On the Statues* 6.
11. Cyril of Jerusalem, *Procatechesis* 13; in *Cyril of Jerusalem*, by Edward Yarnold (New York: Routledge, 2000), 84.
12. John Chrysostom, *To Those Who Had Not Attended the Assembly* 1–2; in *NPNF*[1] 1:223–24.
13. Asterius, *Homily 13: On Repentance*, 3.2.
14. Cyril of Jerusalem, *Mystagogical Catechesis* 5.10; in *St. Cyril of Jerusalem's Lectures on the Christian Sacraments: The Procatechesis and the Five Mystagogical Catecheses* (repr., Crestwood, NY: St. Vladimir's Seminary Press, 1977). Trans. F. L. Cross, Texts for Students 51 (London: SPCK, 1951), 74–75. See also the anaphora in the *Apostolic Constitutions* 8.4.41.
15. See Brian Daley's summary of Augustine's position on the dead, in *The Hope of the Early Church: A Handbook of Patristic Eschatology* (Peabody, MA: Hen-

drickson Publishers, 2003), 138–41; and Augustine, *City of God* 20.9 and 21.24; in *NPNF*[1] 2:1–511). See also Augustine, *Tractates on the Gospel of John* 49.10, where he includes all the dead, holy or not, in a waiting mode of sleep. The righteous already enjoy the promised rest and peace, but await "the resurrection of the flesh, the destruction of death, and eternal life with the angels," even as the unrighteous dead anticipate physical torment when they again receive bodies (*NPNF*[1] 7:274).

16. Augustine, *Sermon 142*, Appendix, "On the Burial of Catechumens," in *The Works of Saint Augustine: A Translation for the Twenty-first Century*, part 3, vol. 11, *Sermons: Newly Discovered Sermons*, trans. Edmund Hill, ed. John E. Rotelle (Hyde Park, NY: New City Press, 1997), 131–34.

17. Cyril of Jerusalem, *Procatechesis*, in *Catechetical Lectures*; in *NPNF*[2] 7:1–5.

18. Paul F. Bradshaw, "The Profession of Faith in Early Christian Baptism," *Evangelical Quarterly* 78, no. 2 (April 2006): 101–15.

19. Everett Ferguson, "Catechesis and Initiation," in *The Origins of Christendom in the West*, ed. Alan Kreider (New York: T&T Clark, 2001), 229–68.

20. Augustine, *On Faith and Works*, trans. Gregory J. Lombardo, Ancient Christian Writers 48 (Mahwah, NJ: Paulist Press, 1988).

21. Everett Ferguson, "Baptism from the Second to the Fourth Century," *Restoration Quarterly* 1, no. 4 (1957): 185–97; on infant baptism, see 191–93.

22. Excerpted from Cyril of Jerusalem, *Catechetical Lectures*; in *Creeds and Confessions of Faith in the Christian Tradition*, ed. Jaroslav Pelikan and Valerie Hotchkiss, vol. 1 (New Haven: Yale University Press, 2003), 95; on renunciation and allegiance, see Cyril of Jerusalem, *Mystagogical Lecture 19* 1.4–9; in *NPNF*[2] 7:145.

23. Ambrose of Milan, *On the Mysteries* 3.15; in *NPNF*[2] 10:319.

24. In the 430s, Prosper of Aquitaine created this maxim, which sums up the role of worship in anchoring knowledge of God in his defense of Augustine's view of grace. See "Official Pronouncements of the Apostolic See on Divine Grace and Free Will," article 8 in *Prosper of Acquitaine: Defense of St. Augustine*, translated and annotated by P. de Letter, Ancient Christian Writers 32 (New York: Newman Press, 1963), 183.

25. Theodore of Mopsuestia, *Catechetical Homilies* 15–16. See Enrico Mazza, *Mystagogy: A Theology of Liturgy in the Patristic Age*, trans. M. J. O'Connell (New York: Pueblo Publishing Co., 1989), 61–65.

26. *Ecclesiastical Hierarchy* in *Pseudo-Dionysius: The Complete Works*, trans. Colm Luibheid and Paul Rorem (New York: Paulist Press, 1987), 209.

27. Frederick G. McLeod, "The Christological Ramifications of Theodore of Mopsuestia's Understanding of Baptism and the Eucharist," *Journal of Early Christian Studies* 10, no. 1 (2002): 37–75.

28. *Egeria: Diary of a Pilgrimage* 25, trans. and annotated by George E. Gingras, Ancient Christian Writers 38 (New York: Newman Press, 1970), 93.

29. Peter R. L. Brown, *Power and Persuasion in Late Antiquity* (Madison: University of Wisconsin, 1992), 29–33, 41–47.

30. On the power of hymns, see Augustine, *Confessions* 9.6.14; trans. Chadwick, 164. On ambivalence of musical beauty, see *Confessions* 10.33.50; trans. Chadwick, 208.

31. *Ecclesiastical Hierarchy* 3 [Synaxis or Communion]–4 (myron, or ointment). See also Susan Ashbrook Harvey, *Scenting Salvation: Ancient Christianity and the Olfactory Imagination* (Berkeley: University of California Press, 2006).

32. Robin Margaret Jensen, *Understanding Early Christian Art* (New York: Rout-
    ledge, 2000), 103–29; Hugh Wybrew, *The Orthodox Liturgy: The Development
    of the Eucharistic Liturgy in the Byzantine Rite* (London: SPCK, 1989), 30–32.
33. Patricia Cox Miller borrows and adapts this phrase from art historian James
    Elkins, in her essay "Visceral Seeing: The Holy Body in Late Ancient Chris-
    tianity," *Journal of Early Christian Studies* 12, no. 4 (2004): 391–411. Asterius of
    Amaseia described this effect upon viewing Euphemia's depicted martyrdom
    in Chalcedon; see "Asterius of Amasea: *Ekphrasis on the Holy Martyr Euphe-
    mia,*" trans. E. A. Castelli, in *Religions of Late Antiquity in Practice*, ed. R. Valan-
    tasis, Princeton Readings in Religions (Princeton: Princeton University Press,
    2000), 464–69.
34. Cyril of Jerusalem, *Mystagogical Catechesis* 5.20–22.

Chapter 8: Cultivating Life in Christ

 1. For the body as a tool for knowing God, see Susan Ashbrook Harvey, "Embodi-
    ment in Time and Eternity: A Syriac Perspective," *St. Vladimir's Theological
    Quarterly* 43, no. 2 (1999): 105–30.
 2. Gregory of Nyssa, *On Virginity* 11; in *NPNF*[2] 5:17.
 3. See the reassessment of Gregory's asceticism at the outset of Martin Laird,
    "Under Solomon's Tutelage: The Education of Desire in the Homilies on the
    Song of Songs," *Modern Theology* 18, no. 4 (October 2002): 507–10.
 4. Gregory of Nyssa, *On Virginity* 11–12; in *NPNF*[2] 5:17–19.
 5. Jerome, *Against Jovinian* 1.36; in *NPNF*[2] 6:374.
 6. Jerome, *Letter 22: To Eustochium* 20.
 7. See Columba Stewart, "Flesh and Spirit, Continence and Chastity," chap. 4 in
    Cassian the Monk (New York: Oxford University Press, 1998), 62–84.
 8. John Cassian's teacher, Evagrius of Pontus, connected *apatheia* (control of dis-
    tractions) and love in the celibate monk. See David E. Linge, "Leading the
    Life of Angels: Ascetic Practice and Reflection in the Writings of Evagrius of
    Pontus," *Journal of the American Academy of Religion* 68, no. 3 (2000): 564–65.
 9. Stewart, "Flesh and Spirit," 74–75.
10. John Chrysostom, *First Instruction* 4; in *NPNF*[1] 9:162–63.
11. John Chrysostom, *Homily 6: On Fasting: Preached during the Sixth Week of
    the Holy Forty-Day Fast* 3; in *St. John Chrysostom: On Repentance and Almsgiv-
    ing*, trans. Gus George Christo, Fathers of the Church 96 (Washington, DC:
    Catholic University of America Press, 1998), 70.
12. See the excellent overview by Cornelia B. Horn, "Penitence in Early Chris-
    tianity in Its Historical and Theological Setting: Trajectories from Eastern
    and Western Sources," in *Repentance in Christian Theology*, ed. Mark J. Boda
    and Gordon T. Smith (Collegeville, MN: Liturgical Press, 2006), 153–86.
13. For example, John Chrysostom, *Homily 1: When He Returned from the Coun-
    tryside* (pp. 24–31); *Homily 3: Concerning Almsgiving and the Ten Virgins* (pp.
    19–23); both in *St. John Chrysostom: On Repentance and Almsgiving*.
14. Basil of Caesarea, *Letter 217 to Amphilochius*, canon 56. See also *Letter 188* and
    Letter 199.
15. Augustine, *Enchiridion* 45, trans. J. B. Shaw (Washington, DC: Regnery,
    1961; repr. 1996), 77.
16. Gregory of Nyssa, *Life of Moses* 10 and 320; in *Gregory of Nyssa: Life of Moses*,
    trans. Abraham J. Malherbe and Everett Ferguson (New York: Paulist Press,
    1978), 31, 137.

17. Basil of Caesarea, *Longer Responses* 6, on retirement; translated in Anna M. Silvas, *The Asketikon of St. Basil the Great* (New York: Oxford University Press, 2005), 178–80. Basil's *Rules* evince the bishop's interest in forming both formal ascetics attached to intentional communities and ascetics in the world. On the fluidity of ascetic life, see Philip Rousseau, *Basil of Caesarea* (Berkeley: University of California Press, 1994), 195–201.

18. Robert E. Sinkewicz, *Evagrius of Pontus: The Greek Ascetic Corpus* (New York: Oxford University Press, 2003), xxvi–xxxii. In the same volume, see also Evagrius's treatises *On the Vices*, *On the Eight Thoughts*, and *Praktikos*.

19. Athanasius, *Letter to Marcellinus* 13; in *Athanasius: The Life of Antony and the Letter to Marcellinus*, trans. Robert C. Gregg, Classics of Western Spirituality (New York: Paulist Press, 1980), 112.

20. *John Cassian: The Conferences*, trans. Boniface Ramsey, Ancient Christian Writers 57 (New York: Newman Press, 1997), esp. mountain of the transfiguration 10.6 (p. 375); fiery pure prayer 9.25 (pp. 345–46); life as prayer 10.7 (p. 376).

21. James E. Goehring, "The Encroaching Desert: Literary Production and Ascetic Space in Early Christian Egypt," in *Ascetics, Society, and Desert: Studies in Early Egyptian Monasticism* (Harrisburg, PA: Trinity International Press, 1999), 73–88.

22. For a good overview of monastic origins and vocabulary, see William J. Harmless, "Monastic Origins: Perspectives, Discoveries, and Disputed Questions," chap. 13 in *Desert Christians: An Introduction to the Literature of Early Monasticism* (New York: Oxford University Press, 2004), 417–58.

23. Basil of Caesarea, *Longer Responses*, Prologue 12; in Silvas, *Asketikon*, 159.

24. Basil of Caesarea, *Longer Responses* 2.67; in Silvas, *Asketikon*, 173.

Chapter 9: Cultivating Humanity

1. John Chrysostom, *How to Choose a Wife*; in *St. John Chrysostom: On Marriage and Family*, trans. Catherine P. Roth and David Anderson (Crestwood, NY: St. Vladimir's Seminary Press, 2003), 96.

2. Asterius of Amaseia, *Homily 5: Against Divorce* 4; in *Asterius of Amasea: Homilies I–XIV; Text, Introduction and Notes*, ed. Cornelis Datema (Leiden: E. J. Brill, 1970), 47.

3. Judith Evans Grubbs, *Law and Family in Late Antiquity: The Emperor Constantine's Marriage Legislation* (New York: Clarendon / Oxford University Press, 1995), 203–60.

4. Asterius, *Homily 5: Against Divorce* 4.

5. Asterius, *Homily 5: Against Divorce* 11.

6. John Cassian, *Conferences* 16.14; in *John Cassian: The Conferences*, trans. Boniface Ramsey (New York: Newman Press, 1997), 565.

7. See Carol Harrison, "Marriage and Monasticism," in *Augustine: Christian Truth and Fractured Humanity* (New York: Oxford University Press, 2000), 159–93.

8. David Hunter, *Marriage, Celibacy, and Heresy in Ancient Christianity: The Jovinianist Controversy* (New York: Oxford University Press, 2007), 280–84.

9. For an overview of the issue in patristic writings, see the passages in "Paradise Lost: Creation, Fall, and Marriage," in *Women in the Early Church*, by Elizabeth Clark, Message of the Fathers 13 (Collegeville, MN: Michael Glazier/ Liturgical Press, 1990), 27–76.

10. For example, Eucharistos the Secular (or "Worldly"), *Sayings of the Desert Fathers: The Alphabetical Collection*, trans. Benedicta Ward (Kalamazoo, MI: Cistercian Publications, 1975), 51.

11. Tyrannius Rufinus, *Historia monachorum* 16.3 and 16.7, my trans.; in Tyrannius Rufinus, *Historia Monachorum sive, De vita sanctorum patrum*, ed. Eva Schulz-Flugel, Patristische Texte und Studien, 34 (Berlin: Walter de Gruyter, 1990), 347.

12. Vigen Guroian, "The Ecclesial Family: John Chrysostom on Parenthood and Children," in *The Child in Christian Thought*, ed. Marcia J. Bunge (Grand Rapids: Wm. B. Eerdmans Publishing Co., 2001), 61–77. Chrysostom's term is "household" and assumed a variety of members, potentially including slaves and clients, but his focus is upon parents and children.

13. John Chrysostom, *Homily 20*; trans. Roth, 62.

14. *Homily 20*; trans. Roth, 61–62.

15. Plutarch, *Advice to the Bride and Groom* 20, trans. Donald Russell; in *Plutarch's Advice to the Bride and Groom, and A Consolation to His Wife: English Translations, Commentary, Interpretive Essays, and Bibliography*, ed. Sarah B. Pomeroy (New York: Oxford University Press, 1999), 8.

16. John Chrysostom, *Homily 12: On Colossians 4:18*; in Roth and Anderson, *On Marriage and Family*, 75.

17. John Chrysostom, *Homily 12: On Colossians 4:18*; in Roth and Anderson, *On Marriage and Family*, 75.

18. John Chrysostom, *An Address on Vainglory and the Right Way for Parents to Bring Up Their Children* 22; in M. L. W. Laistner, *Christianity and Pagan Culture in the Later Roman Empire* (Ithaca, NY: Cornell University Press, 1951), 96.

19. John Chrysostom, *Address on Vainglory* 47–49.

20. John Chrysostom, *Homily 21: On Ephesians 6:1–4*; in Roth and Anderson, *On Marriage and Family*, 67.

21. Evagrius of Pontus, *On the Eight Thoughts*, "Fornication" 6; in *Evagrius of Pontus: The Greek Ascetic Corpus*, trans. Robert E. Sinkewicz (New York: Oxford University Press, 2003), 76.

22. Asterius of Amaseia, *Homily 2: On the Unjust Steward* 6.2; in *Ancient Sermons for Modern Times*, trans. Galusha Anderson and Edgar J. Goodspeed (Chicago: Pilgrim Press, 1904), 58.

23. On Antony and the philosophers, see *Athanasius: The Life of Antony and the Letter to Marcellinus*, trans. Robert C. Gregg, Classics of Western Spirituality (New York: Paulist Press, 1980), 72–80. For Augustine's reaction, see *Confessions* 8.19, trans. Henry Chadwick (New York: Oxford University Press, 1991), 146.

24. Gillian Cloke, *This Female Man of God* (New York: Routledge, 1995), 212–19.

25. Cyril of Alexandria, *Homily 11*; in Luigi Gambero, *Mary and the Fathers of the Church*, trans. Thomas Buffer (San Francisco: Ignatius Press, 1999), 245.

26. Gregory of Nyssa, *Life of St. Macrina*; in Gregory of Nyssa, *Ascetical Works*, trans. Virginia Woods Callaban (Washington, DC: Catholic University of America Press, 1967), 163.

27. Michele Renee Salzman, *The Making of a Christian Aristocracy: Social and Religious Change in the Western Roman Empire* (Cambridge, MA: Harvard University Press, 2002), 205–8.

28. Gregory of Nazianzus, *Oration 14: On the Love of the Poor* 29, in Brian E. Daley, *Gregory of Nazianzus* (New York: Routledge, 2006), 92.

29. *Oration 14* 15; in Daley, *Gregory*, 83.

30. Basil of Caesarea, *In Famine and Drought*, trans. Susan R. Holman, in *The Hungry Are Dying: Beggars and Bishops in Roman Cappadocia* (New York: Oxford University Press, 2001), 77.

31. Holman, *The Hungry*, 77–98.

32. The last two quotations are from Daley, *Gregory*, 90 and 88.

33. Gregory of Nazianzus, *Oration 14* 26; in Daley, *Gregory*, 90.

34. John Chrysostom, *Homily 11: On 1 Thessalonians 5:19–22*; *Homily 1: On Colossians 1:1–2*; *Homily 1: On Philippians 1:1–2*.

35. Gregory of Nazianzus, *Oration 14* 18; in Daley, *Gregory*, 85.

36. Brian E. Daley, "Building the New City: The Cappadocian Fathers and the Rhetoric of Philanthropy," *Journal of Early Christian Studies* 7, no. 3 (1999): 431–61.

37. Peter R. L. Brown, "'Condescension': Poverty and Solidarity in the Eastern Empire," in *Poverty and Leadership in the Later Roman Empire* (Hanover, NH: University Press of New England, 2002), 74–112.

38. Holman, *The Hungry*, 161–162.

Chapter 10: Jesus Christ: Divine and Human

1. Early Christians used language about the intersection of God and Man (roughly humanity). Man/"humanity": Greek *anthrōpos*; Latin *homo*: humanity common to males and females; not the specifically masculine human being, which is *anēr/vir*.

2. Ephrem the Syrian, *Hymn 16: On the Nativity*, stanza 4; in *Ephrem the Syrian: Hymns*, trans. Kathleen E. McVey (New York: Paulist Press, 1989), 149.

3. *Hymn 3: On the Nativity*, stanza 15; in McVey, *Ephrem*, 86.

4. Ramsay MacMullen, *Voting about God in Early Church Councils* (New Haven: Yale University Press, 2006), 24–40.

5. See also Num. 23:19; 1 Sam. 16:7 [1 Kgs. 16:7 in Septuagint]; Job 9:32; in *The Septuagint with Apocrypha: Greek and English*, trans. Lancelot Charles Lee Brenton (London: Samuel Bagster & Sons, 1851; 3rd repr., Peabody, MA: Hendrickson Publishers, 1990).

6. Leo I, *Letter 59* 2; in *NPNF*[2] 12:59.

7. Paul L. Gavrilyuk, *The Suffering of the Impassible God: The Dialectics of Patristic Thought* (New York: Oxford University Press, 2004), 21–46.

8. David B. Hart, "No Shadow of Turning: On Divine Impassibility," *Pro ecclesia* 11, no. 2 (2002): 184–206.

9. Rowan Williams, *Arius: Heresy and Tradition*, rev. ed. (Grand Rapids: Wm. B. Eerdmans Publishing Co., 2001), 108–9.

10. John Behr, *The Nicene Faith*, vol. 2, *Formation of Christian Theology* (Crestwood, NY: St. Vladimir's Seminary Press, 2004), 208–15.

11. In *Creeds and Confessions of Faith in the Christian Tradition*, ed. Jaroslav Pelikan and Valerie Hotchkiss, vol. 1 (New Haven: Yale University Press, 2003), 159, 163.

12. Gregory of Nazianzus, *Letter to Cledonius*, trans. John McGuckin, *Saint Cyril of Alexandria and the Christological Controversy* (Crestwood, NY: St. Vladimir's Seminary Press, 2004), Appendix 2, p. 393; based upon *Letter 101*; in *NPNF*[2] 7:440.

13. John J. O'Keefe, "'A Letter That Killeth': Toward a Reassessment of Antiochene Exegesis, or Diodore, Theodore, and Theodoret on the Psalms," *Journal of Early Christian Studies* 8, no. 1 (Spring 2000): 83–104.

14. Frances M. Young, *Biblical Exegesis and the Formation of Christian Culture* (Peabody, MA: Hendrickson Publishers, 2002), 165–85.
15. John J. O'Keefe, "Impassible Suffering? Divine Passion and Fifth-Century Christology," *Theological Studies* 68 (1991): 52–57.
16. Young, *Biblical Exegesis*, 181.
17. Proclus, *Sermon 1* 1; in *Documents in Early Christian Thought*, ed. M. Wiles and M. Santer (New York: Cambridge University Press, 1975), 62.
18. Nestorius, *First Sermon against the "Theotokos"*; in *The Christological Controversy*, trans. and ed. R. A. Norris Jr. (Philadelphia: Fortress Press, 1980), 130.
19. Nestorius, *Second Letter to Cyril*; in Norris, *The Christological Controversy*, 137.
20. J. Warren Smith, "Suffering Impassibly: Christ's Passion in Cyril of Alexandria's Soteriology," *Pro ecclesia* 11, no. 4 (2002): 469–72.
21. Cyril of Alexandria, *Scholia on the Incarnation* 13; in McGuckin, *Saint Cyril*, 308.
22. Donald Fairbairn, *Grace and Christology in the Early Church*, Oxford Early Christian Studies (New York: Oxford, 2003), 22–23.
23. Ibid., 21–27.
24. Pelikan and Hotchkiss, *Creeds and Confessions:* on Nicaea, 159; on Constantinople, 163; on Chalcedon, 180–81.
25. Fairbairn, *Grace and Christology*, 40.
26. Brian E. Daley, *The Hope of the Early Church: A Handbook of Patristic Eschatology* (Peabody, MA: Hendrickson Publishers, 2003), 111–12.
27. Nestorius, *First Sermon against the "Theotokos"*; in Norris, *The Christological Controversy*, 128–29; emphasis added.
28. Fairbairn, *Grace and Christology*, 26.
29. *The Second Treatise of the Great Seth* and *Apocalypse of Peter*; in *Nag Hammadi Library in English*, ed. James M. Robinson, rev. ed. (San Francisco: HarperOne, 1990), 363–71, 372–78.
30. McGuckin, *Saint Cyril*, 215–16.
31. Cyril of Alexandria, *Letter to the Monks of Egypt 25–26*; in McGuckin, *Saint Cyril*, 260–61.
32. McGuckin, *Saint Cyril*, 201–3, 216–22.
33. On "sonship," see, Fairbairn, *Grace and Christology*, 78–104.
34. "The Fourth Ecumenical Council: The Council of Chalcedon, 451, Definition of Faith," in Pelikan and Hotchkiss, *Creeds and Confessions*, 180–81.
35. Fairbairn, *Grace and Christology*, 200–224.
36. McGuckin, *Saint Cyril*, 235–40.
37. Ibid., 209.
38. Proclus, *Sermon 1 on the Theotokos* 3 and 6; in Wiles and Santer, *Documents*, 63–64.
39. Nestorius, *The Synodical Deposition of Nestorius* (at Ephesus in 431); in McGuckin, *Saint Cyril*, 376.
40. Cyril, *Commentary on John* 3.6; in Norman Russell, *Cyril of Alexandria*, The Early Church Fathers (New York: Routledge, 2000), 110–11.

Index of Names of Persons

Abel and Cain, 123
Abraham
  Christians' view of, 88, 93, 103
  covenant between God and, 6, 8, 9, 16, 36
  and God's mercy, 29
  Gospel of Luke on, 36
  as patriarch, 88
  and Sarah, 104, 190
Adam and Eve
  Adam's dominion over beasts, 20
  first and second Adam (Christ), 134, 220,
    221, 223
  gnostics' view of, 122–23
  Jesus' humanity descended from, 100
  sexuality of, 189
  sin of, 123, 134, 188, 194, 196–97, 199,
    200, 213, 220, 222, 228–29
Alcibiades, 87
Alexander the Great, 2, 14
Ambrose of Alexandria, 88
Ambrose of Milan, 154, 159, 162
Antiochus IV Epiphanes, 14–15, 20, 21
Antony of Egypt, 181, 182, 195–96
Aristides, 56, 57, 60, 78
Aristotle, 78, 192, 194
Arius, 211
Asterius of Amaseia, 152–53, 186–87, 195,
    201–2
Athanasius of Alexandria, 178, 181, 195–96,
    214, 222–23
Attalus, 87
Augustine
  on baptism, 158, 169

baptism of, 155
and catechesis, 154, 155–56
and Christian worship before becoming
    Christian, 140, 162
on church as body of Christ, 148–49
on dead, 153–54, 237n15
death of, 143
and disintegration of Roman Empire, 227
education of, 191
on Good Samaritan parable, 149
on male-female creation, 194
on marriage, 171, 188–89
on Noah's ark image of church, 149
on original sin, 228, 229
pessimism of, about human potential, 229
on sacrament of repentance, 175–76
Augustus Caesar, 2, 47

Barnabas, 50, 56, 99, 103
Basil of Caesarea
  and Alexandrian school, 214
  on ascetic life in community, 182–83
  and care for lepers and the poor, 199–200,
    202
  education of, 191–92
  and episcopal complex at Caesarea, 199
  family of, 55
  liturgy of, 159, 176
  on prayer, 176–77
  and sacrament of repentance, 175
Blandina, 86–87, 197

Caesar, 3, 18, 20

Caiaphas, 37
Cain and Abel, 123
Cassian, John, 171, 179–82
Celsus, 48, 57, 58, 78, 116, 121–22
Cephas, 51
Chrysostom, John
  on attendance at worship, 152
  on baptism and prebaptismal instruction,
    172
  on Bible reading with children, 192
  on caring for vulnerable and needy, 202
  catechetical texts by, 154
  and distractions during liturgy, 176
  on fasting, 173
  on Flavian's intercession before Theodo-
    sius, 151
  on Good Samaritan parable, 149
  on male-female creation, 194
  on marriage and family, 186, 189–90
  on sacrament of repentance, 174–75
  true self at end of life, 195
  on wealthy elites, 202
Clement of Alexandria, 75, 80, 129
Clement of Rome, 94, 98
Cleopatra (of Ephesus), 58, 59
Clovis, King, 143
Constantine I (the Great), 47, 139, 140–42,
  145, 193
Constantius II, Emperor, 141
Cyprian of Carthage, 82, 83, 85
Cyril of Alexandria, 196, 213, 214, 217–19,
  222–25, 229
Cyril of Jerusalem, 152–58, 160, 163–64,
  196–97
Cyrus of Persia, 14

Daniel, 84
David, 8, 15, 19, 20, 22, 30, 35, 36, 41, 50
Decius, Emperor, 47, 73, 74, 82, 83, 88, 106
Didymus the Blind, 214
Diocletian, Emperor, 47
Diodore of Tarsus, 214, 215, 221

Egeria, Sister, 161, 162
Eleutherius, 101
Elijah, 20, 29, 35
Elisha, 29
Elizabeth, 35
Ephrem the Syrian, 206–7
Eusebius (of Caesarea in Palestine), 85, 86
Eutyches, 218, 230
Evagrius of Pontus, 177, 195

Eve. See Adam and Eve
Ezekiel, 12, 20

Felicitas, 197
Flavian (of Antioch), 151
Flavian (of Constantinople), 230
Flora, 119

Gratian, Emperor, 141
Gregory of Nazianzus, 198–203, 213, 214
Gregory of Nyssa
  and Alexandrian school, 214
  on baptism, 169
  on gender, 194, 196, 197
  Great Catechism by, 154
  on humanity created in image of God, 194
  Life of Moses by, 179–80, 196
  on Macrina, 197
  on marriage, 170
  on perfection of human nature, 176
  on virtue, 196, 197

Hermas, 56, 94
Herod Antipas, 18, 31, 33
Herod the Great, 19
Hilarion, 181
Homer, 104–5, 110

Ibas of Edessa, 224
Ignatius of Antioch, 52, 66–67, 84, 87,
  89, 101
Irenaeus of Lyons
  on apostolic tradition, 101, 128
  on gnosticism and other heresies, 117, 119,
    125
  on Good Samaritan parable, 149
  on Gospels, 99–100
  on incarnation, 134–36
  on recapitulation, 134–35
  on salvation, 133, 134–35, 221
  on spiritual disciple, 129–30
  on Treasure Hidden in a Field parable, 107
Isaac, 6, 8, 104
Isaiah, 9, 10, 12, 13, 27–28, 208

Jacob, 6, 8
James (son of Zebedee), 31, 35
James (the Just), 51, 53
Jefferson, Thomas, 105
Jehoiachin, 14
Jeremiah, 5, 9, 12, 19, 27
Jerome, 171, 181, 188, 189

Job, 208
Joel, 50
John (apostle)
   and *Acts of John*, 52–53, 58, 59
   son of Zebedee, 31, 35, 53
John the Baptist, 5, 18, 26–27, 29, 31, 33,
   35–36, 50–51
Joseph (patriarch), 9
Josephus, Flavius, 19, 31
Joshua, 19, 104
Josiah, 9
Jovinian, 188
Judas Maccabee, 14, 15
Julian, Emperor, 141
Justin Martyr
   on baptism, 61
   conversion of, 59–60
   on Eucharist, 63
   on Jesus Christ, 55, 78–79, 103–4
   on Logos, 78–79, 103–4
   on persecutions of Christians, 57
   as philosopher, 59–60, 117
   on Scripture, 103–4
   treatises by, 58
   on worship, 97

Lactantius, 47
Leo I (the Great), 143, 149–50, 173,
   175, 230
Luke, 50
Lycomedes, 58, 59

Macrina, 197
Malachi, 20
Marcion, 99, 103, 104–5, 112, 128, 131
Marcus Aurelius, Emperor, 46
Mary
   Cyril of Alexandria on, 217–18
   Ephrem the Syrian on, 206–7
   obedience of, contrasted with Eve's
     disobedience, 134, 196–97
   as Theotokos, 215–16, 224
   virginity of, and Jesus' conception, 35, 52,
     67, 212
Melito of Sardis, 62–63
Montanus, 96, 118
Moses
   and covenant between God and Israel, 12,
     16, 38, 50
   death of, 16
   and exodus of Israelites, 111
   farewell speeches of, 35

   and God's mercy, 29
   God's presence with, on Mount Sinai, 38,
     179–80
   and idolatry of Israelites, 37, 103
   Jesus associated with, 28, 35, 94, 103
   and tabernacle, 147
   and transfiguration of Jesus, 35
   and YHWH as name of God, 10, 42
   and YHWH in burning bush, 6, 104, 180

Nathanael, 33
Nero, Emperor, 71
Nerva, Emperor, 46
Nestorius of Constantinople, 213–17, 219–
   21, 224–25, 227, 229
Nicodemus, 33
Noah, 61, 149
Novatian, 83

Origen of Alexandria
   on baptism associated with Israelites' exo-
     dus, 169
   on Good Samaritan parable, 149
   on infant baptism, 156
   as influence on Alexandrian school, 214
   life of, 106–7
   and martyrdom, 88, 89, 106
   on miracles, 59
   on monotheism, 78
   on moral community and virtues of Chris-
     tians, 55, 57, 77
   on rule of faith, 129
   on Scripture, 106–12, 115, 178
   on threefold God, 210

Paphnutius, Abba, 189
Paul
   apostolic teaching of, 101
   on celibacy, 57, 170
   on Christlikeness of Christians, 55–56
   citation of Jewish Scripture by, 102
   on citizenship, 76
   on covenant, 43
   on crucifixion of Jesus, 41, 42, 43
   on Eucharist, 61, 63, 206
   on first and second Adam, 134
   on Gentiles, 42–43, 51
   on gods, 77–78
   on God's foolishness as wiser than human
     wisdom, 196
   gospel/good news of, 40–41, 51
   on Holy Spirit, 99

Paul (*continued*)
  imprisonment of, 57
  on Jesus as Lord, 41–43
  on Jesus as Messiah, 5, 32, 40–43
  Letters of, 40–43, 53, 54, 57, 95, 96, 98, 99, 102, 134
  and Marcion, 105
  on membership in God's family, 193
  on "mind of Christ," 177
  missionary activity of, 53
  on pagan origins of Gentiles, 51
  on peaceable living, 45
  on people of God, 42–43
  and Pharisees, 27, 41
  on prayer, 177
  preaching of, and Thecla, 57
  pre-Christian life of, 40, 41
  on resurrection, 40, 42, 51, 148
  on salvation, 42
  on Scripture, 111
  on Spirit-bestowed gifts, 54
  See also specific letters by Paul in Index of Subjects
Paul the Hermit, 181
Pelagius, 228–29
Perpetua, 81, 87–88, 197
Peter
  and *Acts of Peter*, 58, 59
  and *Apocalypse of Peter*, 124, 221
  and crucifixion of Jesus, 124
  and *Gospel of Peter*, 99, 100
  on Jesus as Messiah, 5, 18
  line of apostolic teaching from, 101
  messiah's meaning for, 18, 31
  miracles of, 58
  and Pentecost, 50
  preaching by, 94
  as rock/foundation of church, 31, 230
  and Simon the Magician, 58, 59
  and spreading the gospel, 53
  and transfiguration of Jesus Christ, 35
  on witnesses to risen Jesus, 84
Philo of Alexandria, 105
Pilate, Pontius, 16, 35, 52, 86
Pionius, 74, 88–89
Plato, 110, 120, 161
Pliny the Elder, 70
Pliny the Younger, 70–73
Plotinus, 131
Plutarch, 187, 190
Polycarp of Smyrna, 84, 86, 88, 89
Pompey, 15

Ponticus, 87
Pothinus, Bishop, 87
Proclus of Constantinople, 216, 224
Prosper of Aquitaine, 237n24
Pseudo-Barnabas, 56, 99, 103, 104
Pseudo-Dionysius the Areopagite, 160–63
Ptolemy, 119

Rehoboam, 8
Romulus Augustulus, Emperor, 142

Sabellius of Rome, 210
Salvian of Marseilles, 227
Samaritan woman, 33
Sarah, 104, 190
Septimius Severus, Emperor, 72
Serapion, Bishop of Antioch, 100
Seth, 123
Simon the Magician, 58, 59
Socrates, 77, 84
Solomon, 6, 8, 14, 15, 17, 28
Stephen, 148
Suetonius, 71

Tacitus, 71, 84
Tatian, 98
Tertullian
  on Christian service to needy, 56
  on citizenship, 76
  on gnosticism, 128
  on God, 131
  on heresy, 117–18, 127–29
  on interactions with non-Christians, 80–81
  on Jesus Christ, 133–34
  on marriage, 86
  and Montanists, 97
  on moral community of Christians, 56, 57
  on pagans, 145
  on resurrection, 133–34
  on rule of faith, 127–29
  on scapegoating of Christians, 71
  on spread of Christianity, 67
  on threefold God, 127
  on training of Christians, 85–86
  on worship, 75
Thecla, 57
Theodore of Mopsuestia, 154, 160, 161, 214, 215, 221, 224
Theodoret of Cyrrhus, 214, 224, 227
Theodoric, King of the Ostrogoths and of Italy, 143

Theodosius I, Emperor, 141, 142, 151, 154
Theodosius II, Emperor, 187
Thomas, Apostle, 53
Tiberius Caesar, Emperor 2
Trajan, Emperor 70–73

Valens, Emperor, 142

Valentinus, 118, 119
Victorinus, Marius, 146, 158
Virgin Mary. *See* Mary

Zadok, 15, 20
Zechariah, 30, 35–37
Zerubabbel, 19

Index of Subjects

Acts, book of, xv, 50, 52, 61, 84, 103, 148, 161
Acts of John, 52–53, 58, 59
Acts of Peter, 58, 59
Acts of Thecla, 57
Acts of Thomas, 53
Address on Vainglory (John Chrysostom), 190
Adrianople, Battle of, 142
adultery, 83, 174, 186, 187
afikoman, 62–63
Against Heresies (Irenaeus of Lyons), 99, 117, 129–31, 133, 134
agapē (love), 63–64, 187
Alexandrian school, 213–19, 221–25, 229
anchorites, 181–82
angels, 32, 35, 37, 65, 77, 99, 122, 170, 171, 189, 237n15
Antiochene school, 213–21, 224–25, 227, 229
apatheia (impassibility), 208–9, 214
Apocalypse of Peter, 124, 221
apocalyptic literature, 64–66, 94
Apocrypha, 94
Apocryphon of John, 122–24
apologists for Christianity, 74–79
apostasy, 117
apostates, 82–83
apostles, 53. *See also specific apostles in Index of Names of Persons*
apostolic tradition, 101, 128
Apostolic Tradition, 177
Arians, 211
Aristotelians, 59

ascesis
    communal ascesis, 180–84
    definition of, 168
    and monasticism, 180–84, 189
    ordinary ascesis, 172–73
    and prayer, 176–80
    and sacrament of repentance, 174–76
    and sex, chastity, and love, 170–71, 194–95
    and wisdom, 169
Askētikon (Basil of Caesarea), 182
Assyrians, 11, 14

Babylonian exile, 11–14
baptism
    adult baptism, 156–58, 160
    apostles on repentance and, 50
    of Augustine, 155
    birth at, 151
    and Holy Spirit, 61, 157
    images of, 61, 111, 169
    infant baptism, 156
    Justin Martyr on, 61
    Leo I on, 149–50
    liturgy for, 61, 156–58
    preparation for, 128, 154–56, 172
    renunciation of Satan at, 157, 174
    and worship, 159
Bar Kokhba revolt, 95
Bible. *See* Hebrew Bible; Scripture; Septuagint; and *specific books of the Bible*
bishops, 150–53, 175–76, 203. *See also specific bishops in Index of Names of Persons*

Caesarea (in Cappadocia), 199–200
canon, 100, 101
catechesis, 154–56
Catechetical and Mystogogical Lectures (Cyril of
    Jerusalem), 154
celibacy, 57, 170, 188–89
cenobite, 181
chastity, 57, 170–72
chorbishops, 151
Christ. *See* Jesus Christ
Christianity
    apologists for, 74–79
    and ascesis, 168–76
    and care for vulnerable and needy, 56, 67,
        72, 76, 183–84, 198–204
    categories of Christians, 124–25
    and citizenship, 68, 73–74, 76–77
    and class and gender, 192–97
    communal element of, xv–xvii
    conversion to, 46, 54–60
    creeds of, 52, 67–68, 157, 212
    and cultivating humanity, 185–204
    and cultivating life in Christ, 167–84
    and daily life, 79–81
    defining who is Christian, 79–83
    and *ekklēsia* (church), 139, 145–64
    evaluation of Christian writings, 99–101
    God of, xv, 77–79
    golden age of, 139–43
    and heresy, 115–36
    historical context of, 2–3, 46–48, 140–43
    issues overview on, 1–2, 45–46
    Jewish connection with and Hebrew Bible,
        72–73, 91–95, 102, 111–12
    and Lord's Supper, 60–64
    and love, 56
    and martyrs, 45, 84–90
    message of, 49–54
    and miracles, 58–59
    missionaries of, 52–54
    and monotheism, 45, 46, 67, 72, 78, 210
    moral community of, 55–57
    and peaceable living, 45, 69–90
    and prayer and perfection, 176–80
    and repentance, 50, 51, 174–76
    and Roman Empire, 67–79, 145
    and rule of faith, 126–32
    and salvation, 51–52, 132–36
    and Scripture, 45–46, 89–112
    and self-control, 56–57
    and Spirit-bestowed gifts, 54
    spread of, during first two hundred years
        of, 48–68

and story of Jesus, 50–52, 98, 126
    See also baptism; church; Eucharist; Jesus
        Christ; persecutions of Christians;
        sacraments; worship
church
    architecture of basilicas, 163
    art in, 163
    and bishops, 150–53, 175–76, 203
    as body of Christ, 148–49, 221
    and catechesis, 154–56
    and catechumens, 154–55, 162–63, 172
    and dead, 153–54
    ekklēsia as, 139, 146
    as family, 150–54, 189
    and God's temple, 147–48
    and Good Samaritan parable, 149
    images for being church, 147–50
    lay Christians' responsibilities in, 152–53
    Leo I on, 149–50
    membership in, 154–58
    and Noah's ark, 149
    and patriarchs, 151, 230
    titles and roles in early church, 53–54
    See also baptism; Christianity; worship
circumcision, 3, 6, 15, 17, 42, 43, 61, 72, 104
citizenship of Christians, 68, 73–74, 76–77
class and gender, 192–97
Clement, first letter of, 99
Colossians, Letter to, 52, 66, 190, 221, 222
Commentary on Jeremiah (Origen), 108
Commentary on Matthew (Origen), 107
communication of idioms, 217
communion. *See* Eucharist
Conferences (Cassian), 172
confession. *See* repentance, sacrament of
Confessions (Augustine), 158, 162, 191
confessors, 83, 87, 107
Constantinople, 140, 142, 215, 224, 229–30
conversion to Christianity, 46, 54–60
Corinthians, Letters to
    on celibacy, 57, 170
    on church as body of Christ, 148
    on Eucharist, 206
    on exodus from Egypt as image of baptism,
        111
    on glory of God, 169
    on gods, 77–78
    on God's foolishness as wiser than human
        wisdom, 196
    on Holy Spirit, 54, 99
    on Jesus as Messiah, 32, 41, 42
    on Lamb of God, 62
    on Lord's Supper, 61, 62, 63

on marriage, 190
on moral community of Christians, 56, 57
on resurrection of the body, 132, 133
on salvation, 221
on Scripture, 111
on Spirit-bestowed gifts, 54
on story of Jesus, 51
on sufferings of Paul, 53
Council of Chalcedon, 142, 143, 218, 219,
    223–24, 227–30
Council of Constantinople, First, 142, 211
Council of Ephesus, 143, 219, 224, 227, 229
Council of Nicaea, First, 63, 140, 211–12
covenant
    between God and Israel, 6, 8, 9, 12, 13,
        16–18, 22, 103, 147
    Jesus and covenant relationship with God,
        32, 34–43
    Paul on, 43
    themes of covenant hope, 36–37
Creed of Jerusalem, 157
creeds of Christianity, 52, 67–68, 157, 212
crucifixion of Jesus
    and cry of dereliction by Jesus, 221
    and Eucharist, 62–63, 160
    gnostic view of, 124
    Gospels on, 33–34, 52
    and humanity's disobedience, 134–35,
        222–23
    Ignatius of Antioch on, 66
    and new covenant of the heart, 148
    Paul on, 41, 42, 43
    political reasons for, 3, 31
    and salvation, 124, 134

Daniel, book of, 15, 20, 21, 37, 64, 65
dead, 153–54, 237n15
death of Jesus. See crucifixion of Jesus
demons, 30, 33, 77, 111
Deuteronomy, book of, 7–9, 32, 35, 37,
    42, 56
Dialogue with Trypho (Justin Martyr) 59, 61,
    104, 117
Diaspora, 11, 17, 18
Diatesseron (Tatian), 98
diathesis (love), 187
Didache, 54, 55, 56, 60, 61, 63, 94, 96, 101, 173
Didascalia Apostolorum, 150
distractions, diagnosis of, 176–77
divorce, 186, 187. See also marriage
Donatists, 83

Easter/Pasch, 60, 62–64, 156, 172–73

Ecclesiastical Hierarchy, The (Pseudo-
    Dionysius), 160–61
ecumenical councils. See headings beginning
    with Council
Egypt, 8, 9, 37, 111–12
ekklēsia (church), 139, 146, 167–68. See also
    church
elders, 181
Enlightenment, 105
Enoch, books of, 21
Ephesians, Letter to, 43, 54, 55, 134, 147,
    186, 189
Ephesus, 52–53, 58. See also Council of
    Ephesus
Eucharist
    anaphora prayer before, 153
    and crucifixion of Jesus, 62–63, 160
    Cyril of Jerusalem on, 163–64
    declining participation in, 164, 172
    and Easter, 173
    following baptism, 157
    God's presence in, 225
    as incarnate experience of divine, 163–64
    and incarnation of Christ, 206–8
    and Last Supper, 62, 206
    and Logos, 225
    Nestorius on, 225
    as nourishment, 151
    as thanksgiving, 63
    and union with Christ and communion
        with other Christians, 145, 148, 158, 225
    and worship, 159
    See also Lord's Supper
eupatheiai (good passions), 208, 209
evil
    Christian beliefs on, 130–32
    and demons, 30, 33, 77, 111
    evil thoughts, 177
    gnostics on origins of, 121–24
    and goodness of God, 130–32
    renunciation of Satan at baptism, 157, 174
    See also sin
Exhortation to the Greeks (Clement of Alexan-
    dria), 75
Exodus, book of, 6–8, 10, 16, 62, 80, 129,
    147, 179
exodus of Israelites, 8, 9–10, 16, 37, 61, 62,
    102, 104, 110–11, 169
Exposé and Overthrow of What Is Falsely Called
    Knowledge (Irenaeus). See Against Heresies
    (Irenaeus)
Ezekiel, book of, 12, 21, 100, 147
Ezra, book of, 14

faith, 126–30
families, 189–92. *See also* marriage
fasting, 173, 175
Feast of Dedication (Hanukkah), 15, 16
Formula of Reunion, 224
Franks, 143
friendship, 187

Galatians, Letter to, 27, 42, 53, 193
gender and class, 192–97
Genesis, book of
  on Abraham and covenant promises, 16
  creation story of, 38, 78, 194, 222
  on fall of Adam and Eve, 222
  gnostics on, 122–23
  on Jacob, 5
  on sexuality of Adam and Eve, 189
  in Torah, 7
Gentiles
  as converts to Christianity, 46
  and Jesus on people of God, 38–39
  judgment of, by God, 31
  pagan origins of, 51
  Paul on, 42–43, 51
  and spread of Christianity, 49
gnosticism
  beliefs of generally, 116, 118–20
  and fall and origins of evil, 121–24
  and God, 116, 120, 121–22, 125, 131
  Irenaeus on, 119, 125
  and Jesus Christ, 116, 121–25, 132
  and Nag Hammadi library, 119
  Plotinus on, 131
  and rule of faith, 128–30
  and salvation and orthodox ignorance,
    123–26, 132–33
  and Scripture, 106, 112, 120, 126–27
  Tertullian on, 128
  and unorthodox seeking, 128–30
God
  of action, for Jews and Christians, 16
  agent of, and Jews, 18–21
  anthropomorphic characteristics of, 117,
    207–8
  apatheia of, 208–9, 214
  Aristotelian concept of, 78
  of Christians, xv, 77–79
  covenant between Israel and, 8, 9, 12, 13,
    16–18, 22, 32, 103, 147
  glory of, 169
  gnostic beliefs on, 116, 120, 121–22, 125,
    131
  goodness of, 130–32, 136

holiness of, 209
humanity created in image of, 194, 200,
  203
humans' managing wealth of, 201–2
and Jesus as Word/Logos, 38, 59, 78–79,
  110, 161
Jesus on kingdom of God, 38–39
Jews as chosen people of, 1–2, 5–7
as love, 179–80, 209
prayer and vision of, 178–80
relationship between Christians and, xv
temple of, 147–48
Tertullian on, 131
threefold God, 46, 78, 127, 151, 157, 210
transcendence of, 208, 218, 223
wrath of, 227
as YHWH (Lord), 6, 10, 13, 32, 38, 41–42,
  105, 106, 112, 116, 125
See also monotheism
Golden Rule, 56
Good Samaritan parable, 149
Gospel of Peter, 99, 100
Gospels
  good news of, 25–28, 35–36, 40, 49–50, 132
  inconsistencies among, 98
  Irenaeus on, 99–100
  of Jefferson, 105
  on Jesus as Messiah, 25–43
  and Marcion, 105
  parables in, 39, 107, 120, 149, 198
  as story of Jesus, 50–52, 98, 126
  symbols of, 99–100
  Synoptic Gospels, 25–26, 33, 39, 98
  See also Scripture
Goths, 142
grace, 221, 229
Great Catechism (Gregory of Nyssa), 154

Hanukkah (Feast of Dedication), 15, 16
Hasmoneans, 14–15, 19–20
Hebrew Bible, 7, 91–95, 102, 105, 106, 111–
  12. *See also* Septuagint; Torah; and *specific
  book of Hebrew Bible*
Hebrews, 5. *See also* Israelites; Jews
Hebrews, Letter to, 89, 98, 99, 148, 207, 221
heresy
  definition of, 115
  Greek meaning of, 116
  Jewish "heresies," 116
  and pastoral crisis, 116–18
  Tertullian on, 117–18, 127, 128, 129
  See also gnosticism
hermits, 181–82

Hexapla, 106
holiness
  and Christians, 67
  of God, 209
  and Jews, 17–18, 22, 36
Holy Spirit
  and baptism, 61, 157
  gifts of, 54, 58, 59, 88, 182–83
  and God's covenant through Christ, 95
  and Logos, 104
  and Lord's Supper, 62
  and martyrs, 88
  outpouring of, 50
  Paul on, 99
  prophecy and revelations of, 96
  and psalms, 178
  and Scripture, 108, 110
  and spread of Christianity by missionaries,
    52–54
  and threefold God, 46, 78, 151, 157, 210
  and worship, 65, 66
Homilies (Pseudo-Clement) 94
homilies, 161–62, 197–98, 203–4
homoousios (same essence), 211–13, 215–18,
  223
hope
  and covenant between God and Israel,
    36–37
  and early-Christian views of Jesus, 64–67,
    84
Hosea, book of, 9, 207
humanity
  and care for vulnerable and needy, 56, 67,
    72, 76, 183–84, 198–204
  and class and gender, 192–97
  creation of, in God's image, 194, 200, 203
  as diamonds in the rough, 199–200
  and families, 189–92
  and managing God's wealth, 201–2
  and marriage, 186–89
  seeing and being human, 197–204
  See also incarnation of Jesus Christ
Huns, 142, 143
Hymn of the Pearl,The, 120
hypostases (freestanding individuals), 210, 219
hypothesis (plot), 110

idolatry, 37, 51, 80, 83, 103, 104, 174
Iliad (Homer), 104–5
incarnation of Jesus Christ
  and Alexandrians and Cyril of Alexandria
    on Logos, 217–25
  Arius on, 211

  and Eucharist, 206–8
  and God's *apatheia*, 208–9
  Ignatius on, 67
  Ireneaus on, 134–36
  and *kenōsis*, 208–9
  and Mary as Theotokos, 215–16, 224
  and mystery of worship, 159, 160
  and Nestorius on "assumed man," 214–17,
    219–21, 223, 224
  Origen on, 107
India, 53
Infancy Gospel of Thomas, 99
infant baptism, 156. *See also* baptism
Instructor (Clement of Alexandria), 75, 80
Isaiah, book of
  on Babylonian exile, 13–14
  on disobedience of Israelites, 10, 27
  divine throne scene in, 160
  exilic lament in, 36
  on exodus of Israelites, 12
  on God's rescue of his people, 21, 27–28
  on new heaven and new earth, 108, 132
  on resurrection, 22
  on Suffering Servant, 21
  on vineyard, 39
Israel, kingdom of, 8–9, 147
Israelites
  as chosen people of God, 5
  covenant between God and, 8, 9, 12, 13,
    16–18, 22, 32, 103, 147
  end of kingdoms and exile of, 8–14
  exodus of, 8, 9–10, 16, 37, 61, 62, 102, 104,
    110–11, 169
  idolatry by, 37, 103
  Jesus as vindicated Israel, 37
  plundering of Egyptian goods by, 129
  See also Jews

James, Letter of, 99
Jeremiah, book of, 12, 19, 27, 108, 148
Jesus Christ
  Alexandrian and Antiochene debates on,
    213–25, 227, 229
  and beloved disciple, 187
  church as body of Christ, 148–49, 221
  and covenant, 32, 34–43
  demons controlled by, 30, 33, 111
  divine-human status of, 66, 203, 205–25,
    228–30
  as failed Messiah, 29–31
  and forgiveness of sins, 29
  gnostic beliefs on, 116, 121–25, 132
  good-news ministry of, 26–28, 49, 50, 132

Jesus Christ (*continued*)
  historical context of, 2–3
  and hope for early Christians, 64–67, 84
  identity of generally, xv–xvii
  Ignatius of Antioch on, 66–67
  issues overview (520 BC–AD 70) on, 1–2
  as king, 35
  on kingdom of God, 38–39
  as Lamb, 64–66, 104
  and Last Supper, 62, 206
  as Lord, 41–43
  martyrs' imitation of, 86–87
  as Messiah/Anointed, 1–2, 5, 18, 25–43,
    64–66, 84, 94
  miracles of and healing by, 29, 58
  as mystery, 33
  as Pantocrator, 163
  parables of, 39, 107, 120, 149, 198
  Paul on, 32, 40–43
  and people of God, 38–39
  and the poor and unclean, 38–39
  as prophet, 26–28, 34–35, 94
  reasons for linking Jesus to Messiah,
    26–29
  resurrection of, 33–35, 37, 41, 50–52, 62,
    66, 84, 99
  as sacrifice and sacrificer, 89
  as second Adam, 134, 220, 221, 223
  second coming of, 103
  and Sermon on the Mount, 28, 56
  as Son of God, 33, 38, 41, 52, 126, 128,
    209–13
  as Son of Man, 20–21, 29, 37
  story of, and early Christians, 50–52, 98,
    126
  as teacher, 28–30, 34–35, 209
  and temple, 30, 31, 34, 37, 39, 147
  Tertullian on, 133–34
  testing of, in wilderness, 37
  transfiguration of, 35, 179, 180
  trial of, before Caiaphas, 37
  typology of, 102, 134
  as vindicated Israel, 37
  See also Christianity; crucifixion of Jesus;
    incarnation of Jesus Christ; Logos;
    salvation; and *specific Gospels*
Jewish Scripture. *See* Hebrew Bible
Jewish War (AD 70), 19
Jews
  Babylonian exile of, 11–14
  as chosen people of God, 1–2, 5–7
  Christians' connections with, 72–73, 91–95,
    111–12

  and circumcision, 3, 6, 15, 17, 42, 43, 61,
    72, 104
  confession of Jewish faith, 42
  and covenant themes, 16–18, 22, 32
  and Diaspora, 11, 17, 18
  and different perspectives on Judaism, 6,
    22–23, 43
  and God's agent, including messiah, 18–21
  Hellenizing Jews, 14–15
  historical context of and timeline on (520
    BC–AD 70), 2–3, 23
  and holiness, 17–18, 22, 36
  hope for restoration of, during, and after
    Babylonian exile, 11–14
  and Jesus Christ's identity, xv–xvii, 18
  knowledge of religion by, 7
  literacy of, 7
  and Maccabean interlude, 14–16
  monotheism of, 3, 46, 72, 210
  and priesthood, 6–7, 15, 17–19, 89
  relationship between Christianity and,
    72–73
  and resurrection, 21–22
  and Roman Empire, 3, 14, 15–16, 19, 72
  and salvation, 16–22, 43
  and Scripture, 7
  and Second Temple, 6, 14, 17, 20, 21, 22,
    43, 95
  and Solomon's Temple, 6, 14
  See also Hebrew Bible; Hebrews; Israelites
John, Gospel of
  beloved disciple in, 187
  characteristics of, 26
  on Creator as Savior, 52
  date of, 26
  on death and resurrection of Jesus, 33–34,
    35
  on Eucharist, 158
  on Holy Spirit, 183
  Irenaeus on, 99–100
  on Jesus as Son of God, 33, 38, 211
  knowledge of, at mid-second century, 98
  on Lamb of God, 62
  lion as symbol of, 100
  on Logos, 38, 78, 100, 103
  on messiahship of Jesus, 35
  on miracles of Jesus, 31
  on salvation, 222
  on shepherd and sheep, 151
John, Letters of, 99, 209
Judah, kingdom of, 8–9, 11, 12, 14–16, 19,
  147
Judaism. *See* Hebrew Bible; Jews

kenōsis, 208–9

Lamentations, book of, 11
Lazarus and the Rich Man parable, 198
Lent, 173
leprosy, 199–200
Letter of Pseudo-Barnabas, 56, 99, 103
Letters of Paul. *See specific letters, such as Corinthians, Letters to*
Letter to Diognetus, 56, 77, 97–98, 148
Letter to Marcellinus (Athanasius of Alexandria), 178
Leviticus, book of, 7, 89
Life of Antony (Athanasius of Alexandria), 181, 182, 195–96
Life of Moses, The (Gregory of Nyssa), 179–80, 196
liturgy. *See* worship
Logos
    Alexandrians and Cyril of Alexandria on, 214, 217–25
    Athanasius on, 222
    and crucifixion of Jesus Christ, 221
    and Eucharist, 225
    and God's *apatheia*, 214
    Gospel of John on, 38, 78, 100, 103
    and Holy Spirit, 104
    and incarnation, 217–23
    Jesus Christ as Word/Logos, 38, 59, 78–79, 100, 103–4, 108, 110, 131, 136, 161, 213–22
    Justin Martyr on, 78–79, 103–4
    and *kenōsis*, 208–9
    Nestorius on, 215–17, 220–21, 224–25
Lord's Prayer, 178
Lord's Supper, 60–64. *See also* Eucharist
love, 56, 179–80, 183–84, 187, 209
Luke, Gospel of
    on adultery, 186
    on caring for vulnerable and needy, 202
    on disciples' view of Jesus' reputation, 5
    Good Samaritan parable in, 149
    on Holy Spirit and spread of Christianity, 52
    Irenaeus on, 99–100
    on Jesus as Messiah, 25–28, 30–37, 39
    on Jewish heritage of Jesus, 103
    on John the Baptist, 51
    knowledge of, at mid-second century, 98
    Lazarus and the Rich Man parable in, 198
    and Marcion, 105
    ox as symbol of, 100

Maccabean Revolt, 15, 21
Maccabees, 14–16, 21–22, 84
Maccabees, books of, 15, 22
Malachi, book of, 20
Manicheans, 47, 120, 155
Marcionites, 131
Mark, Gospel of
    on adultery, 186
    on disciples' view of Jesus' reputation, 5
    eagle as symbol of, 100
    Irenaeus on, 99–100
    on Jesus as Messiah, 25–27, 30, 31, 34, 35, 37, 39
    Jesus' expelling of demons, 111
    knowledge of, at mid-second century, 98
    on Peter's view of messiah, 18
    on resurrection, 189
    on taking up cross to follow Jesus, 84
marriage, 57, 86, 170–71, 186–91. *See also* families
Martyrdom of Perpetua and Felicitas, The, 81
Martyrdom of Pionius, The, 74, 95
Martyrdom of Polycarp, 55, 89
martyrs
    artworks on, 163
    as Christian par excellence, 89–90
    and imitation of Christ, 86–87
    and intercessors and patrons, 87–88
    and Jews, 21–22
    and limits of being Roman and Christian, 45
    origin of term, 84–85
    resurrection of, 88–89, 153
    training for, 85–86
    women martyrs, 86–87, 197
    See also persecutions of Christians
Masoretic text, 7
Matthew, Gospel of
    on adultery, 186
    on baptism, 61
    on care for vulnerable and needy, 184, 203
    on disciples' view of Jesus' reputation, 5
    human as symbol of, 100
    Irenaeus on, 99–100
    on Jesus as Messiah, 25–32, 34, 35, 37, 39
    on John the Baptist, 18, 51
    knowledge of, at mid-second century, 98
    on Last Supper, 62
    on marriage, 186
    Origen's commentary on, 107
    on Peter as rock/foundation of church, 230
    on pure heart and seeing God, 108, 169

Matthew, Gospel of (*continued*)
  on "search, and you will find," 118, 125,
    128, 183
  on Sermon on the Mount, 28, 56, 57
  on spread of Christianity, 49
  on taking up cross to follow Jesus, 84
  Treasure Hidden in a Field parable in, 107
Messiah
  arguments against Jesus as, 29–31
  different meanings of term, 18–20
  early Christians' views of, 32–43
  Jesus as, 1–2, 5, 18, 25–43, 64–66, 84, 94
  John on, 38
  and John the Baptist, 31
  Paul on Jesus as, 32, 40–43
  perspectives on, before, and after Jesus' res-
    urrection, 32–34
  Peter on, 18
  warrior image of, 30–31
metropolitans, 151
miracles, 58–59
missionaries, 52–54
Modalists, 210
monastery, 181
monasticism, 180–84, 189
monks, 180–84, 189
Monophysites, 229, 230
monotheism, 3, 45, 46, 67, 72, 78, 210
Montanism, 96–97, 118
murder, 83, 174–75

Nag Hammadi library, 119
Nehemiah, book of, 14
New Prophecy, 96–97, 118
New Testament. *See* Gospels; Scripture; and
  specific books of New Testament
Nicene-Constantinopolitan Creed, 212, 219,
  223
Numbers, book of, 7

Odes of Solomon, 94
Odyssey (Homer), 104–5
Old Testament. *See* Hebrew Bible; and *specific
  books of Hebrew Bible*
On First Principles (Origen), 106–10
On the Generation of Animals (Aristotle), 194
On the Incarnation of the Word (Athanasius of
  Alexandria), 222
On the Mysteries (Ambrose of Milan), 154
On the Pasch (Melito of Sardis), 62–63
On the Sacraments (Ambrose of Milan), 154
On Virginity (Gregory of Nyssa), 170
original sin. *See* sin

orthodox, 116
Ostrogoths, 143
ousia (essence), 210, 211, 223

pagan revival, 141
parables, 39, 107, 120, 149, 198
parenting, 190–91
Passover, 8, 30, 62, 160
pastoral care, 116–18, 167, 176, 178–79
pathé (passions), 208, 209, 217
patriarchs, 151, 230
Patripassionists, 210
Paul's Letters. *See specific letters, such as
  Corinthians, Letters to*
Pax Romana, 2
penitential process. *See* repentance,
  sacrament of
Pentateuch, 7
Pentecost, 50
perfection and prayer, 176–80
persecutions of Christians
  and adverse conditions, 71
  and apostasy, 117
  and cost of fidelity, 81–82
  "Great Persecution" (303–312), 47, 83, 86,
    139
  Jews' offer of refuge during, 95
  Justin Martyr on, 57
  and martyrs, 45, 84–90
  and Origen, 106
  and Pionius, 74
  Pliny the Younger on, 70–71
  and political and economic conditions,
    46–47
  and postpersecution trauma, 82–83
Persia, 14, 15, 19, 46
persons
  personae, 210
  prosōpa, 210, 219
Peter, Letters of, 61, 95, 99, 149, 222
Pharisees, 27, 39, 41, 116, 152
Philippians, Letter to, 27, 41, 52, 121, 208,
  217, 221
physis (nature), 216, 219, 224
Platonism, 59–60, 78, 103, 168, 209
polytheism, 77–78
poverty and suffering, 56, 67, 72, 76, 183–84,
  198–204
praxis (disciplines for developing stillness),
  179, 180
prayer
  contemplative prayer, 139, 178–79
  for dead, 153–54

and diagnosis of distractions, 176–77
Lord's Prayer, 178
and perfection, 176–80
and Scripture, 177–78
and vision of God, 178–80
priesthood, 6–7, 15, 17–19, 89
Prodigal Son parable, 39, 120, 152
Proof of the Apostolic Preaching (Irenaeus of
    Lyons), 127, 134
prophets
    Didache on, 101
    of Hebrew Bible, 7, 9, 11–13, 18, 19–20,
        29, 84, 102, 103
    Jesus as, 26–28, 34–35, 94
    John the Baptist as, 26–27, 36
    *See also specific prophets in Index of Names of
        Persons*
Prophets, books of, 7, 36, 94, 103, 117, 195
    *See persons*proto-orthodoxy, 116, 124,
        126–28, 130–35
Proverbs, book of, 7
Psalms, book of
    category in Jewish Scripture, 7
    and Christian worship, 162
    and Christ's cry of dereliction at crucifix-
        ion, 221
    connections between Jesus and, 20, 34, 37,
        94, 221
    and devotional practices, 178, 192
    on disobedience of Israelites, 10
    exilic lament in, 36
    on exodus of Israelites, 102
    on God's anointing of Christ, 211
    on God's covenant with Israel, 9–10, 12–13
    on righteousness versus wickedness, 56
    on salvation, 222
    on son of man, 20
    on true status of rich and powerful, 195
Pseudepigrapha, 94
Pythagoreans, 59

Q, 26
Qumran Scrolls, 7, 16, 18, 19, 20, 102

recapitulation, 134–35, 222–23
Recognitions(Pseudo-Clement) 94
renouncer/renunciant, 181
repentance, 50, 51
repentance, sacrament of, 174–76
resurrection
    of body, 88–89, 132, 133, 148, 153, 221
    of Jesus Christ, 33–35, 37, 41, 42, 50–52,
        62, 66, 84, 99

Jews' belief in, 21–22
of martyrs, 88–89, 153
Paul on, 41, 42, 148
Pharisees' belief in, 27
preparation for, 169–70
Tertullian on, 133
Revelation, book of, 64–66, 84, 98, 100, 132,
    160
Roman Empire
    Bar Kokhba revolt against, 95
    and Christianity generally, 67–68
    and christological controversies, 228–30
    and citizenship of Christians, 68, 73–74,
        76–77
    Constantinople as capital of, 139, 142
    destruction of Second Temple by, 6, 72, 95
    disintegration of, 142–43, 227–30
    and divorce, 187
    eastern and western divisions of, 2, 47,
        227–30
    emperors of, 46–47, 140–43
    and Jews, 3, 14, 15–16, 19, 72
    and Jews' longing for warrior-king Mes-
        siah, 30–31
    and legal toleration of Christianity, 145
    and non-Roman gods, 2–3
    and Pax Romana, 2
    and Pliny the Younger, 70–73
    slaves in, 193–94
    wealthy in, 201
    See also persecutions of Christians; and
        *specific emperors in Index of Names of
        Persons*
Romans, Letter to, 41, 42, 43, 45, 49, 76
rule of faith, 126–32

Sabellians, 210
sacraments, 60–64, 136, 154, 159, 161. *See
    also* baptism; Lord's Supper; repentance,
    sacrament of
Sadducees, 19, 21, 116
saints, 66, 153–54
salvation
    Alexandrian view of, 221–24, 229
    Antiochene view of, 220–21, 229
    Athanasius on, 222–23
    Christian beliefs on, 51–52, 132–36
    and Christ's second coming, 103
    and covenant hope, 35–37
    gnostic beliefs on, 121, 123–26, 132–33
    Irenaeus of Lyons on, 133, 134–35, 221
    in Jesus Christ, 51–52, 103, 132–36
    and Jews, 16–22, 43

salvation (*continued*)
Nestorius on, 220–21
Paul on, 42
and recapitulation, 134–35, 222–23
and sharing God's life, 221–24
Satan. *See* evil
Scripture
Antiochene and Alexandrian schools on, 215
canon of, 100, 101
and children, 192
and Christianity, 45–46, 89–112
contents of Christian Scripture, 97–99
etymology of term, 92
and evaluation of Christian writings, 99–101
and gnosticism, 106, 112, 120, 126–27
God as author of, 110
Hebrew Bible and Christians, 91–95, 102, 111–12
interpretation of, and Jewish heritage, 101–6, 112
Irenaeus on, 99–100
of Jefferson, 105
Justin Martyr on, 103–4
literal and nonliteral meanings of, 109–11, 112, 214
mainstream versus marginal texts of, 98–99
mysteries in, 107–8
and new Christian traditions, 95–96
New Testament of, 96
Origen on, 106–11, 112, 115, 178
Paul on, 111
and prayer, 177–78
and *testimonia*, 101–3, 104
and typology, 102–3, 134
and Valentinians, 118
and worship, 96–97, 111
as written subset of tradition, 92–93
See also Gospels; Hebrew Bible; Septuagint; and *specific books of the Bible*
Second Temple, 6, 14, 17, 20, 21, 22, 43, 95
Second Treatise of the Great Seth, 124, 221
Seleucid Empire, 14–15
self-control, 56–57
Septuagint, 7, 38, 72, 92. *See also* Scripture
Sermon on the Mount, 28, 56, 57
Servant Songs, 21
sexuality, 67, 170–71, 188–90, 194–95
Shepherd of Hermas, 56, 94, 99, 174
sin
of Adam and Eve, 123, 134, 188, 194, 196–97, 199, 200, 213, 220, 222, 228–29

and evil thoughts, 177
forgiveness of, by Jesus Christ, 29
light and heavy sins, 174–75
and sacrament of repentance, 174–76
seven deadly sins, 177
See also evil
Sirach, 18
skopos (purpose of text), 110
slaves, 192, 193–94
Solomon's Temple, 6, 14, 17
Sophia (Wisdom), 122
Stoicism, 59, 78, 103, 131, 168
substantia (essence), 210
Suffering Servant, 21
Synoptic Gospels, 25–26, 33, 39, 98. *See also* *specific Gospels*

Ten Commandments, 56
Testimonia, 101–3, 104
Theodosian Code, 187
theoria (contemplation), 179, 180
theōsis (divinization), 160, 223, 228
Theotokos (God-bearer), 215–16, 224
Thessalonians, Letter to, 40–41, 51, 177
Timothy, Letters to, 54
Titus, Letter to, 54
Torah
Antiochus' outlawing of, 15
content and themes of, 7, 9
and covenant between God and Israel, 6
and Diaspora, 18
and Exodus experience, 16
and Gospel of Matthew, 99
and holiness, 17
and Jesus, 25, 29, 35
and *Letter of Pseudo-Barnabas*, 103
Marcion on, 105
as presence of God, 91
on purity, 30, 94, 95
secondary texts to, 94
See also Hebrew Bible
transfiguration of Christ, 35, 179, 180
Treasure Hidden in a Field parable, 107
Trinity, 46, 78, 127, 151, 157, 210, 219, 229. *See also* God; Holy Spirit; Jesus Christ
typology, 102–3, 134

Valentinians, 117, 118, 119, 124
Vandals, 143, 227
Vineyard and Tenants parable, 39
virgin (parthenos), 181
virginity, 57, 170–71, 186, 189, 196
virtue, 74–76, 196, 197

wedding, 191. *See also* marriage
Wisdom literature, 7
Wisdom [Sophia] of Jesus Christ, 123
women, 193–97
worship
  and art, 163
  and chrism, 163
  definition of liturgy, 159
  Eastern liturgies of, 176
  of first-century Christians, 60–64
  and homilies, 161–62, 197–98, 203–4
  and incarnate experience of the divine,
    161–64
  and incense, 162–63
  Justin Martyr on, 97
  and music, 162
  mystery of, 159–64
  and ritual encounters with God, 160–61
  and Scripture, 96–97, 111
  Tertullian on, 75

Zechariah, book of, 19

green press
INITIATIVE

Presbyterian Publishing is committed to preserving ancient forests and natural resources. We elected to print this title on 30% post consumer recycled paper, processed chlorine free. As a result, for this printing, we have saved:

8 Trees (40' tall and 6-8" diameter)
6 Million BTUs of Total Energy
639 Pounds of Greenhouse Gases
2,890 Gallons of Wastewater
337 Pounds of Solid Waste

Presbyterian Publishing made this paper choice because our printer, Thomson-Shore, Inc., is a member of Green Press Initiative, a nonprofit program dedicated to supporting authors, publishers, and suppliers in their efforts to reduce their use of fiber obtained from endangered forests.

For more information, visit www.greenpressinitiative.org

Environmental impact estimates were made using the Environmental Defense Paper Calculator. For more information visit: www.edf.org/papercalculator